AMERICA AND COSMIC MAN

AMERICA
and Cosmic Man,

BY WYNDHAM LEWIS

KENNIKAT PRESS/PORT WASHINGTON, N. Y.

AMERICA AND COSMIC MAN

Copyright O 1949 by Wyndham Lewis
Reissued in 1969 by Kennikat Press by arrangement with
Doubleday and Company, Inc.
Library of Congress Catalog Card No: 76-86569
SBN 8046-0570-X

Manufactured by Taylor Publishing Company   Dallas, Texas

ESSAY AND GENERAL LITERATURE INDEX REPRINT SERIES

CONTENTS

PART 1

PART 2

AMERICA AND COSMIC MAN

PART 1

This people (the American) is the hope of the human race.
—Turgot

---

1 INTRODUCTORY

I do not see how England and America as nations can ever have a very close understanding, the incompatibilities are too numerous. Both have what might be called the champion-complex. Bossiness is not extinct in the English, and the average little American derives much satisfaction, still, from the bigness of the U.S.A. Purely as competing nations, and until that type of relationship is superseded by something more intelligent, it is a waste of time to "explain" them to each other with a view to establishing an *entente*. I commit myself to this expression of opinion lest people at the start suppose I am engaged upon some good-will mission, which is not the case.

I am not here to sell America to you. But I should like to sell *something* that is to be found there, and not here in Britain, that is very impressive; so much so that once you have grasped what it means, it must affect profoundly your outlook. For my own part—ensuing upon travel in "those United States"

11

which never seemed to have an end—it will influence everything I think and write henceforth. It has tended to transform me from a good European into an excellent internationalist.

In writing of America one has of course to remind oneself how intimately the American is now known to the inhabitants of these islands. He is known in all his varieties: Hoosier, New Yorker, Texan, demi-Mexican, and high-yellow—little gentleman from "Harvard," and little thief just out of a penitentiary. But he is known in a military disguise, far from his habitat, under conditions calculated to bring out all that is most irritating in the American.

The presence of great numbers of United States troops in England for so long a period, it is better to admit, has not been politically helpful. Such contacts rarely prove to be that, especially where one set of people is so much better supplied with cash than the other and is not exactly disposed to conceal the fact, or the less fortunate inclined to be philosophic regarding his economic inferiority.

So on the more primitive levels mass-contact has left in the main antagonism, though do not let us exaggerate. The popular Press does not diminish this by its reports, in which the United States figures as an economic bully, ordering Great Britain about; when she's in Carey Street, as she is today, refusing to lend her money, and at the same time scolding British miners for not working hard enough. Politics is a melodrama for teen-aged minds: America has not *le beau rôle* over here, and the British are the invariable recipients of a bucket of dirty water or a derisive howl in the silly old thriller as played by any American, whoever he may be. Who, for instance, were these words written by? (I take them from a book review.) "We broke away from the English and beat them and sent them back to their island; and they have never forgiven this." By Mr. Edmund Wilson. That garish jingo lining to quite a worldly little bag of tricks is typical.

In a mild way it is a case of cat and dog, for neither English nor American has a monopoly of prejudice, and I have seen Englishmen considerably more intelligent than Mr. Wilson display just as raw a chauvinism. On both sides this indicates the "big-shot" complex, which is of course a pity. It manifests the sublimest indifference to history, this applying, if anything, rather more to the English than to the American.

Toward America the English stand in a very special relationship. Its birth as a Whig baby (unnaturally large) in the eighteenth century induced in us formerly feelings of rather quizzical parenthood. But, like babies, and other things, in the pages of *Alice in Wonderland,* as we gazed at it across the Atlantic this baby changed. It was still a baby, it continued to express itself in English, but it took on a more swarthy complexion, and it became obvious it was no longer in the main our child.

The fact, however, that America and England have a common tongue, that their respective institutions derive from a common source, and that in the past they were so closely related by blood, and have innumerable ties, historically, morally, and intellectually, means that America is for us theoretically in a class all by itself among states.

In another way it has played a very profound part in our life as a nation. The influence America has exerted all along upon England is enormous; a fact that is generally forgotten. England would not be the place it is today had there been no America. Almost certainly there would be no social-democratic government at this time—no Mr. Attlee or Mr. Bevin—but some regime such as the Dutch still have, or like that obtaining in Hungary prior to World War I.

When Morley was engaged in refuting Maine's onslaught upon popular government in the 'eighties, he brought out this point very well, tracing the growth of "English Liberalism of a radical democratic type" to the influence of America. "The success of popular government across the Atlantic has been the strongest incentive to the extension of popular government here." To the example of the United States he adds that of the overseas commonwealths. "The success of popular self-government in these thriving communities is reacting on polit-

13

ical opinion at home with a force that . . . is every day increasing."

It continually increased until Lloyd George's innovations in the field of social insurance went farther along the Liberal road than America had thought of venturing; and today, in beginning the change from private ownership to public ownership of key industries, we have indeed left our great model of "multitudinous government" behind. But the first and most powerful impulses in that direction came from the United States. Without the experience of American prosperity and stability, the English would hardly have broken away from the general belief that no government of the Many can be stable or be conducive to prosperity, or nothing like so soon.

In our broken world there are two great States which remain intact, namely the U.S.A. and the U.S.S.R. These two gigantic nations tower above our famished slums (one of them, paradoxically, itself a slum, almost as ill-fed and ill-clothed as any). For a considerable time to come, these two dominant Powers will, between them, exercise almost complete control over our national life. Consequently what they *are* is a matter that must invite our anxious attention. I have done my best in these pages to show what one of them, the U.S.A., *is,* as State and as human organism, in this connection bleakly distinct.

For Russia much less antagonism is felt in England—partly, of course, because there is no ruble problem as there is a dollar problem. Yet the popular ecstasies of the war-years are not even a memory, no trace is left at all: Russia is seen now as the perpetual obstructor in peace conferences, and even as a potential war-maker. It is considered by the average Briton that she does not observe the terms of pacts and treaties, and that she has contracted the odious habit of hanging iron curtains around those states she has politically raped and in some cases murdered, or bits of which she has lopped off.

There has been no contact, except between troops. That has had the worst possible effect. English soldiers returned from Austria and Germany, who have lived in daily touch with the Russian soldiery, have not a good word to say for them. An

14

image remains, from the stories they tell, simple in outline, and it never varies: a dirty man at the end of a tommy-gun asking violently for something to which he has no right. (Our man with the property-complex would be just as unsympathetic as viewed by the other.) To set against such adverse pictures, a photograph of "Uncle Joe" with his mustache and his pipe still draws a kindly smile from the newspaper reader.

But what must always keep Russian-British relations on a rather artificial plane, far from passion—real sympathy, or real dislike—is the fact that Russians are too remote a species to have personal feelings about in Lancashire and Gloucestershire; they are not trade rivals as the Germans were, nor rivals in the financial field as were the Americans—in the days when we were the great "clearinghouse" and the Old Lady of Threadneedle Street richer than she is at present. As to their Communism—about which ninety per cent of Englishmen have the haziest ideas—that would have no effect one way or the other on feelings about Russians now that they have been our allies in a victorious war against a despot and aggressor.

So there is no question of powerful emotions here where Russia is concerned. The Englishman is just shocked every time he opens the paper to learn that his ally has smothered another small state. And he wishes he knew how peace-loving the Russians were! He feels uneasy—there is anything but enthusiasm or cordiality. That is all.

In any case, there, roughly, is the position; the Englishman's relations with the two mammoth States whose good will, or ill will, must mean so much to him are not very satisfactory. He is himself an ex-giant, with still some pretensions to being in the "giant" class, which complicates the situation. He has, in fact, all the disadvantages of being "great" and none of the blessings of second-rateness. Then the white man's burden has not grown any lighter, but the white man has not as of yore a beefsteak under his belt. He becomes a poor white—with a burden, which is the remnants of an empire.

To turn now more specifically to the United States, it is unfortunate that Britain in its distressed condition—with its huge population and diminished power to make provision for it—should be so exclusively dependent upon a nation with which it has so many incompatibilities, and which it finds so difficult to understand. One thing I can say of this book is that, since it is the work of a great friend of America, it will not embitter relations with that country. If what I say could not be published in the United States by a foreigner (and indeed it is a fact that what you read has been refused on those grounds), Americans themselves are free to transgress—though no doubt each arriving at his own conclusions—and the subject matter is the merest commonplace of conversation or Press comment. You cannot build so vast a state at top speed out of a wilderness *prettily;* and the horrid building proceeds.

There is much beauty in America: of course unbelievable physical beauties, and a population with the highest percentage of physical perfection that can ever have been attained by men of European stock. Yet you could say, metaphorically, of America that what you see there is as yet perhaps an unsightly enough grub—if one thinks of its rackets, or of Hollywood, of all the Teapot Domes that never break—of "Murder Incorporated" and Sindlinger's *Workshop.*

But what you must divine is the imago that will one day burst out—at the end of these preparatory phases—the first entire cosmopolis. Whether that disastrous power which the splitting of the atom has made available will precipitate this evolutionary process, or whether things will follow a more normal course, is a matter of speculation.

It is, I believe, the destiny of America to produce the first of a new species of man. It is the first of the great "melting pots." The pots take a long time to melt. Beneath this titanic human caldron is nothing more incandescent than an old-fashioned campfire, or the ritualistic sticks brought in from a sacred wood and periodically rekindled into token flames. So the pot does not melt very fast. Americans actually are quite unconscious what a novel kind of people they are. On the one hand they wrestle reverently with a reactionary Constitution, they darkly hide away their hoarded gold underground, and aggressively practice an antiquated economy. That State structure and that fairy gold are the campfire alluded to above. To place against that, their techniques race ahead, leaping the centuries into the future. Further than that, they are, it seems to me, dedicated to the future more than any other people: and it is my argument in this book that we can read *our own* future by an imaginative scrutiny of what is occurring, and what is so plainly destined to occur there in America.

Politics can only be judged by results: who, then, upon the world scene, has been smart since 1939? That is answered by the landscape, from the Iron Curtain to the Shetlands, or from the Channel to the Bosporus. Not many signs of foresight and acumen there! To turn from that scene to the American might incline us to suspect that that country had outsmarted us all. But Americans do not have to be smart to be prosperous —they cannot help it. It is the *lack* of smartness of which I have been speaking, rather than its aggressive presence. It would be a pity for anyone to feel they had been outsmarted— but it would be terrible (with one shirt on and one at the wash) still to feel they were smart. Domestic politics apart, wrestling hopelessly with the demoniacal conundrum of *sovereignty* and of racial pride, the older nations must be more and more persuasively affected by the example of America. Then although in the externals of popular government we have left the Americans far behind, they greatly excel us in what might be called the raw human material of Socialism.

2 A NEW KIND OF COUNTRY

The United States is the most aggressive national personality
extant: but in a certain sense it is not a country. The fact is, it
is a *new kind of country*. It is better than a country. The Greeks
of antiquity only dreamed of Cosmopolis: but the European
discovered an enormous continent upon which to set one up:
America. It was not his conscious intention at all, but that was
what happened.

"America is not a boardinghouse." So blustered Theodore
(Teddy) Roosevelt. He meant, of course, that it was more than
just a place to go and secure board and lodging in. It had to
be taken seriously if you took up your quarters there, he meant
—as *a country*.

The President's words were addressed to Americans, mainly
immigrant. But by no one, native or foreign, is the United
States taken otherwise than very seriously today. Very few see
beyond its power, wealth, youth, and size. However, it con-
ceals strange vistas beneath the outward trappings of twentieth-
century power. In political interest it outstrips Russia (which
it resembles), more especially in political possibilities. Admittedly it is in a crude and raw-material stage. Even it struggles
violently against its destiny—seeks to evade the logic of fact,
racial and other. The Americans who, like Henry James, have
abandoned the American scene altogether are the extreme
exponents of this evasion. But the extraordinary incubation
proceeds, beneath the surface of the orthodox machinery of
State and the panoply of Business power.

As to the Russian parallel, it is important. Generally people are inclined to regard America and Russia as both *large,* but in other respects *dissimilar.* To give an instance of this, the following is from an article by the late Mr. J. L. Garvin: "These two gigantic societies [the U.S.A. and the U.S.S.R.] are as dissimilar as can well be conceived. They are not only contrasting, but opposite. They differ diametrically both in principle and practice. Russian 'state capitalism,' that 'no less dynamic system,' is the antithesis of the American system."

In contrast to this view, what strikes me is their resemblances much more than their differences. Mr. Garvin was, I believe, speaking without firsthand knowledge of the Russian scene. It interested me to see Mr. Malcolm Muggeridge (who has) quoted recently as saying that the United States had reminded him more of Russia than of any other country he knew.

In the U.S.S.R. State capitalism is productive of conditions in which the individual has less liberty than anywhere. With the individual in the U.S.A., it is quite the opposite—he has more liberty than anywhere else: which applies to the socially unimportant—the circumstance which astonishes people most about this country. So the actual political and social core of his life is in absolute contrast to the Russian. For I did not say that in everything these two nations resembled one another. That in so many respects they do is a paradox—so many, in fact, that in spite of their being poles apart in their attitude to the individual, it is curious how easy it is to think of them together.

Both are very large and very dynamic countries, as Mr. Garvin wrote; both occupy a continuous land-bloc of very great extent. But you can go on from that to other profound similarities. Both have at the base of their system, as a political rationale, man's brotherhood. Unlike the military aristocracies of Europe, which effected a transformation of themselves into bogus "democracies," the U.S.S.R. and the U.S.A. *start* from that. The life of both is involved ideologically with industry. (England, traditionally, has always regarded industry as a grimy and socially inferior partner: *they* think of it as a steel-limbed god.) Both are gang-minded, collectivist. America is a big club: a Women's Club and a Rotary; community life in Russia lives up to the doctrine of Communism. The "solitary" does not thrive in either system, as he has in the past par excellence in England. And both are power systems.

Were the United States to nationalize its great industries—and they are so large as already to be highly impersonal—and were it controlled by a New Deal type of bureaucracy, it would be exactly what Russia would be like, barring accidents, after a century or two of peace and technological progress, barbarism overcome. In other words, we have a Russia, only immeasurably better fed, better dressed, with car, washing-machine, refrigerator; living upon a higher plane of social evolution, as far as all material things are concerned.

I have used the expression power systems; by that I mean that both these rival giants are States about which the adjective "dynamic" is apt to be used (as we have seen it used above): both are skyscrapers, as it were, among State structures, still building. And a skyscraper is a form of architecture designed to dominate neighbors and to impose by its towering volume. It is sometimes an almost demented impulse to power which projects such monsters.

All governments, it can be argued, of course, are power systems, and so they are; and "law" is legalized force. But these two vibrate with the dynamism of growth—they are the only places where our world is in that vibrant condition. (No one could say of Great Britain that it vibrates.) In the case of the United States, its short history has been that of an aggressive body charging itself with more and more power, until one almost feels it lives for power alone. It is one immense power-house, to which has now been added atomic power.

If you look at North America on the map of the world, you see a very uniform mass. It is more concentrated and uniform than any other land mass. You see an immense area full of people speaking one tongue: not a checkerboard of "united states" at all, but one huge State. "United States" is today a misnomer. And since plural sovereignty anyway—now that the earth has become one big village, with telephones laid on from one end to the other, and air transport, both speedy and safe—must be a little farcical, the plurality implied in that title could be removed as a good example to the rest of the world, and the U.S.A. become the American Union.

Not only one tongue, but one standard thought about almost everything is the sort of unity you find there. The British Isles, even, that small, ragged shape broken off from Europe, insignificant as it is in extent, is much more differentiated. One does not have to point to the Welsh, still jabbering a foreign tongue, or mention Gaelic or Erse: you need go no farther than the Yorkshireman and he from Dorset, and note how differently these two men speak, look, and think. No such starkly differing types exist inside that Union, which Lincoln died for, known as "America." This spectacular unity is spiritual, produced out of the most diverse stocks. It is still a union of men gathered together to be free. And this particular collection of men do keep reminding each other that they are there for that purpose.

Standing on America (one feels greatly magnified while there gazing out at other lands), one sees nothing but *disunity*. No "united states"—only "disunited states." So gazing out of America, one realizes one day that what this nation stands for is unity, just that, as no other does—even to the point of uniformity; with all the irresistible power that oneness bestows. And its very name conduces to that understanding and makes one see how lesser Union may, snowball-like, lead to a greater Union, until there is no disunion any more on earth. The term "United Nations," however tentatively, is symbolic of that future: so American Union would perhaps not be so good. That it is "American" is not important; that it is so United *is*.

Lincoln did not die for Yankee capitalism, but to preserve the Union. Why did he so object to secession: was it for the reasons Webster clothed in such flamboyant language, in 1850, a decade before the Civil War?

"Sir, he who sees these states, now revolving in harmony

around a common center, and expects to see them quit their places and fly off without convulsion, may look the next hour to see the heavenly bodies rush from their spheres, and jostle against each other in the realms of space, without producing the crash of the universe. . . .

"Peaceable secession! Peaceable secession! The concurrent agreement of all the members of this great Republic to separate! A voluntary separation, with alimony on one side and on the other. Why, what would be the result? Where is the line to be drawn? What states are to secede? What is to remain American? What am I to be? An American no longer? Where is the flag of the Republic to remain? Where is the eagle to tower—or is it to cower, and shrink, and fall to the ground?"

The cultivation of that eagle—the breeding of larger and larger birds, for today the bird has become a bomber—has been the sentimental aim of most Americans, with such notable exceptions as Jefferson: the eagle being the symbol of ferocity and power. "What am I to be? An American no longer?" is a *cri de coeur* that would find echoes in Lincoln's heart, of course: "the supreme American of our history," according to Woodrow Wilson. A model American could only be dedicated to one thing; to building America, and building it *big*.

It may be fanciful, but I think that Lincoln was a man of sufficient imagination to see that *union* was a political principle of universal worthiness, and universal application. He secured peace forever upon the North American continent. Even were Lincoln—a statesman, after all, a man of government—unconscious of anything but the problems of force and power, uniquely American: and even if no American, past or present, had ever been aware of it, yet America's greatness as a state is in the interest of everybody; its continued union, and even peaceful expansion, everybody's affair.

Were Lincoln alive today he would be gazing across at us— at our slums and ruins—with astonishment. The terrible fruits of the insane opposite of Unity he would note: States, going concerns in 1939—"great nations" and all that—today bankrupt dumps, infested by the black-marketeer, with the

22

usual three political factions squabbling for control of the site. He would not have been prepared for so tremendous a collapse.

Actually Lincoln's successors are now addressing themselves to the austere, if eccentric, task of taking over the world (as an American friend of mine puts it) and running it as a sort of poorhouse, disciplined by atomic fission. Their great predecessor would only have agreed to that proceeding in so far as it offered the possibility of the various inmates abandoning their pauper pride and becoming part of the American Union: which is to say he would not have agreed, for he would have known they would never have been so sensible.

Of all the downcast powers, England is in a way the worst off of any, because she is so great a war victim but does not know it. The spectacular activity of Labor, profound alterations in the economic structure of society, the confidence and gusto of Ministers, the sense of liberation displayed by the English working class, all conspire—unconsciously of course—to mask the true situation of the country, which must constantly deteriorate unless recognized and provided for. This bulging population, swarming upon its insufficiently spacious island coal mine, has priority as a problem, of those swamped in the exuberance of our austerity.

England's position has changed with such suddenness that for a while it will be possible for ambitious public men to behave as if it had not changed. Yet common sense dictates the halving now of the number of its inhabitants—for rather than fifty million people to be reduced to permanent undernourishment, would it not be better for half of them to go and form self-supporting colonies (such as the Germans founded in Brazil, Uruguay, Chile) or (always keeping together, which is best for the English as settlers) establish new towns and communities in Africa, Australia, or even Canada? Or perhaps—why not—the United States of America? England's position after World War II—Socialist or whatever it may be—is nowhere clearly presented to the people; from neither Press nor Radio does one ever hear a whisper of it.

The fact is that, if you cannot win a war without the help of

23

some other country richer and stronger than yourself, you cannot win it. The country which helps you wins it, if anybody does: although you may have been most gallant, bled much more than she, and even have expended all your patrimony in the effort. The Germans had not the power to secure the empire they coveted, no more in 1939 than in 1914, but they always had the power to ruin England unless that country was very smart indeed. All people with eyes in their heads could see that.

3 THE AMERICAN AND THE OLD WORLD

The position upon the planet of the different countries determines something about their outlook, as it does about the picture we have of them. Russia's position, for instance, high up toward the top of our world: Asia and Europe merging at their summits, from which elevation Russia looks down into both. In thinking of Russia one always has this geographic page in the foreground of one's consciousness, just as anyone whose mind turns to England sees an *island*. Contrariwise, from the English consciousness the same physical fact is never absent.

With people it is much the same thing. I can never read an anecdote about Napoleon without seeing, mistily, in the background of the mind, a diminutive and corpulent figure, nor could Napoleon fail to be intellectually conscious of this external self that I indistinctly discern: though obviously it would be of far less significance to Napoleon that he was diminutive in stature than it is to England that it is an island. This question of the degree-of-the-significance is quite distinct.

These facts belong to psychology: bearing them in mind, America may be regarded as a solitary. Stuck out there in the midst of the oceans, between two worlds, for all its immense size it is uniquely insular. The earth-view which I felt I was acquiring is American. A President of the United States, for example, is possessed of this politically: just as America is a good place for observation of the eclipses of the sun, the White House is a kind of political observatory.

Such geographically imposed isolation may lead to too abstract a temper. There was something chilly and unearthly about President Wilson's approach, or that is what other nationals felt at the time. But the occupant of the White House during the second of the world wars—as a good and typical American, calmly surveying mankind from China to Peru—was more human. The immense convulsion—which it was his destiny, more than that of any other single person, to direct—was guaranteed, however, before it was done, to melt an iceberg.

With Americans in general, though detachment, if not aloofness, characterizes them, that does not at all prevent them from displaying a feverish interest in the affairs of Europe. They are apt to take a change of government in England, if it is the sort of change they do not like, as a personal affront. They are very much more interested in the affairs of Asia than is any British empire-builder. Theirs is the spirit of the spectator: one who has paid a great deal for his seat and brought with him a profuse supply of rotten eggs and bouquets large and small.

Except as a very privileged spectator, Americans really want to have nothing to do, more than they can help, with Europe. For all serious practical purposes America seems to have its back turned to Europe. It faces west: a permanent return to the lands overseas—the lands *behind* them—from which all Americans come, is impossible. For the American, this seems to have the force of a biological law. After all, mankind, regarded as a migratory horde, started in Asia and followed the sun. "Go West!" something whispered within the first man to start the ball rolling—where was it? Perhaps in the Caucasus or Pamir. Wherever it started, it wound up on the Pacific Coast of the U.S.A.—America is the end of the road. There is nowhere else to go to—that you could possibly call a "new" world, at least.

There is something final about America. For an American to move eastward, in reverse, is like swimming against the tide or cutting against the grain: like putting back the hands of a clock (which is said to be bad for the clock), revisiting scenes of your childhood, and thinking back to that barbarous epoch of knee pants and yo-yos. I always feel sorry for an American friend settled in Europe or in England: and if they are women it is worse. They never reconcile themselves to it, however beautiful their surroundings. They go around all the time hungrily looking for other American exiles of their own sex to talk to: to get back to America with for an hour or so. For "America" is wherever Americans are: America is much more a psychological something than a territorial something. That is the first thing, of major importance, to realize about it.

Patriotism, again, in America is structurally different, if I am not mistaken, from the more traditional varieties. It is the very opposite of *Blut und Boden*. In a sense it may be said to be abstract. The United States is rather a site for the development of an idea of political and religious freedom than a mystical *terre sacrée* for its sons, upon the French model. They will fight for brotherhood, rather than, possessively, for a mother earth. Brotherhood is rather a good thing to fight for. And with them it is really the brotherhood of man, since they are so mixed in race.

America is a man with his back forever turned. The English should not forget this. They should recall that he is not an Englishman either—perhaps an Irishman or German, a Swede or a Swiss, but seldom an Englishman: and that, if not antagonism, at least indifference must always be expected of this man whose back is turned. A farmer in Iowa or Idaho, a workman or executive in Washington, is no more interested in England than the Britisher is in what is going on at the South Pole, or at Minsk or Mexico City. They are usually not violently hostile —unless their name is O'Brien or O'Connor. They just take no interest at all, they live in another universe. Since in their foreign relations Americans are instinctively "tough" and aggressive (and thereby they constantly antagonize their Latin neighbors to the south) one must always expect them to be "tough" and unaccommodating, except at such times as England is functioning as an "outpost" of American capitalism:

and even then they are really none too polite. There is the truth of the matter. If the average Englishman feels indignant, he should ask himself if *he* experiences a warm interest in America and the Americans. What you do not give, nor have ever given, should you, in all fairness, expect to receive?

In a *Herald Tribune* review of the Beards' book, *The American Spirit,* occurred the following passage: "The Middle West was anti-European because most Americans were anti-European in their blood. They had come to the United States because they were Europe's rejected or because, as conscious rebels, they had forsworn European values."

The past tense is quite unnecessary here. Substitute "are" for "were" in "most Americans were anti-European," and you have a true statement of the position today. (England is of course regarded as an integral part of Europe.) Many intelligent Americans are to be found today who think very differently from the Beards—and many existed before Charles and Mary R. Beard first saw the light in Indiana. But it is of the very nature of Americanism that it *should not change.* A static principle is inherent in that particular *ism,* for it exists that it may achieve the static.

A new nation—especially one that is not really a nation—has first of all to provide itself overnight with a Constitution. It must also have characteristics which differentiate it from other peoples. At the founding of the American Republic the leaders in the War of Independence were bewigged replicas of English polite society. No marked difference to be found there! But the farmers and storekeepers who composed Jefferson's powerful political clubs, the "democratic societies" (which transformed the new nation from a rather Tory into a sentimentally radical community), readers of Tom Paine and the literature of "rebel" Enlightenment—these people were really something *new;* it was a novel mixture, at all events.

It was a mixture of militant puritans, bog-trotters, indentured servants or "white slaves" (come as human chattels from many nations): they were charged to their bearded muzzles with libertarian uplift and fierce Hebrew mysticism: Rousseau's "natural man," replete with virtue, and dark visions of Original Sin were forced into a mad union in their consciousness.

This novel confusion took on the fixity of tradition overnight. A Constitution had been composed for all time: and an "American" had been created, for all time, likewise. You have to make a start *somehow* and with *somebody,* in suddenly founding a state like that.

Americanism may not have been conceived in this way: but that is the impression it conveys. America's geographical isolation from other nations would almost account for it. But there is that relentless fidelity to the State-framework bequeathed it by the eighteenth century: and the inflexibility of many American modes of feeling is the *identity complex of a new society,* it is permissible to guess.

This intense identity possessed by the American has been put to good use by the centralizers. It has assisted unification: was even a major and essential ingredient. On the other hand, when the American comes to universalize himself—as is much more his "manifest destiny" than the shoddy imperialism immortalized by that phrase—Americanism will not survive. A tendency to de-Americanization, I believe, is already present Even in America's furious cultural eclecticism is implicit such a movement. And you hear more disobliging, even scornful, remarks about the American ethics in New York than you do in Paris or London.

4 AMERICAN CITIZENSHIP

Nationalism, as understood in Europe, or in the British Isles, would be impossible for the American. With us, the core of nationalism is invariably racial: it is not too difficult for the Irish to pretend to be all of one racial stock, and even the Germans succeeded—to the satisfaction of their own people, though of no other—in basing their nationalism upon a blood-tie, uniting the entire *Volk*. The Russians have the Slavic rallying-cry, the South American republics the Latin. Only the Americans are debarred from such emotional delights. Even religion offers them no foothold, for they are committed to the protection of every sect on earth; and all are there, in a flourishing condition. In this dilemma, is it to be wondered at that, as a nation, they should have cast around for something to fill the void?

The way in which this *something* manifests itself is in the rite of citizenship. Citizenship is, of course, so much taken for granted by the American-born that I doubt if the curious importance of this instrument of identification is fully grasped.

U.S. citizenship is something as unique as it is extraordinary; it differs radically from what in Europe is understood by "nationality." The United States is a fragmentary, most imperfect, and in some respects grotesque advance copy of a future world order, as I have already indicated. It is a Brotherhood rather than a "People." Americans have something *more* than nationality. In its place they have what amounts almost to a religion; a "way of life." It is one of the most important spiritual phenomena in the world today. If you match it with Russian Communism you will find it held to with just as impressive a tenacity, by a people almost equal in numbers. To Shintoism, or any State-cult, it is not inferior in quality. And the present condition of the planet does not weaken it, but quite the reverse.

Without running too great a risk of confutation, the American might claim that in his case "citizenship" exists, theoretically, upon a more intelligent plane than that of older models. The man of these new lands is traditionally suspicious of anything too rooted. Living as he does in a country that is too big for him, he tends to rocket about in it as a foot does in a shoe that is too large. But in any case, attachment to one place —or, for that matter, to one person—he indulges in with a certain misgiving.

American citizenship takes with it, of course, a whole system of ethics and politics: of puritan ethics and revolutionary politics. Both the ethics and the revolutionary principles are a little archaic and also dilute. However, today this particular citizenship's major interest for everybody lies in the fact that America stands out as the one great community in which race has been thrown out, and the priests of many cults have been brought together, in relative harmony—in a world in which obstinate bottlenecks of racial and religious passion, whether in Europe, Asia, or Africa, are in process of being overcome, or at least have reached the showdown stage. The United States is for Europe as well as for India, for instance, not to mention Palestine, an object lesson in how to make the lion lie down with the lamb.

Let us compare American citizenship, however, with some other kind: the classic method of analysis. There are only two sorts of citizenship of *universalist* character, as one might call it: British and American. These two orders of citizenship may be readily grouped together.

British citizenship is hard-boiled: pseudo-Roman. You could become, until the start of the late war, a British subject for ten pounds. It was as simple as that. You neither had to be able to read or write, nor to speak the English language particularly well. Just make yourself understood. Like Rome, Great Britain in the past spread its great tolerant wing over all those, irrespective of color, creed, or tongue, who possessed forty bucks and a clean collar.

In its abstractness, or at all events in its freedom from racial bigotry (for the Englishman, like the American, sets his face against that), British citizenship is analogous to that of the United States. But there the resemblance ends. There is nothing of that hard-boiled matter-of-fact British quality about the American variety.

In considering what is peculiar to America—its quite extraordinary contribution to the problem of human identification—it must be remembered that the U.S.A. is not a dispersed colonial empire, but a mammoth expanse of territory with no territorial ambitions outside itself. Consequently it is unable to confer so abstract a national status as Rome, or as nineteenth-century Britain, which aimed at being universal systems.

American universality is of a different kind. The universe comes to it, and is gathered into it, instead of America going out to absorb other species. Itself a conglomerate of many nations, there is no metropolitan race as such. So it does not merely hand you something like a luggage label, but, rather, an authentic soul. Naturally, if you have got a soul already, you do not need this. But if you come from somewhere where you haven't been able to call your soul your own, it must be enormously welcome.

John Bull's problem has been a very different one, necessarily, from that of Uncle Sam. People never crowded into England as they did into the States. You cannot make yourself an Englishman really by signing a paper. You become "British." It is legally and contractually the same thing: but I am speaking realistically. What, on the other hand, you become upon receiving your citizenship papers in the U.S.A is as valid an American as if your forebears had been with Washington at Valley Forge. That is what it took me a long time to understand.

No man who merely regarded America as a convenient place of residence—"a boardinghouse"—good opportunity for business, and so forth, and took out papers as he would sign a lease, would ever become an American, in the proper sense. This is the land given up to a cult, that of Demos. The mystique of America is an act of faith in tomorrow, in something vaguely millennial. Such is the nature of the revolutionary universalism of the American.

You are a Slovak shoe-factory hand, or a Welsh miner, say. The idea enters your head that you will emigrate to the States. Well, that is not just an idea like another, though you may not quite grasp this at the time. It is like "seeing the light," a little. It is even a little like death. You commit suicide, in the nationalist or tribal sense: you say good-by forever to Cambria or to Slovakia (and to all tribal or national ideas as well) and sail away into an abstract Goodness—or into something better, at all events, than the land of your birth. Even you are followed there, as a rule, by a number of your relatives. It resembles death in many respects—but death for the devout; a rebirth, and reunion, in a better world.

The United States is not a substitute for other states. Russia will go on being Russia: England persists in itself, with a great release of energies, formerly bottled up in class, to be effected by Socialism, but otherwise true to the pattern: France goes its intelligent way, among its vines and sunlit factories: even Germany will survive, dismembered and penniless. America, rather, is a new sort of state altogether, entirely unlike those in a fundamental manner.

A group of chapters which now follow are concerned with the kind of State-religion which underlies everywhere the noisy pagan crust of American life. It is the crude emotional makeshift, provided by American nationalism, attempting to rise to the occasion, but with no understanding of what the occasion is: namely, the birth-throes of a new type of society.

The core, as it were, of this group of chapters is a study of three great figures in the State-religion. I do not take them

chronologically, but start with that fascinating political conjuror, Franklin Delano Roosevelt. Next I turn to his namesake
and relative, Theodore Roosevelt. Last comes Woodrow Wilson. In these three men I shall be able to display the mechanism of this political idolatry in action. In the chapter you
have just read, the sacramentalism evidenced in the act of becoming an American has been described. And we now pass to
the high priests, the hierarchical summit of this politico-reli-
gious order—the occupants of a magistracy comparable with
that of the Dalai Lama and nothing else extant.

But before we can reach these great figureheads, we have to
pass through a tropical undergrowth, for which I must really
apologize, but there is no other way of getting there. Their
function is complex. They are the exponents of an extraordinary parliamentary Party-game—something like poker
champions, whose poker faces and power of fooling their ad-
versary are greatly admired and relished—as well as semi-
divine officers and pontiffs. It has become their habit to run
with the hare and hunt with the hounds: or, rather, loudly
announcing themselves on the side of the hare, to tag along
pretty consistently with the hounds. This applies even to the
best of them, and my first subject, according to my computation, is *very good*. The hero-cult indwelling in this spectacular
office makes of them mythological figures whose cunning is
almost as prominent as their valor and strength, as we find
when consulting the legends of primitive people: so those
habits of theirs are not reprobated except by the most class-
conscious of hares. But the real difficulty is the Party-game,
which has to be fairly carefully explained, since it has nothing
to do, except indirectly, with the power-mysticism of which I
speak. And with the Party-game goes the atmosphere this
game has generated in the course of decades.

Until you know something of the medium—the political
and social atmosphere—in which these great figures live and
have their being, it would be useless to attempt to delineate
them for you: just as no one will be able to explain Queen
Victoria to future ages, without first mastering the chemistry

34

of the stuffiness without which such a creature could not live a minute. Water is a very different medium from air: and if you had never seen water in any but minute quantities, it would not be easy to explain to you about the life of a fish. But the medium I have to re-create is rarefied rather than opaque and very unreal: it affects one sometimes like laughing gas. They are tragic gusts, it is true, which can be seen sometimes to convulse the lonely figures of the great Magistrates. Before coming to the latter, however, we have, as I said, to acquaint ourselves with "Party," as that is practiced in the U.S.A.: there is no short cut, I fear.

5 THE PARTY SYSTEM—WESTERN DEMOCRACY AND EASTERN DEMOCRACY

In the United States a President wears a Party-label, just as does a British Prime Minister. A French President is elected by the legislature; the title to power of an American President comes direct from the people—or that part of the people which approves of his Party. His great power is said to derive largely from that fact. When a U.S. President wields unusual power the fact that he is put there by the people is his moral, if not his constitutional, sanction.

In truth, however, he holds his power from the Party, rather than from the people: that is, unless he chooses to make a great point of his relationship to the people, as did the two Roosevelts and Wilson.

First of all let us ask ourselves what "Party" is: for as Anglo-Saxons, we are so accustomed to it that most of us have never stopped to ask ourselves exactly of what ideas it is composed.

"Party" is not a glorification of disagreement: but it is an open recognition of the fact that men do not agree and are not obliged to do so. It is also a discouragement of the view that government is an art, like playing the piano or writing an epic.

How much it is reasonable for men to disagree is another matter. They are not expected to disagree too much. This point is of the very essence of parliamentary democracy. Irreconcilable opposites have no place in a parliament.

"Party," then, is that technique of government in which

the nation is invited to divide itself up into two or more sections and, in the U.S. presidential election, to cast votes for one or more politicians. The politicians may be the champions of nothing-in-particular, or just the same thing, made to look a little different. Or they may stand for opposing types of political thinking (but that gets rarer every day).

In the latter case one side may, for example, be extremely averse to "government interference" in the nation's economic or social life. The other side may be great believers in a "planned economy": in maximum government control.

In practice in democratic politics issues are rarely so clear-cut. The essence of the democratic system is compromise. But in the case of two such starkly opposed Parties there might be a third: one of mild planners, but with a soft spot for individualism. Or you can have a third Party who are utterly uninterested in such problems. The promotion of intercourse with other planets might be its plank: or to revive Little Englandism and promote a large-scale exodus.

Party in the United States is unlike Party anywhere else. It began as in other countries as a parliamentary framework for two or more main groups in the nation, divided upon clear-cut issues, as above. One advocated, for instance, the slave-economy; the other was for abolition or at least for no extension into newly formed states. One wanted a tariff wall against foreign goods, the other a greatly reduced tariff. The manufacturing North was for the former, the South (the raw-material states) for the latter.

National political Parties in the United States "never quite lose their essential character as a bundle of local factions and interests," it has been said. Yet there *is* one clearly established difference between them. The Solid South and Tammany always put in the Democrats, and although neither the Solid South nor Tammany is remarkable for its liberal policies, the Democrats are less illiberal than the Republicans. And liberal principles are not dependent upon geography.

The Solid South puts in the Democrats for the same reason that the French-Canadians always put in the Liberal Party in

Canada: not because they themselves are particularly liberal (indeed, except for the Solid South there is nothing so conservative on the North American continent as French Canada); they just regard the Liberals as their best bet. After the Civil War the South decided to vote Democratic because they hated the Republicans (Lincoln's Party) more than they did the Democrats.

So it is a settled convention, the Democrats always put in a more liberal President, but the rich Southerners make it their business to see that the man they are mainly instrumental in electing does not observe the tradition too zealously. Often they threaten to vote Republican, to go mugwump—which would be the end of the Democrats.

There is, therefore, a sort of irrationality at the heart of Party business—rather as if a man voted Socialist because he was allergic to Mr. Churchill. This detachment from strict Party-meaning, which has prevailed since the Civil War, may have helped: but whether that is so or not, Party, having started to subserve some distinct end, at last came to exist for its own sake: rather as gold started as a mere medium of exchange and ended as a commodity, which was bought and sold like wheat or butter. Often the Party-rivals had planks identical in all respects, but developed just as much bitterness as if one had stood for death and the other for life.

In the way that many Socialists grow so absorbed in the political power-game that they come altogether to forget what Socialism is all about—namely, the working masses—so the American Parties became engrossed in the Party-game and forgot the State. Both lost sight of the fact that democratic politics, with its "Parties," is supposed to be a device for eliciting that illusive quantity, the Will of the Sovereign People. They forgot about the people.

So "Party" superseded the institutions which had brought it into being. As Bryce says of the monstrous growth of Party and Party organization in America: "They constitute a sort of second non-legal government which has gained control of the legal government."

38

Party became a game, bigger than all the sports-rackets put together. The money involved is past counting. Reminiscent of the Byzantine factions which grew up around the chariot races in the Hippodrome, it is a parasitic sport draining the political energies of the community.

For a contemporary parallel to this remarkable situation let us imagine that in Spain the *aficionados* of the bull ring had divided up into two nationwide factions: each faction maintaining its own teams of bullfighters and armed partisans. Then, at a Grand Fiesta every four years, one or other would be declared the victor, and would rule the country. Add to this that most of the civil and diplomatic services and government offices changed their personnel every time one set of bullfighters lost and another government came in, and you get a feeble idea of what U.S. Party organization became. Such matters as peace and war, capital and labor, grew to be secondary and, as it were, academic issues.

This is what Party may become: but what Party theoretically *is* occupies me more particularly in this chapter. Since Party has, however, suffered such strange distortions—especially in America, as the original English influence faded out —I shall later, mainly with the help of *Modern Democracies,* give some details of this fungoid metamorphosis of institutions which are no longer suited to the populations to be found there.

Party-politics is very generally accepted as the *sine qua non* of political liberty. In a London Sunday newspaper—to take an example—in the course of an article discussing happenings in Eastern Europe, was the following summing up:

". . . with all its seamy side, free party politics remains the only effective means yet devised to keep at arm's length and to protect the individual against the omnipotent State. To preserve the freedom of parties becomes more, not less, important, the more widely the powers of the State expand in the Socialist age."

That is a clear statement of the parliamentarian case for Party-politics. The great enemies of Western democracy—who claim to be themselves a better variety of democrat—are the Russians. Communist methods outrage me, and always have. Of late they have aroused violent resentment everywhere. However obnoxious other features of their doctrine, their theory of Party is deserving of study though.

The "omnipotent majority" of de Tocqueville, the "omnipotent State" (especially when Socialist) of the above columnist are objects disposing of the strength of a thousand dragons, and so causing alarm. But there are other dragons: the ones who are there in the beginning. The Socialist State comes into being after all to resist other tyrannies.

That that State in turn may grow oppressive is true, like all human institutions. But it is not an argument for Party-politics to say that the system that has kept the class superstition intact in England should be preserved in the name of Freedom. That sort of Freedom has resulted, for instance— and that is fresh in all our minds—in the shamefully ill-paid English soldier (still a "King's Shilling" soldier) being an object of contempt, socially, for the troops of other English-speaking countries: not good publicity for England, among other things.

If the above is not a good argument, what would be one? I am afraid I don't know; except that some kind of democracy is desirable: and if Party were prevented from deteriorating, as it shows a violent tendency to do everywhere, under modern conditions, and were intelligently framed in the first instance, it is a notion that deserves respectful attention.

It is a fact of some significance that the nation which many excellent judges have regarded as the model democracy, Switzerland, has been no great lover of Party. It is not the Swiss Landesgemeinde that is most impressive, but the methods of direct popular legislation which survived in the Referendum, and in some cantons the Initiative. Any grave questions of policy would still be submitted to the people by way of the Referendum. It is usually argued that everywhere the people are so conservative that it is undesirable to resort to this device. This is a highly undemocratic argument. If the Sovereign

40

People are always conservative, that is too bad: but if you do not allow them to speak, then the term "democracy" ceases to apply to your administrative procedure.

Jean-Jacques Rousseau's insistence that no government deserves the title of "popular government" unless the people participate directly in the law-making and *not through delegates or representatives* should command attention. In societies so large as ours it is only by the Referendum that direct popular action can be compassed. Without that, democracy is an anachronism. Government by "primary" assembly, in which all the adult males have their say and cast their vote, as that prevailing among the early Teutonic tribes, is today impossible. So we work along artificially, in politics, just as in economics we retain the fiction of gold. We suffer much waste and hardship because of our accumulation of fictions, at the very heart of our social life. I do not think we should object to fiction and artifice, in reasonable proportions. It is when there is nothing that is what it affects to be any longer, and our institutions and beliefs are weighed down under a murderous load of symbolism, that it is "time for a change," as Thomas E. Dewey, Governor of New York, chanted at the microphone in vain in 1944.

This, it is understood, is being very fussy about your democracy. I have mentioned these conditions for the perfect functioning of a popular government, in order to show how little what we call "democracy" or "popular government" deserves that name, more often than not.

Here is a British official statement of the case in a recent controversy. It will provide another view of the Party-system, more authoritative than my last quotation.

"The Russian system of One-Party democracy is regarded in the West as a contradiction in terms, and the divergence is accordingly fundamental."

So, in the eyes of this British spokesman, you can have no true democracy without Party. The Russians, I think the exponents of what could be called Eastern Democracy—could answer that you can have no true democracy *with* Party, unless the Parties were true Parties, which is apparently impossible in a large industrial State.

Their sincerity is not here involved: only the theory, not their usage of it. Seeing that their own system was attacked because it had only *one* Party, they would mean that the two Parties of our system had really to stand for *distinct* policies, sharply contrasted. Otherwise, they would argue, in what way was it superior to their system?

It would be a valid argument. There should be, certainly, a true polarity of opinion. The two Parties ought to represent standpoints impossible to merge. Can we decide at what point a Party attains a sufficient degree of divergence from its rival to satisfy the requirements of authentic democracy? At least we can explore this question.

6 THE DISINTEGRATION OF PARTY POLARITY

In every political belief its opposite is implicit, one dogging the other as the night the day: just as white is logically involved with black: or as the idea of heat is contingent upon the idea of cold, and vice versa. This dialectic affinity is at the basis of all affirmation of that order. And "Party" ideally would be the mustering of opposite views, and opposite interests, in any given society in two distinct camps.

In an ideal parliamentary democracy, the object would be to reach a compromise between two radically opposite standpoints, by means of public debate, resolved by the method of voting upon the matter at issue. The entire nation would adhere to one or other of these two conventional extremes. It would go to the ballot boxes to elect representatives upon one side and upon the other. But the nature of the polarity needs to be carefully defined. Such would be a rigidly logical form of the Two-Party system.

The parliamentary system in which many Parties exist, as in France, is more individualistic. It is felt—in countries where this plurality obtains—that the simplicity of the Two-Party system makes no allowance for all shades of opinion in between these conventional extremes. A voter might feel that he would sacrifice too much of his narrow personal interests by adhering to whichever of these two technically polar opposites was nearest to him. Although A might be nearer to him than B, he might nevertheless feel that neither one was quite near enough to satisfy his very special and fastidious requirements. Were he somewhere near the halfway mark, he might feel that there was not much in it. For one side would be as good, or as bad, as the other. In general his feeling would be that this was too abstract a division. At least there should be a third Party *in the center,* and preferably two more between the center and the respective extremities.

The weakness of this Multi-Partied system is that, taken to its logical conclusion, each individual citizen would be his own Party. There would be as many Parties as there are voters. In contrast to this, the Two-Party system, with its certain impersonality, seems highly acceptable. It has, as much in Great Britain as in the United States, a fluctuating character. In the present era of social and economic change the division tends more and more to conform to a class polarity. But it is never the same from one decade to the next. All that is constant is the ostensible duality: its "Two-Party" character.

In Britain today the last General Election brought Labor into power in the most decisive manner. At last we have a genuine cleavage between the two main Parties. The Labor-Capital issue is a very different one from the vague Liberal-Conservative one which preceded it. It is obvious, in a democracy, that it should be specifically stated, to begin with, *what the Parties are to be about.*

In the United States the Republican and Democratic Parties stand for no Class issue, for the Solid South, the mainstay of the Democratic Party, is at least as conservative as the Republican. From the Marxist point of view the all-important issue of Class has no part anywhere in that ostensibly "Two-Party" system. Therefore, as those people judge it, it is merely a very hypocritical *One-Party* system. It only masquerades as an inclusive system, allowing free play and open debate to the whole nation.

Again, the Communist would say that since all Russians are agreed upon the Class issue—the only issue that matters—more than one Party would be meaningless. All minor, non-Class issues can be decided, in friendly debate, within the framework of the single Party. But Class has become for a Russian a word charged—swollen—with magic, in a fairy-tale vocabulary. It is at least as unreal as the Parties of the U.S. The reality is *Power*. Power—an even worse abuse—so obviously in the Russian system has come to occupy the place vacated by Class.

The purely logical object of a Two-Party system, I have said, is to *reach a compromise* between two extremely opposite interests. The purpose of all government being *peace*—there is no other possible object, since for a permanent state of war no government would be necessary—compromise is the object of Party.

But true, irreconcilable, polar opposites know no compromise. In a parliament separated upon some fundamental issue the extremists would find themselves watered down by a majority on their side of the fence: milder people than themselves, nearer the comfortable middle than the extreme limits. In effect, then, the two Parties would not be polar opposites at all. Each would be *half-opposite,* as it were. Each would represent a standpoint halfway between a neutral center point and the extreme end of the pitch. A would not be boldly confronting B, eternally and irreconcilably opposite. It would be Ab confronting Ba.

In practice, however, retaining this linear picture of a line terminating at one end in a big B, and at the other end in a big A, bisected at a point ab, halfway—in practice the two opposite Parties, in a modern parliamentary democracy, are far nearer to ab than they are either to A or to B, probably containing no extreme elements in either. And in the United States of America—substituting the letters D and R (Democrat and Republican) for A and B—the two parties occupy positions on the line D—R, at times, which are well over the center. Mr. Dewey passed clear across the dividing mark and into the half of the line belonging to D. In fact, he was maneuvering about to *try to get in between* Mr. Roosevelt and the big letter D which stood at the far end of the Democratic section of the line: to be more democratic than the Democrats.

When this point of confusion is reached, a Two-Party system ceases to be that in anything but name. Its polarity would have disintegrated. It becomes so near to a One-Party system that the difference is really academic. The Soviet retort, outlined above, would be difficult to meet.

For a long time past, both in America and in England, people have felt that this was the position, and that the noisy partisans who spring to life at the time of an election, and denounce each other so roundly, are in reality separated by no vital issue: are playing only at being political antagonists. Whoever you vote for, you get the same thing. In the United States at the time of the Roosevelt-Willkie campaign, it was remarked by many that very little difference existed between the platforms of the two candidates. The Roosevelt-Dewey campaign was marred by the same indulgence in protective coloring (on both sides).

It is not necessary to multiply instances. Apathy was met with everywhere prior to the war. For this the public were scolded at election time by the newspapers supporting the rival candidates: in Mr. Baldwin's time it was suggested that people should be fined for not voting.

The Western Nations, on the whole, have not been good enough democrats to lecture anybody (we are born scolders), any more than our bloodstained and grasping Christianity entitles us to sit in judgment in the way we never fail to do. A moral watchdog would be of great use internationally: but we too often are like a man with a suspiciously red nose, denouncing indulgence in alcohol: we turn a stern and censorious eye upon offenses of the same character as our own.

In America the passion for *unity,* which is so striking a feature of American national life, would tend to harmonize, to the point of identity, Party differences. But it is not that which has been mainly instrumental in causing the policies of American statesmen, like those of the Republicans Willkie and Dewey, on the one hand, and those of the Democrat Franklin Roosevelt on the other, to draw so near to each other

46

that in many respects it would be difficult to tell them apart. In England any Conservative statesman of the future—should Conservatives ever enjoy another spell of power—would have to model his program so closely upon Labor policy that "Conservative" will have become a meaningless term.

7 THE NOVELTY OF THE
AMERICAN PARTY SYSTEM

When he had written his account of the American Parties, James Bryce evidently felt that what he had said would provoke incredulity. For no one has paid the attention Bryce has to this extraordinary subject. "It may be thought," he writes, "that the description here given exaggerates the novelty of the American Party system." Anyone acquainted with the United States will know that there is on the contrary understatement, if anything. A great *novelty* the American Party system certainly is.

The American no longer sees these things around him. "Evils of long standing are taken for granted." "The standard custom has set comes to be accepted; it is only the stranger who is amazed. . . ." The American takes everything for granted, from Elsie the Cow to the uproarious juvenility of the National Conventions of the Party, at which a nominee for the Presidency is elected.

Sir Henry Maine, where he was examining the Constitution of the United States, invites his readers to "clear their mental view" by adopting the Aristotelian analysis: namely the classification of all government as governments of the One, governments of the Few, and governments of the Many. As to whether government by the Many is really possible, he expressed the gravest doubt; for "wherever government by the Many has been tried, it has ultimately produced monstrous and morbid forms of government by the One, or government by the Few."

48

Bryce's description of the American Parties seems to bear out this conclusion of Maine's. It shows an attempt at government by the Many resulting in "a monstrous and morbid form of government by the Few." I have no polemical aim here, I should perhaps say. Democracy is my subject only incidentally.

There is the law that "the larger the body, the fewer those who rule it." A very handy law, for the student of institutions. And America is one of the largest countries, and its dual Party-organization represents a huge aggregate of people. All of these people, from the biggest shot of all down to the smallest, is thirsting for place and power, or just for money. "The main inducement is Office, or the assured prospect of receiving an office when the Party one serves is in power. 'What are we here for except the offices?' was the oft-quoted deliverance of a politician at a National Convention."

The Party Conventions provide the equivalent of a vast Christmas tree, upon which are hung glittering little prizes for good little boys—magistracies, inspectorships, *jobs* of every size, shape, and hue. And the whole of this national fun-fair, never stopping all the year round—for an election is always going on somewhere—is in the hands of a few men.

Here is Bryce again: "The two great Parties in the United States, counting their members by millions, have long been ruled by small cliques: and in every huge city the Organization has its Great General Staff or Ring of half a dozen wire-pullers, usually with a Boss or chief."

Most Englishmen have heard about the city Bosses so much a feature of life in the U.S.A. Their Organization is known as "the Machine." More generally, the Party Organization everywhere, in all its manifold activities, is known as the Party Machine. "It is largely self-supporting, like an army that lives off the country it is conquering, but while the Party forces are paid, by salaried posts, the funds of the Organization are also replenished by contributions exacted from business firms or corporations which its power over legislation and administration can benefit or injure." Routine blackmail of this order degenerates, in the poorer wards of the great cities, into the violence of armed gangs.

Party is everywhere: it covers the country with a close network of Committees, Primaries, and Conventions. It fights endless elections, raises money in every imaginable way. "The machinery of [Party] control in American Government" (says Henry Jones Ford) "probably requires more people to tend and work it than all the other political machinery in the rest of the civilized world."

The Party supports its Machine Organization through evil-doing and well-doing. Machines, unlike men, are not troubled with consciences. Some of its deeds are very dark. It is, however, a wonderful recruiting sergeant. It is on the lookout for immigrants, lately arrived. It turns into fervent Republicans or Democrats masses of brand-new citizens who, neither knowing nor caring what the tenets of the Party are, like to be associated with a body which brought them into the life of their adopted country. They become partisans without principles, "the solidest kind of voters."

The immigrant, whom we saw, in the chapter which described the mystical character of citizenship, being made into that novel thing, an American, we now find "joining up" in the ranks of the Democratic or Republican army: a recruit who asks no questions as to why he fights upon this side rather than upon the other (which in any case would be fairly difficult to define): who is totally without interest in policy or principle. The perfect mercenary—"the solidest kind of voter."

Each of the forty-eight states of the Union have, in miniature, the same government as has the nation. They have their individual constitutions (and their constitutions were the model of the Federal one), their own Senate and House of Representatives. The amount of electioneering and electing that is proceeding without let, in the United States, is staggering to contemplate. It is as if all the counties of England, Scotland, and Wales had a small replica of the House of Commons and House of Lords; all the year round elections proceeding up and down the land.

The Party Machine likewise—without technical justification or official sanction—is installed in all the state legislatures. This came about because the Federal senators were selected by the legislatures of the states: consequently it was necessary for each Party to fight every election of a state legislature, on Party lines, so that it should have a majority in the local legislature and secure the election of senators of its own faction to the Federal Senate at Washington.

This explains how the obsessional duality of Party—almost an Oxford and Cambridge boat-race type, of those exhibiting the Dark Blue and those the Light Blue favors—penetrated into the local governments, and eventually the city governments too. Even in hiring a charwoman, it is necessary to find out first what ticket she votes. Many Republicans would not buy meat from a Democratic butcher.

Although these great armies of people have come to be at the mercy of small political gangs, or "cliques," as Bryce tells us, all this sprang most ironically from a fanatical zeal for democracy, and the principle of popular sovereignty. That is how the Primary came into being—which became, with great rapidity, a gathering of yes-men. "Wishing to make sure of a subservient primary, the [local] Committee took care to place on the rolls only those whom it deemed to be trusty Party men, so any citizen suspected of independence was not likely to be enrolled."

To bring Bryce up to date—for he wrote before all the safeguards against the encroachments of capitalism had materialized—the Initiative, Referendum, and Recall were adopted. Twenty states have the legislative Initiative; in twenty-two there is the Referendum; and in twelve the Recall of elected officials obtains. So the Sovereign People cannot say that it is not protected. But how little difference these safeguards make is sadly apparent. Such devices merely serve as fresh opportunities for the display of corrupt and lawless ingenuity.

Even the law courts are not free from Party: the inferior quality of the judges in many states laying them open to every influence. No able advocate, learned in the law, would take

51

a common or garden judgeship. There is so much money in the law—everywhere except on the Bench. Slapstick at the expense of the judge of earlier days, who knew less law than the men haled before him, has no contemporary verisimilitude any more than the Mr. Justice Thrasher of *Amelia* could be matched today in England. But the administration of justice over large areas is still of dubious equity and mixed up with so many things that have nothing to do with justice that if in a smaller city you had occasion to employ an attorney, you would first have to inquire which Party-gang was at the moment running the city; discover to what Party the person belonged with whom you were involved in litigation—inform yourself what pull he would be likely to have in the court, and probably pick an attorney of an opposite Party to that of your antagonist. I am speaking here *en connaissance de cause,* for once I picked an attorney of the wrong color.

The Machine rules the courts, has the chief of police in its pocket. Yet these conditions, too, began in an outburst of popular democratic fervor. Again let me turn to Bryce.

Between 1830 and 1850 a wave of democratic sentiment swept over the nation. The people, more than ever possessed or obsessed by the doctrine of popular sovereignty, came to think that they must be not only the ultimate source but the direct wielders of power. The subjection of all authority to theirs was to be expressed in the popular choice of every official for a term of office so short that he must never forget his masters, and with a salary too small to permit him to fancy himself better than his neighbors. The view has persisted, and still governs men's minds in most states. It is not argued that the plan secures good judges. Obedience to a so-called principle disregards or ignores that aspect of the matter. Being in Kentucky in 1890, attending a State Convention called to draft a new Constitution, I inquired whether no one would propose to restore the old method of appointment by the Governor, and was told that no such proposal would be listened to. It would be undemocratic. In California in 1909 when, after hearing severe comments upon most of the judges, I asked whether the citizens could not be induced to secure better men by larger salaries and longer terms, the answer was that the only change the citizens would make would be to shorten terms and reduce salaries still further in order to prevent the judges from feeling class sympathy with the rich and the business corporation.

A red-hot "wave of democracy," coming from the European continent, hit America about a hundred years ago. All the countries of Europe were experiencing more or less severe attacks of social unrest, and the "wave of democracy" coincided with a wave of refugees. But this excitement died down. It left nothing behind except the instinct to boss, and new "democratic" means of satisfying those instincts, and all man's usual repertoire of uncivilized emotions.

"It is time to face the facts and be done with fantasies." So concluded James Bryce, the best-known historian of democracy, who was profoundly attached to democracy, but believed it was impossible, à l'état pur. So by "fantasies" he meant the nonsense resulting from a mixture of two opposites: egalitarian intoxication (democracy à l'état pur) and the irreducible bossiness and insincerity of man, producing a scene of chaotic comedy, punctuated with salvos from submachine-guns.

These are farces which are blood-relations of those with which the history of the Christian nations abound. Military aristocracies adopt, or rather inherit, a highly emotional religion of mercy and of love. In trying to reconcile the doctrines of the gentlest of Teachers with their violent impulses and actions, replete with everything except Christian charity, they were the cause of a vein of bloodthirsty buffoonery running through European history. As colonizers, of course, we have nearly driven mad race after race, all over the world, by the nonsense that we talked about "love" as we planted our heel on their necks.

The kind of entire democracy which Bryce considers impossible is so involved with Christianity that it is difficult to tell them apart. And all less entire and whole-hogging democracy is something else. It is only called "democracy."

53

But Bryce made use of a word, in that connection, which has a remarkable appositeness, applied to the mental habits of the American. He is not, as we find him, at all averse to *fantasy*. The farcical and violent texture of his life provokes only feebly the ethical and critical reactions which people expect.

8 AMERICAN APPETITE FOR THE INCONGRUOUS

Americans—sometimes in a sedate and morose manner, more generally with a robust matter-of-factness—have acquired even an appetite for what is always there. It was there when they were born: they have identified themselves with it. They are not more violent or dishonest than other people, just inured to breaches of the peace, to peculation and illicit spoils.

If you are disrespectful about a really atrocious murderer they will become offended. When a man is engaged in a wife-beating we recognize it as unwise to interfere. Both of them might turn on one. In much the same fashion it is better, if in the States, to affect not to be aware of a crime-wave, say, or to discuss the gang-shooting of a state senator. The latter signifies Party activity. This is very dangerous ground. Learn to take these things for granted, as does the native.

As a matter of fact, there is no doubt that it amuses them to see their city is governed by a kind of rogues' gallery, or that the "grand old Party" is living up to its tough tradition. For they are very intelligent and fatalistic, and far prefer to be amused than shocked. And when they reflect that Einstein or the Duke of Windsor has his fingerprints taken when he enters or leaves the United States—why, that improves the joke.

They have developed a great appetite for nonsense. And there is more sheer non-sense of that order in America than almost anywhere. All the hens of unreason of "civilized man" seem to have come home to roost in those parts.

No country need resent the imputation of the presence of

a great deal of unreason. It is ubiquitous: it is the lot of all of us to propagate it. There is more that is irrational in America, merely because it is the place where all the irrationality is being worked out of the transplanted European system. In the process, a great plethora of absurdity is induced.

"Graft" is an American word, again, and to be just untidy about money is a characteristic of all administrations, except the highest, in the U.S.A. In the disorder of its great and headlong growth the habits were contracted. As such it is accepted by the most unimpeachably honest, and the disorder is chronic, because such men as a crooked mayor perpetuate it. Disorder is always more amusing than order. Let us confess that a train journey is made more memorable for us if amid scenes of great confusion a thief is apprehended. Do not let us pretend that irregularities in conduct—wife-murders, arson, bank robberies, black-market shootings—are not the backbone of the newspaper Press and for most of us the salt of life. Does that make us criminals?

I do not, of course, mean that the average American is impervious to the promptings of the moral sense. But he is not such a fool as not to get fun out of a "gorilla," his pockets full of knock-out drops and lead-piping, or the fascinating grotesqueries of graft.

Again, as to the incongruous: that the American should develop an appetite for it is natural enough, since he is more alive than we are, and so outside it. It is something to be aware of the incongruous.

Let us take a few classical examples of violent incongruity: of situations that make no sense. In the past, religion—or to be more strictly accurate, irreligion—provided some of the best examples. Here is one. In every prison of, say, the sixteenth century, "the crucifix and the rack stood side by side." This was a glaring incongruity upon which the enemies of religion have naturally seized.

Next select a couple of incongruities from the present age. Simultaneously expert doctors are patching up and bringing back to life human bodies wrecked by bombs invented by other scientific experts. A man's nose is blown off by one of our fellow-men and put on again by another, both of the same fraternity. Men of science supply us with many a grand joke.

Here is another fine example of the incongruous. In the nineteenth century men looked forward to a time when our "command over nature" would be so great—our technical, "labor-saving" devices be so spectacular—that instead of the mass of men having to slave all their lives to keep body and soul together, they would at last have all their animal needs satisfied, so great would be the abundance, and leisure would be secured to them to enjoy the sweets of life; the intellectual satisfactions, the sensuous delights. But, though productive power has been multiplied a hundredfold, man is no better off. Half the population remain underfed and underclothed.

There is, of course, nothing really funny about the instances I have given. Yet this type of violent incongruity (and there are few things today, anywhere, that do not exhibit it), which seems inseparable from our half-animal existence, provides a situation which, no doubt, "makes the angels weep," but is a source of sardonic amusement here on earth. Weeping does not change anything. The angels have been weeping a long time.

Probably it was unfair to say that the United States has a finer crop of these mad anomalies than other lands. It may be an optical delusion, for which publicity is responsible. But I experienced a sympathetic appreciation of the way Americans take them: just as those who mourn at weddings and wear a complimentary smile at a burial put these events in a better perspective. I give this crude illustration in the interests of starkest clarity. One is always in danger of being thought ironical when dealing sympathetically with a paradox.

American publicity is a bizarre fairyland. It should, of course, be stamped out, and all its practitioners hanged, for lèse-majesté. (Here Majesty being the People.) But I confess to having myself developed a taste for such imbecility, as no doubt a psychiatrist succumbs to the lure of the nonsense to which he is obliged from morning till night to listen.

Much light may be thrown upon this difficult subject, and upon all its ramifications, intellectual and moral, by the contemporary art of painting, or equally that of the impressionists. For preference these painters have used the vulgarest objects of everyday use. In their pictures we are shown the mass-produced eyesores of modern life, the cheap carafe, crockery and cutlery of the dime-store type: the bright little matchbox, the repulsive print tablecloth. They would have been embarrassed by such beautiful stuff as classical Chinese ceramics. That there is politics implicit in these aesthetics is true enough, the politics of the Plain Man. But most of the practitioners were unconscious of that.

For some it would be an egalitarian assertion of the importance of the common life, a doctrinal acceptance of its unpretentious accessories. But if I interpret correctly, it was with the majority a fatalistic aesthetic rather than Socialist politics. Our civilization, compared with those of the Extreme Orient (prior to our arrival and destructive influence), is visually of the utmost vulgarity. Do not let us *pretend*—these men would say —as did the neo-classicists. Let us embrace this triviality and ugliness (it is all that there is) and transmute it into something fair, in its rough way.

Upon anyone quite unfamiliar with painting, the accuracy of this apposition may be lost. It might, in such a case, be of assistance to think of the "hideous" images, as it seems to him, which today are put on exhibition as examples of the "Fine Arts." There are many educated people who applaud and defend these "monstrosities." The American is like a grimace of Picasso's—who is endowed with a tremendous macabre humor.

For the best Americans, Elsie the Cow is on the same footing as a National Convention: they class these things together, as features of their nonsense-life. Their "love-life" often is part, too, of their nonsense-life. Their attitude is reminiscent, I think —to approach the problem from another direction—of the English fondness for nonsense in literature: as demonstrated in such popular classics as Lear's *Nonsense Rhymes,* or *The*

Hunting of the Snark, or *Alice through the Looking-Glass,* or
In Wonderland. A taste which is fundamentally anarchic: and
many an educated Frenchman has puzzled himself over this
childish lunacy.

In the case of the Englishman such hysteria is confined to
the bookshelf. The radio-active thinking stops when he puts
Alice away where she belongs, on the shelf. Not so with the
American. In his daily life he accepts upon equal terms the
rational and the irrational. Life is decidedly "screwy": instead
of trying to compel it to make sense he laughs and goes about
his business. If he sees someone killing somebody else, he may
quite likely make himself scarce. He feels these guys know their
own business best.

He lives—some more, some less—*inside* the looking-glass,
too. Politics is a Mad Hatter's Tea Party: and if there happens
to be so disturbing a figure as the Mad Hatter presiding, in
any walk of life, he likes it all the better. He craves to see the
Dormouse thrust into the teapot. He has, in his daily life, no
real Red Queens or Jabberwocks, but he has quite a nice assort-
ment of City Bosses, "gorillas," jailbird mayors, "Czars" of all
sizes, from Petrillo downward; Movie Stars as "Wolves" (with
gold-digging Red Riding Hoods), the Zootsuiter "cutting a
rug," and the Killer, pistols strapped under his armpits, wor-
shiped by the little children; the Soap Opera, with its gurgling
organ; Crooners with their sickly bleat, Radio prophets,
screaming like birds of prey; post-mortem exhibitionism in the
Funeral Parlors and the sacrificial "hot-squats" when the Law
offers up the criminal in Chthonian expiation.

More thoroughly to disinfect this of suspicion of national
bias, let me quote from an old issue of a London newspaper
(*News Chronicle,* November 7, 1945) a report of a visit to the
amusement arcades, wax-work shows, "Wonders of the World"
which had sprung up in the heart of the city. In the gaping
cavities of blitzed shops they found their opportunity.

" 'Those are cultural shows,' said George Honiball, manager
of 'Wonders of the World,' standing beside posters advertising
the 'Giraffe-necked Woman.' On the site of a blitzed furniture

shop in Oxford Street . . . for sixpence you may see wax-works of the Teheran conference . . . for a further sixpence 'flogging with a barbed-wire lash,' 'stamping to death,' 'tree-hanging,' and other horrors of the German atrocity camps depicted in wax.

" 'People love it,' Mr. Broadey, the manager, told me. 'No one more so than the men who have been prisoners themselves. They bring their wives and families here. Everyone says the models are most lifelike. We shall go on showing war scenes indefinitely, and I do not think people will tire of them for a very long time.' "

There are plenty of funny things in England, too. But one of the showmen said, "Britain needs a show-street, something like Coney Island." So we get back to America, where, as I have said, the fun has got out of the wax-work shows into real life.

A rich and crazy existence, in which anyone might meet himself coming down the street chained to another man; or as one watched the smoke pouring out of the top of the tower of Baal (the local republican skyscraper), see it turn a bright green to court the Irish vote in the near-by slums. People (big, frenzied, front-page people, and all get influenced, down to the bums) are drunk there with ideas of power all the time—mentally they live on top of skyscrapers, a little hysterical with vertigo, and they live beyond good and evil, of course. They are not as a rule critics of their civilization. Most take hot music for granted, and race-riots in which Negroes are shot up, too, not liking them, but taking them as what life is like. They are the best-hearted people in the world. But they get very easily tired of their emotions. They are only intermittently conscious. Much is automatic.

This, and the preceding chapters, has been rather like laying down an emplacement for a large gun. As it happens, it is an emplacement that will serve for three large guns: my three Presidents.

Unless you know something, as I said before I embarked on this subject of the Party soil out of which Presidents spring (to change the figure from a gun to that of a flower), it would be impossible to understand them: and not only the soil, but the rich manure I have just now been analyzing, all the detritus of the wild city life, which causes them to bloom with so violent a vigor. "Teddy" reeked almost of that thick tangy life out of which he came. His more elegant cousin was redolent of the choicer *parterres* of the country-house life of the richest Americans. But to him I now will turn.

9 THE CLUBMAN CAESAR

Franklin Delano Roosevelt was the third greatest American President. Jefferson, the originator of democratic America, the hero of the Bill of Rights; and Lincoln, who saved the Union, are the two who excel him.

No scarred and beetling figurehead for the ship of State, like Abraham Lincoln, almost a "city slicker" by comparison; beside Jefferson's intellectual endowment, a mediocre mind, however nimble. It does not even seem very certain that the late President was an extraordinary Democrat, though I say this under correction. But his non-stop Presidency effected great changes—almost, one felt once or twice, was going to slip over the invisible line dividing politics from something else. He remained, however, the politician: but so important a one that no other President except the two mentioned above (neither of whom were politicians to the same extent) deserved so high a place.

The great Party Machine, which was my subject throughout three chapters, strained, and roared, and gave off dense clouds of steam, and at last it put this man, with his terrible physical handicap, into the White House. Then really remarkable things began to happen, and continued to do so up to the moment when he put his hand up to his forehead and said, "I have a perfectly terrific headache!" and collapsed.

It was almost as if the strenuous, cunning, stupid Party junta, ignorant of the nature of their gift, had presented the nation with a Poltergeist for a President. Things began at once to fly about, at all events. And they had an uncanny habit of hitting the right people.

A radio-active something was secreted in the tall, stately interior of this bland, calm, too generously chinned figure, perpetually seated: reaching up to pin medals upon people's bosoms, or to extend a dignified glad hand and a beautifully dentured welcome—who began in the most well-mannered and easygoing way possible to govern with a witchery that made the most violent measures appear much less out of the ordinary than they were. In the end he put a spell upon the Congress: there seemed to be nothing he could not do, and at last there was nothing they would not let him do.

A man hardly above the average in visible ability, what was the secret of his success? I make the suggestion that the answer is to be found mainly in his *receptivity*. To magnify (and exaggerate) for analytical purposes, he was a tactful medium who knew his place. Add to this two assets: (1) his social position, and (2) that remarkable woman, his wife. And not to leave that out, though that alone would account for only a fraction, he was a very smart politician.

Belonging as he did to one of those not very numerous American families with a historic name, with the "backgrounds" of established wealth and, so, social position, Roosevelt brought to his great office the outlook of the "man of society." He was daring where less plushily backgrounded politicians would be cautious. He flung billions about light-heartedly, since he had no craven superstitions regarding money. His flippancy was proverbial. He was capable of frivolous decisions: he loved to astonish: the more he confused people, his supporters as much as the public, the better pleased he was.

On this side of the picture there was more than a reminder of Frederick the Great, one of whose favorite pastimes (war, of course, being sport No. 1) was ragging or hazing his entourage. But Frederick had a very vicious streak, whereas F.D.R. seems to have been kind. It was only in that one particular he was like Frederick.

He was a typical modern American of the "clubman"

species: extremely fond of the absurd, and getting a big kick out of all that was inconsequent and irrational. Out of nothing more mischievous than "mischief" he would stick a square peg in a round hole and observe its antics (for the peg, of course, was human). Often it was rumored he had lost his reason. The slander of enemies, doubtless, or else a conventional or provincial reaction to an "illogical" proceeding of his or some horseplay of his off-stage satellites.

The country had never been so lively a place, and probably never will be so lively again. Often he turned the United States up on its head, which is the best possible thing for any country. Most people forget that half of us living so eccentrically upon this spinning globe are walking upside down all the time, though which half it is who knows? Mr. Roosevelt never forgot that. Such was the kind of thing about him which makes him stand next to Lincoln, in the Presidential hierarchy, and above Jackson, who took great liberties, as did he, with the Constitution, but was not a sorcerer.

His ease and disinvolture were perfect. He conducted himself at times as would the stereotyped "cynical clubman" were that gentleman called upon suddenly—as the result perhaps of a bet—to desert momentarily his exclusive clubs, yachts, racecourses, boxes at the Opera, and govern an enormous nation. Poker-faced, without the flicker of an eyelid, he would take the controls. As one would anticipate in such circumstances, the nation shot ahead, in the most sporting style. It would have reached the goal of an intelligent, American Socialism, had not —how shall I put it?—the clubman been also a politician.

Mr. Roosevelt was a capital actor. He had one notable impersonation, namely that of his erstwhile master, Woodrow Wilson. It was uncommonly lifelike, even down to the austere Wilsonian mask. In some of his photographs at Big Three meetings it could be the "Presbyterian Priest" himself one is looking at; as also in his paraphrases of the Gettysburg Address, he walked in the footsteps of a hero of his youth.

In the interesting European groups (though I am afraid this will make it seem as if I were always ranking him *below* somebody else) it was Stalin, unassuming, matter-of-fact, without any theatricals, who makes the best impression. Mr. Roosevelt by any computation was what we call a great man. But he wanted too much to look it. For the Russian, "greatness" would seem anyway a romantic superstition of Westerners.

When Franklin Roosevelt came to power he plunged in straight away, in approved Roosevelt style; declaring he was going to be either "the best or the worst President the United States had ever had." Actually he was one of the most dazzlingly successful. With him the United States moved forward a century or so. This was, of course, the work of many people: but, as impresario, he gave them every encouragement, up to a point. No one since Jefferson had given encouragement of that type.

First he had a "brain trust," and latterly what in Jackson's day was called a "kitchen cabinet." Hopkins, Judge Rosenman and the rest, the cabinet behind the scenes, were the true Administration, much more than the big foreground figures in the ministerial limelight, who came and went.

Often they went with a farcical suddenness, as they would in a Groucho Marx film—shooting out of sight unexpectedly down a trapdoor; or after a violent altercation before the footlights, to the amazement of the spectators, a *couple* of them would be hustled off, waving their arms and protesting, never to reappear. These noisy disturbances became quite frequent toward the end. Into the showmanship crept a note of nervous violence. His pathetic chuckling "I can take it" speech, during his last election campaign, reminiscent of the final phase of Wilson's career, enlightened the audience as to the condition of the showman himself. By that time he was a dying man. And those who knew all that Roosevelt had meant for America held their breath. His disappearance would leave a dangerous vacuum.

Franklin Roosevelt undoubtedly became more frolicsome as he went on; for his appointments had a deliberately facetious look at times. Sometimes an angry frolicsomeness made itself

65

felt: his jokes were of an insulting kind, now and then. No politician *loves* his public—or only during the honeymoon period. He of course carefully peruses every morning all the insults leveled at him in the Press, daily more bitter: it is but natural, after, say, ten years of it, that he should insult back. One could only wonder how the President was able to keep his patience as well as he did. And prior to this last period of his life his equanimity was one of his most striking attributes.

This is a largish thumbnail sketch. Its aim is to bring out certain specific things about the American system, that and nothing else: regarding that aim, the character of Mr. Roosevelt, the nature of his success, and of his endowments, are invaluable evidence.

No greater centralizer than he—in an age of centralizers, or would-be ones—existed. He almost succeeded in splitting the Constitution—that most obstinate of atoms. Of the famous check-system of triune government of the United States there was not much left when he was through with it. The Supreme Court, packed with his appointees and stout Party-men, ate out of his hand. The Congress, which once had climbed up on top of the President, had never been so powerless.

No contemporary statesman was so confirmed an internationalist. He, more than any man, was in the secret of the peculiar destiny of his country.

All that he did, whether wittingly or not—and much he was personally responsible for—was *good*. He was, however, the archetype of the democratic autocrat—the "Czar" or "Caesar." Though—typically—not a New Dealer, he was firmly cemented into a Caesarian power by that remarkable organization—since Jefferson's democratic societies the greatest revolutionary phenomenon in the United States.

When, in retrospect, one considers what the New Deal accomplished, one is astonished that so great an event was not better understood in other countries. One reason was, no doubt, that it was obliged in its own country to conceal its real character, all the time. Publicists like Pegler (a first-class journalist) kept hammering away at it. From a selected batch of

Pegler's articles anybody could see exactly what the New Deal was far better than from material favorable to it. These massive polemics, invariably amusing, sometimes scurrilous, you would receive, naturally, with a shovelful of salt. Some of this columnist's conclusions you would simply reverse. Pegler has always thought the Employer infallible. If a workman asked for more pay, he must be wrong: the Employer would give it him if he ought to have it. His feelings about the New Deal may be imagined. Mr. Roosevelt was for him something like a Leader of the underworld. But he had a sharp eye for a Marxist tucked away in a Ministry.

The New Deal, however, did show a way how a civilized country could be ruled: not a new feudal world like Russia, or a military Caesarism like a Hitler. It turned the U.S. on its head. F.D.R. lay back and laughed to see such sport. It sent troops into the offices of the dread lords of industrial capitalism, picked them bodily up, carried them outside, and deposited them, speechless with rage, in the street. Within a decade this new bureaucratic power had put the big-business world under its spell. Could Roosevelt have lived a few years longer the New Deal might, for better or for worse, have effected a complete break in American tradition. They might have rewritten the Constitution—not of course torn it up—so that it harmonized with contemporary economic conditions.

The Party-system might have been superseded by the New Deal bureaucratic organization throughout the States. For it, like Party, was, strictly speaking, an illegal excrescence. And when two excrescences, both of which have usurped the functions of the legal government of the nation, come face to face, one disappears.

The greatest advertisement of Mr. Roosevelt is the New Deal: by that he will always be remembered. How could it be, then, that he was not a New Dealer? For I do not believe that he *was* anything, in that positive sense—in the sense that Stafford Cripps is a Fabian State-Socialist. One explanation is the fact that the New Deal and the Constitution could not co-exist, and F.D.R. enjoyed playing the great historic part of U.S.

President. The New Deal proposed a new kind of play altogether. Many people, of course, would say that he was, quite
simply, a New Dealer—or that he was the New Deal. That
would involve, to my mind, a shade too much seriousness for
our clubman.

When Roosevelt became President, he probably had in mind
a program of revolutionary window-dressing on the Wilson
model. He intended to go one better, of course. His aim was
not a profound revolution or revaluation, but a demagogic
power within the conservative fold. He and his wolves would
not eat up all the sheep, because they would not be wolves
but some other animal masquerading as such, in a more or less
polite terrorism.

When Wilson came into power he started something he
called the "New Freedom"—he christened his program that.
Roosevelt, his admiring disciple, started the "New Deal." But
it is unlikely that he had any idea of the energies his rallying-
cry would attract. Having opened the gates to all that was
intelligently radical, a mob of young men rushed in, and
thenceforth, smiling with a sardonic suavity, he was carried
along to ends he could not have foreseen, since he did not know
enough to be able to do that.

But he loved power as a schoolboy loves candy: he had
behind him the vast and elaborate Machine of Party (see the
chapters devoted to Party): but *that* might grow cold toward
him. Why not build up another Machine of his own, or let these
people build it up for him? He need not utterly commit himself
to it. And that is what happened: and this new Machine—
backed by the more serious labor organizations, aided still by
the Party Machine—it became practically impossible to defeat,
in the end, by democratic means. It was, of course, all highly
"undemocratic," in the ordinary Party-sense.

Conceived on the pattern of the Anti-Saloon League, the
"Political Action Committee" (a near-Marxist outfit), plus an
army of Roosevelt-appointed Federal agents in every state,
formed a solid foundation. Millions literally of these Federal
agents, many more than there was any reason for, in most states

68

exceeding in number those in the state service, were the President's private army: a great body of votes. The power of appointment—what was the old "spoils system"—is recognized as the President's greatest source of power. He did not neglect to use it. In all the forty-eight states of the Union there were Roosevelt-appointed judges; so that in his disputes with outraged magnates, in the last phases of the World War, it was not easy to find a judge willing to adjudicate against the President. And the Supreme Court was as I described it just now: solid for its patron or its Party leader. Leagues of Woman Voters and such-like agencies, in the great provincial cities, worked upon the electorate in the Roosevelt interest. There was superb Radio support, and for the war-time Press, of course, he became the war-leader: much of the sharp edge of opposition disappeared automatically. None of the violent criticism of his policy and motives which have since been heard found expression in those days. All these and many other adjuncts of democratic power (as that functions in our mass-civilization) proved irresistible at the ballot-boxes.

This is a Caesarism of an oddly elaborate and roundabout kind. It is a product of the famous "rigid Constitution" of the United States, when that instrument is sufficiently boldly interpreted. An elective kingship, it insures enormous power to a skillful politician, with few scruples about "democracy," and not afraid of Wall Street.

Roosevelt had, of course, the best legal minds at his disposal, to tell him just how far he could go. It was as far as any ruler can go, short of open despotism, or totalitarian or Cromwellian "Protectorship" or Führership. But it is really more rule by a group than by an individual. Alexander Hamilton would have delighted in this "elective king," as a brilliant exponent of the principles of personal power, and consummate centralizer. But his economic escapades would have broken Hamilton's heart, could he have witnessed them.

This kind of ruler is a peg on which to hang power. When he is receptive and accommodating he can be a Trojan Horse for a democratic group, ruling collectively inside his hollow frame. Before proceeding to what I now am arriving at, let me put it in this way. F.D.R., it appears to me, was a great frame, rather than a great picture. But much upon which we bestow that flattering epithet of "great" is just that. And to be a *great frame* is not so easy as it looks. It is extremely praiseworthy.

In the States it is regarded as bad form to be perfectly idle. They have to "work." But Roosevelt was born potentially one of this "idle rich" class of privileged "workers," and he possessed what is a marked characteristic of that class, he was no great scholar; passing his law exams, for instance, with considerable difficulty.

He did not, however, shy away from learning in another man, as do most of those conscious of limitations in themselves. On the contrary, he used brains wherever he found them and would even get these brainy fellows to write his speeches for him. (The public were always told, semi-officially, who had written such and such a speech of the President's.)

Perhaps the "man of society" came in here again. He was so well satisfied with being what he was that he despised, in true American fashion, all the things that make a man a "brain-truster": was that it? However that may be, beaming at them with his big animal chin and extending his hand in a welcoming sweep of "well-bred" patronage, he sucked in anything that displayed the glitter of vitality. He had a veritable genius for assimilation. In the end there he sat, a composite colossus, his Presidential stature growing daily. His Presidential throne was surrounded by human shells he had thrown away.

All are agreed that this glamorous Chief Executive was the reverse of unattractive. One of Mr. Truman's supporters, referring to his association with the late President, observed that being with him was like making a meal off nothing but caviar. For his part, he declared, he was glad to get back to ham and eggs. (This fare, of course, was Mr. Truman.)

Mayor La Guardia, one time, on leaving the White House, was reported to have shaken himself, inhaled a deep draught of fresh air, and exclaimed: "After spending a few hours like that with the President is like coming away from a necking party." His clubmanesque, his Rooseveltian charm was from all accounts overpowering.

He was a Democrat in one sense, in contrast to Wilson. He worked readily with and through other people. He could never have performed what he (ostensibly) did without the daily and hourly co-operation of a staff of people often far more individually gifted than himself, as well as possessed of special knowledge he had never troubled to acquire. But it seemed to him this was just as it should be. A President of the United States is the creation of many minds and wills. He is a *collective* phenomenon. That was thoroughly understood by Roosevelt.

Few men so placed, however, would have picked assistants so self-effacingly (or so smilingly have allowed himself to be picked): with so fine an instinct for this queer collectivist game. His "build-up" of himself was slick and deft. Who would have picked, or let himself be picked by, the New Deal except F.D.R.? Though even he got frightened now and then by these dynamic associates.

Finally I arrive at that part of my Presidential portrait-sketch where what seems to be a blemish must be dealt with. This blemish has a most obvious bearing upon his radicalism. It raises the question of his sincerity.

He and his predecessor and relative, "Teddy" Roosevelt, both started with a most valuable contempt for the rich. This was very rare even in F.D.R.'s generation, and was a first-class asset. In his autobiography the first Roosevelt wrote: "Of all forms of tyranny the least attractive and the most vulgar is the tyranny of a plutocracy." He was in some ways an even more extraordinary demagogue: I think that F.D.R. at no time referred to a capitalist he had gone after as a "fat spider." His exuberant relative did, however. "Why did you call Mr. Hill a fat spider, sir?" another spider demanded of the President. "That is *my* way of putting it," the President blandly answered. James Hill was the rail-king, and hero of "the Bum Song."

This detachment from the world of wealth was perhaps Franklin Roosevelt's greatest asset. Without that—no New Deal! But of course history will recall—and here I am afraid objective criticism supervenes—that both he and his Republican relative, Theodore, remained rich men; enjoyed all the advantages without stinting themselves of being rich, with the prestige that riches gave in a "plutocracy," while at the same time enjoying the advantages of being anti-riches.

You overawe people with your clubmanesque airs and graces, you live at Hyde Park (the name of his estate) in seigneurial style, *and* you derive great fame and personal advantage from denouncing the rich and all their works. That was no doubt to be wanting in entire honesty: the thoughtful historian of the future will conclude that, I am afraid. Again the late President liked rich men all right, to share his "old-fashioned" and enjoy some pleasant company; but for him there were *the right rich,* and *the wrong rich.* For Lenin, let us say, there was no such thing as *right rich.* All were wrong. But, of course, the statesman we are discussing was a demagogue, in a different universe from Lenin. He was a middle-class demagogue, a very recognizable product of the old Party-system. The "forgotten man" got something out of him. But he got far more out of the "forgotten man."

One does decidedly have a rather disagreeable sense of snob-appeal throughout the Roosevelt showmanship—even down to the naming of his property Hyde Park. The "aristocrat" notion was played up, heavily, all along, it cannot be denied: and one would meet in America many a little reactionary who, though he or she winced at the thought of the New Deal, and loathed most of his politics, spoke with a crooning deference, a complacent affection for this great gentleman in the White House, naughty radical though he was!

No picture of Mr. Roosevelt would be complete or truthful without some special stress on this—that he owed almost as much to the snob-appeal as to the appeal to the underdog. One hesitates to say this, because he *was* of great use to the underdog.

The English reader, accustomed to aristocratic Prime Ministers, will not see the full force of the above remarks unless he is made acquainted with a cardinal fact of American political life. I refer to the noticeable absence or scarcity of the rich class in politics. Leaving out, of course, the earliest days of the Republic, the plutocracy, who have always ruled America, do not go into politics at all, which they regard as degrading and "second-rate." They prefer to work behind the scenes. The Presidents have almost invariably been poor men—professional politicians. Whereas in England politics has traditionally been a playground of the rich, the aristocratic.

The same rule applies to the American Army or Navy. As there is no money to be made in either of these callings, they have always been despised, like the teaching profession. Under such circumstances it was a great novelty, in the case of both the Roosevelts, to have a rich man in the White House. The financial oligarchy must have greatly disliked Franklin Roosevelt's candidature: and it is most unlikely that the Republicans would have tolerated a second Roosevelt after all the trouble they had had with Teddy.

Let us at the last, however, forget this blemish. F.D.R.'s services to the United States were of such magnitude that this personal frailty is unimportant—if it was a frailty, for he may just have played up his "background" for all it was worth to outwit the snobbish element, and so camouflage his dark designs against them. The First Lady could have got away with murder in the Back Bay or in the snob-troughs of the half-gilded end of the remoter cities.

I think we had better leave Franklin Roosevelt out of the count and concentrate on the other two Presidents, even if he is evidence for what I am trying to prove.

And how joyously he piloted his way, in the seething sea of unutterable nonsense in which all popular statecraft in America has to navigate, with a bump here, and a bump there, as his administration collided with some hoary absurdity. He understood no other President had the really irreducible nature of those barnacled superstitions and crazy prejudices which clutter the waters athwart which the ship of State is obliged to direct its course. With that rag-time thinking which, in one form or another, since the early days of this century, has been recognized as what is most essentially American in America (over against, for instance, the *bel canto* spirit of Italy, the proud Berber stamping, guitars and castanets of the Spanish world, or the martial crashing of Germanic orchestras which emotionally fastened upon the Teuton that heavy dream of Power) —with that transatlantic philosophy this great American man of action was imbued.

10 WORSHIP OF THE EMPIRE-BUILDER

The genial autocrat with whom the last chapter was concerned
and the other autocrats to whom I shall turn in a moment
could have been as powerful as they were solely by virtue of
two things, (1) the great powers secured to the President of the
United States by the Constitution; and (2) conditions, obtaining in any great industrial State, whereby unprecedented power
is enjoyed by government, to which the highly centralized
organization of so vast a country as the States must be added.

There is, however, in America a third factor, favoring the
development of autocracy. This is the hero-cult which has
grown up around the figure of the President. The most mediocre little provincial politico, once he steps into the White
House, as the "ruler of America" (the words of Roosevelt II's
First Lady), is spoken about with a quite different intonation
by everybody; with a quiet but solemn deference for which
nothing but some kind of "divine right" would account.

Macaulay (as quoted by an American historian) wrote:
"Every political sect has its esoteric and its exoteric school, its
abstract doctrines for the initiated, its visible symbols, its imposing forms, its mythological fables for the vulgar. It assists
the devotion of those who are unable to raise themselves to
the contemplation of pure truth by all the devices of . . .
superstition. It has its altars and its deified heroes, its relics
and its pilgrimages, its canonized martyrs and confessors, and
its legendary miracles."

These words, applied to sect, or to Party, could be endorsed by a profusion of evidence. The Communist Party, with its Lenin mausoleum, its many saints and martyrs, provides a striking instance. But a great State, in process of militant growth, as much as a sect or Party, or more so, can supply us with the same mythical accessories, celebrating its triumphs and its power.

From Abraham Lincoln to Franklin D. Roosevelt, American history betrays a remarkable continuity. The same pattern of events seems, under various guises, to be repeated: the same order of personality makes its appearance, to preside at the unfolding of exceptional events. It is not just a repetition, however; it has the character of a progress toward something or other.

From Lincoln onward this progress is easy to trace, particularly with respect to the "high spots" and big figures, especially wars, or war-leaders, or would-be war-leaders. It is abruptly halted—history goes into reverse—as at Pueblo, Colorado, on September 25, 1919, when President Wilson suffered a paralytic seizure from which he never recovered, occasioned, it was said, by the popular hostility with which he had everywhere been met, as he toured the States and expounded his ideas regarding a Society of Nations, which America, he argued, should join and underwrite.

The force which opposes it—for its progress has been painful and forever under heavy attack from within—sometimes violently registers its opposition, as when, on April 14, 1865, Abraham Lincoln was assassinated by the actor John Wilkes Booth—no one knows why, apparently, except the historian with a sense attuned to the dramatic logic of events.

At the ceremony of inauguration as President, Theodore Roosevelt wore a ring sent him by John Hay, containing a lock of hair cut from the head of Abraham Lincoln on the night of his murder. This rather savage relic, casketed upon the tanned fist of the incoming rancher President, was rightly seen by the latter to be ceremonial and symbolic. In having this ring on his hand he regarded himself bound, in his own words, to "treat the Constitution after the manner of Abraham Lincoln, as a document which put human rights above property rights when the two conflicted." The Rights of Man come first in this ritualistic way of thinking. But the "great Presidents" will always be the war-Presidents: war always being prosecuted against a background of the Rights of Man.

What makes this—whatever it is—keep on coming back, realizing the same type of action, and making the successive high priests take on the same moral attributes, use the same gestures, hark back to the same evangelistic vocabulary, is an evolutionary-historic phenomenon. It first got itself described as "Manifest Destiny": "an irresistible impulse in the racial life." That was long before Lincoln, when America incorporated a third of Mexico into the ever-expanding bulk of the master-State of the Western hemisphere.

A phenomenon of growth and crystallization accompanied by incantations which have long since ceased to correspond to contemporary realities; by blood-sacrifices ordained almost, but which are modest in dimension, having regard to the scale of the operation: this is what it is. For America is an uncompleted organism still. It will continue to grow, to "expand," on the one hand, and to suffer alteration and internal adjustment, on the other, until it reaches its preordained limits, and takes on what is to be its final shape and character. For we do not know what it is quite or where it begins and ends, as yet. It will reach perhaps someday from Ellesmere Land to Tierra del Fuego. Such a destiny—"manifest" or otherwise—is no trivial affair. It calls for ceremonial. Even, it has its temples.

"The obelisk to Washington and the memorial to Lincoln on the Mall of the capital of America express the judgment which has been worked out from the American culture to which so many inscrutable things have contributed in the last sixty-five years." So writes Mr. Lee Masters, an enemy of that culture. But there are many, of course, who blaspheme.

Lincoln is the object of the most elaborate cult of any of America's political demigods. The great sanctuary of this cult is at Washington: the Lincoln Memorial. The capital city bears the name of Washington, and he has his obelisk: but the

Lincoln Memorial is its major shrine. As to this famous sanctuary—in which, uncovered, stand hushed groups of pilgrims —"analysis reveals significant characteristics," says Professor Gabriel, of Yale. "It is a Greek temple. Within it is a graven image. [This] is a romanticized Lincoln. Three devices enhance the religious atmosphere; on the walls in bronze are the words of the hero; a light falls from the ceiling upon his forehead; and above the brooding figure is an inscription. It reads: 'In this temple as in the hearts of the people for whom he saved the Union the memory of Abraham Lincoln is enshrined forever!' "

What Mr. Bernard Shaw spoke of somewhere as "the most celebrated birthplace of the Western World," is at Stratford-on-Avon, Warwickshire, and is that of a poet.

This is a quite extraordinarily significant fact. Neither Pitt nor Cromwell, with us, nor for that matter the famous Queen, who was the sovereign of our national poet, attracts so much popular veneration.

The English built something, too, about which any other people, large or small, would have made a monstrous fuss. But the builders of the British Empire—Clive, or Wolfe, or Cecil Rhodes—occupy a very secondary place in their homeland compared with the man who wrote plays for Londoners three centuries and a half ago.

Even a famous President of the United States—who might himself have been a candidate for political apotheosis—expressed himself as follows: "I would not have you think that the writer of books is less steadily in search of reality than the builder of states or the builder of great material enterprises or the man who is in the midst of action."

But these are the exceptions: the exoteric in this cult has an unusually high percentage of clients.

Had the English acquired their empire in a similar spirit to that in which the United States has expanded, certainly it would not be a great humanistic poet, but a great empire-builder, whose birth-town would be the show-place of England. And perhaps a group of temples would have risen along the banks of the Thames, beyond the Houses of Parliament, in which crowds would stand bareheaded before colossal statues of the superman who acquired Rhodesia, or him who was mainly responsible for the British Raj. But the Whigs and Liberals saw to it that nothing of that kind happened—the same Whigs who assisted the Americans to secure their independence of a Tory Britain: the same Liberals who did their best to stop the plunderings of nineteenth-century English adventurers.

Anyone who has taken the trouble to read the story of British colonial expansion is aware that it was much against their will (and often they resisted with great spirit) that the English received the present of so unbecomingly large an empire. They were Romans *malgré eux*—whether it was the Whigs who impeached Warren Hastings, or tried to put a brake on Clive: whether the unlikely Lord Glenelg or Mr. Gladstone, the English statesmen who had enormous slices of empire suddenly thrust upon them—wet with the blood of Kaffir or of Fuzzy-Wuzzy—were at least as shocked and disturbed as was the late Mr. Willkie, when he contemplated the compromising spectacle of this imperialist anomaly—of one of the main partners of the United Nations engaged in a "war of liberation"—still possessed of all this ancient loot. We should be doing Mr. Willkie less than justice if we recalled in this instance that Great Britain is the principal trade rival of the States: that, minus its Empire, it would be commercially and financially pretty small beer. Finally, the secession of the American colonies in the eighteenth century was warmly applauded by the English Whigs, the predecessors of the Liberals: and the Americans received at the hands of Whig ministers most generous terms, almost as if to reward them for having been so Whig as to rebel against that Tory monarch George III. To this I shall return in a later chapter.

Reverting to the American sanctuaries, the fact is that the creation of this New World, this super-State, America, is generally regarded as an event of such exclusive importance that its political architects—to the exclusion of any other type of man—have been invariably selected for apotheosis. Washington is a demigod of equal though not superior status to Lincoln: for Washington it was who started the building, and Lincoln it was who prevented it from falling apart, at a most critical period of its construction.

This great material task, the building of a State—to be the biggest, most powerful, richest State on earth; the increasing of the power of that State in every direction, expanding it from coast to coast, filling it up with people, consolidating its "missionary" temperament, as the metropolis of the Free, concentrating control of it in the industrial area (the North), building up the power of the central Executive as against its semi-sovereign sub-states, and of the political as against the juridical: this is what counts to the mind of the American, and it counts so much that scarcely anything else counts.

Unquestionably there is something obsessional in Americanism. Its zealots are not as other men. This great communal enterprise, like the erection of a cathedral in the age of faith, has functioned at the expense of the individual. But it is quite certain that, had the citizens of this new nation not concentrated fanatically upon the making of America, it would have grown up a rather ramshackle, patchwork polity—if it had not long ago fallen apart into a number of independent republics, as it threatened to be going to do on December 20, 1860, when the South Carolina convention met at Charleston, and proclaimed that "the Union now subsisting between South Carolina and other states under the name of the 'United States of America' is hereby dissolved."

It is easy for anyone to see the sacrifice entailed in the narrowing down of human life, where material power is the sole aim. Personal freedom, that great luxury, has to be largely forgone. The conditions, to some extent, of a police-state supervene. Standardization compels all those non-conformities we speak of as "freedom" into a single giant mold. Mass-production has as its corollary the mass-mind—"syndication" is productive of the syndicated mind. Anything comes to be denounced as "un-American" which does not respond with a zealot "Yes!" to some fiat of government.

In Germany an effort of the same kind, which built up the Reich in a few generations into a great industrial and military State, had analogous results: docility, in the land of Luther, became a byword throughout Europe. Rapidly it put a stop to the cultural output which in the peace of the sleepy courts of grand-duchies and small kingdoms had made the German name synonymous with the life of thought and feeling. "Guns are better than butter" is a slogan which can be adapted to include all the other things that guns displace. "The music of the guns," as an example, "is preferable to that of the finest fugue." By the time the National Socialists arrived on the scene the Germans had so deteriorated that few could any longer play an instrument, as formerly most could: they read no books; their philosophers had turned into Gestaltists: their personal creative passions had shriveled to the roots. They were creating, with a collective passion, not a cathedral but a Festung Germania, a mighty totalitarian machine. The National Socialists were the last insane throw of the dice, in the game called *Machtpolitik*.

With the German nation, as with the American, *union* was the master aim, to which everything else was sacrificed. The State-cult of Hegel, the nationalism of Fichte, the blood and iron of Bismarck, the martial orgies of Wagner, conjuring up legendary hosts, have had no parallel, of course, in America. And there is this great difference between the two cases: *union* spelt different things in Germany and in the United States respectively. In the former it was a feudal hangover: union and the power so secured had for its end domination. Whereas the only person an American has ever wanted to dominate is another American: Union was ideally to assure adequate strength to maintain inviolate what is still called the "American way of life."

It is deplorable, but so innocent a motive has not left America in a much better case, culturally or socially, than Germany: for which, however, the blight of the plutocracy is as much to blame as the demands of an infant-state, growing at a record speed.

We are so used to the United States that we cannot imagine its not being there. We forget what a mushroom it is. Yesterday it was not there (in the "yesterday" of historic time). A realization of the immense speed at which it has shot up, assuming the proportions of a giant among States, as it were overnight, induces in the observer a sense of great instability.

At the time of the death of Queen Elizabeth in 1603, England did not possess a square inch of territory outside itself. Yet in 1775 a country a hundred times its size parted company with it—a country which *in the meanwhile* it had brought into existence. In the natural history of nations that is a speed record, surely.

Some American cities provoke the same kind of impression. Detroit, for instance, is enormous. Splendid hotels, one or two even betraying signs of imminent decay; streets in formerly fashionable quarters taking on a venerable pathos already—altogether it looks anything but *new,* except a little at Grosse Point, where the richest people now live. Yet this city is coeval with Henry Ford; with the motor industry. Fifty years ago it was not there. People remember Henry Ford coming round to fix their electric light, when Ford was the employee of an electric lighting plant, and Detroit quite a small place.

It is paradoxically the absence of any signs of youth—the fact that nothing looks *fresh* or *new* in the cities of the New World—that is responsible, more than anything else, for this strange impression—the sense of an apparition.

The "ghost-towns" are phenomena of a similar order: Cobalt in Ontario is an excellent example. The presence of a mineral deposit causes a city to spring up out of the earth, complete with central heating systems, hotels, churches, poolrooms, drugstores, taverns, and so forth. Something goes wrong: the mines close down, and in a few weeks the town is a "ghost." It begins to sink back into the earth.

It is a commonplace, of course, that everything in the United States has a short life, lacks continuity: dwelling houses, as much as factories, spring up, of enormous size, for a short spell of life—like the life of a dog, short and of feverish vitality. The quick-growing vegetables, for nature participates in these modes, lack the flavor of the European species (with some exceptions, like the Idaho potato).

In general, the form of this community is not the final form. It is something that is subject to sudden and to violent alteration. It came into being violently, and waxed very quickly. Its capacity for dynamism has not been exhausted, it is obvious. Its destiny is a great question mark.

The political mythology, fixity of its traditions, adherence to the letter of its written Constitution—that is the principle of permanence in this flux. Someday—any day—these may suffer profound alteration, even be discarded, in favor of some other framework. Meanwhile, they are a spine existing in the midst of a very active jellyfish.

These propensities of the American mind, which I have been attempting to analyze, almost invite Caesarism. It would be difficult for an ambitious man not to avail himself of the opportunity. The religious conception of the State, the idea of a messianic destiny which is implicit in a cult of the young, superlatively powerful commonwealth produce of their own accord, almost, the autocrat.

The subject of the next chapter, Theodore Roosevelt, is related to Franklin Roosevelt in more ways than by the blood-tie. The former was the first of the three world-famous American twentieth-century demagogic Caesars. And he prepared the way for his successors.

During the period of Woodrow Wilson's governorship of New Jersey, when he first stepped out into the political limelight, and began publicly formulating his policy, he took almost automatically the demagogic path. "Part of Wilson's success . . . was due to an electorate aroused by years of agitation by the Muckrakers, by Roosevelt's stirring appeals, by La Follette's spectacular struggles in Wisconsin, by the unremitting campaigns of William J. Bryan."

"Muckrakers," it is interesting to note, was a word coined

(in contempt, curiously enough) by Roosevelt I. The mere fact that a Republican President had indulged in denunciations of corruption, of Boss-rule, of the intrigues of great finance corporations, imposed upon his successors, especially a Democrat like Wilson, some show of "idealism." More "idealism" than he would perhaps under other circumstances have exhibited was forced upon Wilson by what had gone before. The shadow of the egregious Teddy's "big stick" fell across all his doings from the beginning. Even, according to Mr. Lippmann, Theodore Roosevelt had to *jog* him into going to war.

11 RANCHER-CAESAR, OR THE MAN WITH THE MIND OF A BOY

The fluctuating emotional cycle, of alternations of self-centered passivity and of great spasms of aggression, by which the political life of America has been characterized, offered in the year 1898, to the inquiring student, a perfect opportunity for field-work. Spain, in Cuba, had been stamping out the fires of insurrection less than a hundred miles from the coasts of the U.S.A. Theodore Roosevelt had declared, in his inimitable way, "McKinley has no more backbone than a chocolate éclair." No one should stamp on anyone smaller than himself in Uncle Sam's back yard!

McKinley played the chocolate éclair as long as he could: the fire-eaters in his Party, thirsting for profits or for glory, were difficult to withstand. But someone, or something, blew up the U.S. battleship *Maine* in Havana Harbor. Two hundred and sixty lives were lost. There was nothing much the most backboneless man could do after that. It was war. Theodore Roosevelt, dressed as a cowboy, started, in a blaze of publicity, on his road to the presidency.

That same year a somewhat prophetic book was published called *Rise and Growth of American Politics,* by H. J. Ford. It was an "Idea of a Patriot King," for the *fin de siècle* Americans, about to be born into the twentieth century: "the American Century."

(The American Presidency is, of course, an elective kingship. Secretary Seward, asked about the American system of government, was succinct on this subject. "We elect a king for four years, and give him absolute power within certain limits.")

Ford had a tiresome mind, was a reactionary: nevertheless, he was a force in his way. Considering what happened immediately afterward, his book strikes one as uncannily à propos. It appeared in 1898: three years later Theodore Roosevelt entered upon his "messianic" Presidency. It is amusing to speculate whether the new President by any chance had had his thoughts turned in the direction of a Chief Executive very near to the people, whose idol he was; naturally a "patriot"— ready to go to war at a moment's notice, with anyone so foolish as to give him the shadow of an excuse; and of course a bulwark standing between the Trusts and the millions of forgotten men threatened by them.

Bolingbroke wrote, "a patriot king, at the head of a united people." In order to be truly *united,* according to Bolingbroke, the Party-system (which had not long before come into existence) must be abandoned, or reduced to a minimum. Since this "miracle" king would be the enemy of Party or of faction, his would be in effect the One-Party State. This was the inspiration of Ford: was it to any extent a stimulus, via Ford, for the Bull Moose?

Theodore Roosevelt, though ruling over a Two-Party State, was no friend of Party—in the end breaking away and founding a Party of his own, since the Republican Party was too narrow to contain him. This was named the "Bull Moose Party." But since Bull Moose was synonymous with Roosevelt, it might as well have been called the Roosevelt Party, as any Party to which he adhered would in fact become.

He was a novel kind of Republican. For was not the Party which he was supposed to represent that of the "malefactors of great wealth"? Such was his customary way of referring to the Republican magnates who had put him (a fellow-capitalist) into power. It was much as if a Tory Prime Minister indulged in philippics against "landed parasites," occupying millions of acres in an overpopulated island, which, if taken from them and rented out to farmers, could provide food for those under-privileged masses, who at present are so ill-fed that they are scarcely able to get through the day's work: or against "those fat spiders, the insurance companies," say, with their bloated surpluses, running into millions a week, who "batten upon the poor." That, as a parallel, is not far off the mark.

Or focus your mind, in fancy, upon a "trust-busting" Mr. Baldwin. A Tory Prime Minister, developing unexpectedly those proclivities, could not remain in office a fortnight. Even in America, accustomed as they are to emotional outbreaks, people rubbed their eyes in astonishment, until they decided that his bark was worse than his bite, and that he was just a very smart politician. But those he barked at got very tired of his barking.

Of inherited riches he had himself taken the fullest advantage from an early age. His biographers show us the young Theodore at Harvard, smartly hatted and gloved, driving a phaeton along the banks of the chilly Charles into Boston (with or without groom, I forget). Very much the rich young man: with a beautiful patroonish name and, although a sickly youth, addicted to every sport, as should be the young blood. It is a *snobbish* picture. And it is hardly the kind of beginning you would expect for a political moralist, a crusader against the selfish rich.

Political opponents were, of course, well aware of the confusion imported into politics by this new crusading technique. They knew that their own promises of reform were never fulfilled, any more than he intended to fulfill his: but oh, what a complicated game it must become if everyone were to start in promising the same beautiful impossible things! Bryan ruefully declared that Mr. Roosevelt had "bodily stolen every plank in his platform." Governor Dewey, to whose electoral techniques I have already alluded, incurred the same criticism, namely that he was trying to out-New Deal the Democrats.

But Theodore Roosevelt had thought out a plan of action, as when he wrote—later on, it is true, but such had always been his idea: "I wish to do everything in my power to make the Republican Party the Party of sane, constructive radicalism, just as it was under Lincoln." Like F.D.R., he felt himself all the time as standing in some especial relationship to Lincoln.

The "theory" of Lincoln and Jackson he took as his model: by which he meant that in certain cases it was the President's duty to disregard the Constitution and act on his personal initiative. The word "constructive" usually connotes "conservative," and his radicalism was noisy, nothing more. Yet it startled the privileged classes, as it won him the adulation of the "one-suspender" type.

"A Republican President is a President of things as they are. A Democratic President is a President of things as they ought to be." This handy formula, for which a Mr. Baker was responsible, applied to that first of three twentieth-century messianic Presidents, would make nonsense. He was *a Republican President of things-as-they-ought-to-be,* a contradiction in terms.

"Another phase," writes Ford, "of popular sentiment in our own times that has its prototype in English politics of the eighteenth century is that which may be described as the Messianic Hope of politics—expectation of the advent of some strong deliverer. The ideal President or Governor who rises superior to Party, and calls all good citizens to his support, is Bolingbroke's 'Patriot King' in republican dress."

Whether Theodore Roosevelt had derived inspiration from this book or not, as I have said, I do not know, but certainly he regarded himself as a Messianic Hope—a "strong deliverer" from "the Romanoffs of our social and industrial world," the Hills and Morgans. His relative and namesake, three decades later, felt just the same about it. But whereas T.R. accomplished nothing, F.D.R. shook the world of "malefactors of great wealth" to its foundations. He was, however much or little he really deserved to be, a deliverer.

Theodore's views upon war were identical with those of Adolf Hitler: namely that there was nothing in the world could hold a candle to it. It brought out all that was best in you! In his biography Roosevelt wrote: "Love of peace is common among weak, short-sighted, timid, and lazy persons." But most Americans are "short-sighted" like that, and let him down badly a number of times: one even shot him. On one occasion he became "sick at heart" at "the way that the country as a whole evidently approves of them [Wilson and Bryan] and backs them up." "My belief is," at another time, "that the country is not in heroic mood." The slogan "He kept us out of war" was what assured the re-election of Woodrow Wilson. What can you do with a people like that—timid and lazy?

It is needless to say that the *cause* (a good cause or a bad cause) did not enter into the picture. Only "heroism." "Heroism," of course, stimulated by the boyish desire in the bosom of the common man to demonstrate that he is not a chocolate éclair—a sissy or a quitter. (There are a whole battery of schoolboy epithets to bring about the desired result.)

Under analysis I do not feel sure that Teddy's boyishness would prove to be authentic. His official biographer, J. B. Bishop, writes: "The peculiarity about him is that he has what is essentially a boy's mind." But since this public man recognized that his Public was immature, is it not probable that he arranged for his mind to remain that of a boy, in order to fit himself for his part in public life, that of the strenuous rip-snorting demagogue?

Against that theory it must be agreed that one would have to have a distinct appetite for what is childish to play the part so thoroughly. This type of man always presents a big psychological problem, however. There are many varieties of the boy-man: Kipling was one, for instance. It is a problem of the same order as the red-nosed clown who sends all the children into fits of laughter, but who in private life is reported as being of a melancholic turn.

As to his morbid pugnacity, that, under analysis, would be shown to be authentic: of glandular origin, probably. War of any kind was very dear to him. Jefferson said, "Peace is my passion." With this great twentieth-century sportsman it was just the other way round. So naturally it would be a matter of indifference what a war was about. Ethics would spoil the sport: a "good cause"—anything *good*—might have a dampening effect. One needed no excuse for *"la bonne guerre."*

While World War I was in progress (into which he had

"jogged" Wilson) he never ceased to be "sick at heart": for no one would let him get any publicity out of it. It was the most wretched period of his life: the whole world resounded with the roar of guns and exploding bombs, and he, the "Colonel," in spite of all his appeals, out of it all! To this "sickness at heart" in the end he succumbed.

When he went stalking lions and other big game in 1908, had one of them got him instead of his getting it, would not that have been a better end? Then he would not have come back to watch Taft enjoying power, and he out of it all: not have seen himself rejected as a Bull Moose: nor eventually have experienced the mortification of seeing another man (a college president!) take the United States into a war of epic proportions.

This college president, one of the three political messiahs who have occupied the White House in this century, was upon a higher human plane than this obstreperous vulgarian. Wilson needed no "tennis cabinet," like Theodore Roosevelt. He was his own brain-trust. His speeches abound in happily turned phrases and massive literate eloquence. Not since the early days of the Republic had there been so literate and completely educated a President, not since Jefferson or Adams. Whereas Teddy was the *énergumène,* as the French call it, standing for all that is immature and violent in America.

Teddy was the crazy extrovert: although much shrewder than he would seem to anybody watching him flinging himself about and mouthing imbecilic slogans, he was not an exponent of "Italian policy," like his namesake. And to turn back to F.D.R. for a moment, *his* war was one that had to occur, as part of the universal purgation. It was conducted with great firmness, and without heroics. (Imagine what an unseemly uproar there would have been had Teddy been at the helm.) So there is no point of comparison there between the two Roosevelts. War did not mean for one what it did for the other. And as we come to consider Wilson, it is necessary to remember that the work of Franklin Roosevelt's administration in the domestic field was really revolutionary.

The weak spots in F.D.R. belonged to his office and are inseparable from it, and from the routine of a democratic politician: which is why I included him at all in this grouping.

Woodrow Wilson, equipped with a specialist's knowledge of American history—and armed with an invincible sense of superiority to the ignorant multitude—left the governorship of New Jersey to occupy what he described as "the most perilous helm in Christendom," with all the frigid ardor of his nature. His mind was made up: he was determined to do or die, knowing the risks for a man of his inflexible mold in mounting so haunted a throne—so deceptively commonplace and homely a one in appearance. All right if you did not sit down on it too heavily, or exact from it more than a modest measure of authority. But he went to it as a messianic king and, as it proved, martyr.

12 THE "PRESBYTERIAN PRIEST"

Erect, professorial, reeking of integrity, Woodrow Wilson, at the age of fifty-four, suddenly deserted his quiet study at Princeton University, and strode out into the fierce world of American politics, like a figure from the pages of Bunyan. The inmates of the thieves' kitchen into which he so unexpectedly burst—and Jersey City ranks with the toughest America can show—looked up in amazement and alarm.

His "high-principled" eyes level and stern behind coldly glittering glasses; inner rectitude imparting a prim starching to the outer man; the bland glare of the dominie intimidating only the more because of the frosty political smile which, as a candidate, he wore: he must indeed have spread consternation. For he was there to propose himself as next Governor of the state. They did not know what to make of it at all, the myrmidons of Boss-rule. No man of the type of the "Presbyterian priest" had ever done this before. Had he come there to reform them? Or was he a paradoxical recruit to the racket? Some approached him gingerly, to try to find out what was at the bottom of this unwelcome intrusion, and then, still baffled, went away to report to their superiors. Others laughed derisively.

But he began his campaign for the governorship of New Jersey, great success attending his first public appearances. The novelty of his personality and high-sounding language captured the attention of his audiences. Instead of having their emotions appealed to—and as a rule their less edifying ones— here for the first time it was their reason that was the object of a dignified attack. Their conscience, too, was dragged into politics—as if it had been Sunday, and their favorite curly-haired preacher raving away about being good. They got quite a kick out of it.

Their emotions, of course, via their reason and conscience, were not neglected. He would not have been averse to intoxicating his audience, with irreproachable elixirs, of course. Once he said: "I wish there were some great orator who could go about and make men *drunk* with this spirit of self-sacrifice." He no doubt tried to do that too: for of course his speeches would generally be sermons—in that he set a fashion: the Christianity lurking beneath all politics was his theme.

But the novelty wore off. And in the end the more politically serious would want to know—Christianity apart, for it might be their experience that Christians were people of words, not deeds, and so they were prejudiced against the Christian approach—what side he was on in politics, that of the rich or the poor: how far in the matter of "self-sacrifice" he was prepared to go. Was he, in other words, a "phony," or was he an authentic man of the political Left? They soon discovered the answer.

These genuine men of the Left became irritated with him, with his "academic lectures on government." They found him evasive, if nailed down to any particular point. Naturally he was very afraid of them. For, ultimately, in order to win the election, and the other more spectacular one beyond it, he had to satisfy quite a different type of person from those persons with addresses in Wall Street.

But the Party zealots nearer home were important. They made him feel an impostor, yet could not be ignored. They *were* what he was playing at being. "Men like George I. Record, who had been working, agitating, organizing, against the evils of the body politic, who knew specific conditions as Wilson did not, and who had certain clearly defined legislative objectives, considered that Wilson's speeches were 'glittering generalities, beautifully phrased, but having nothing to do with the political campaign in New Jersey.' They wanted him to 'come out' for direct primaries, a corrupt practices act, employers' liability, and other advanced measures. These remedies struck at the roots of Boss-government and privilege in New Jersey. The reformers had been advocating them for years and Wilson . . . had never helped them, never even shown any interest. . . . He was now appealing to the progressive spirit which they had been so active in arousing and yet refused to declare himself on specific measures."

Wilson appealed to the progressive spirit, that is he appealed for progressive *votes*. The word "progress" possessed an emotional attraction for him, certainly. But the Governorship and the Presidency exercised an even greater. He was a man of conscience, not of "Italian policy." But his fastidiousness naturally was adulterated with ambition.

The position in America was this: the time had come around for the Democratic Party to have its turn of power again. As the great interests saw it, it was essential to find a President who would satisfy the people by a show of zeal. They were all afraid of Bryan, who was so dangerous because, to their minds, a fool.

A certain Colonel Harvey, an influential political wire-puller, was on the lookout for a *safe* Democrat. This gentleman was supposed to be working in the Morgan interests. Hearing of this college president who had turned up and was described as a likely man, he proposed that he enter the Presidential race: and here is a passage from a letter of Wilson's, to the editor of the Brooklyn *Eagle,* offering enlightenment regarding his qualifications:

". . . the possibility of putting in nomination somebody who held views . . . which would hold liberal and reforming programs to conservative and strictly constitutional lines of action, to the discrediting of rash and revolutionary proposals."

The Constitution is a State paper, the motivating spirit of which, it has been said, "was to make the nation safe *from* democracy." Great fidelity to that was one of the first pre-requisites for a safe candidate. Wilson promised to be strictly constitutional. Was this merely to secure the support of Colonel Harvey and his friends? For he had men of the George Record

94

type to satisfy, if possible, on the one hand, and the Colonel Harveys on the other.

His biographer, Ray Baker, puts the matter in this way: "Wilson was never opposed to great wealth," except where used to corrupt the State. "To the end of his life some of his warmest friends were men of great wealth." He began like Gladstone a conservative—"a man naturally of the conservative class, with conservative friends. But like Gladstone, he was *also* an independent thinker." That *also* speaks volumes.

To paraphrase the above: Mr. Wilson approved of great riches. He recognized, however, that money had its dangers, since cads got hold of it sometimes. But anyway to be "progressive" you had to be a little rude about money. Trust-busting was obligatory. (It did no harm to the Trusts.)

As he was pushed into war in 1917—when reports of England's weakness alarmed American finance, with its great investments in this country—so with his "reforms." He was not a leader: he was a follower. For a "progressive" cannot be a leader: in nothing can he be an initiator. (That would throw the whole thing out of gear.) His Federal bank reform was the opposite of what it looked like to that gull, the public: it secured far greater power to finance instead of reducing that power as it affected to be doing. Typically, the drafting of the bank "reform" he entrusted to a banker. The latter made a wonderful job of it—for his fellow bankers. If you want to rent a house in an American city today you go, not to a house-agent, but to one of the banks. They own the houses. They did not do so in 1913.

Here is a note of Wilson's for a speech, January 1, 1911: a table of definitions of political terms:

RADICAL—one who goes too far.
CONSERVATIVE—one who does not go far enough.
REACTIONARY—one who does not go at all.
PROGRESSIVE—one who (a) recognizes new facts and adjusts law to them; and (b) attempts to think ahead, constructively.

The wording of this table is worthy of study. Does not this "adjustment," resulting from the "recognition of new facts" merely signify *being pushed?* As the "new fact" jogs you, you "adjust" yourself. It is possible to respect a Reactionary (one who indulges in strict immobility): one can respect a Radical (who goes too far for the majority of the electorate Wilson had his eye on). But it is very difficult to respect a Progressive.

The man who does not want to go anywhere we can understand—who does not want to go places, because all places at bottom are much the same. We can understand the man who wants to go where no man has ever gone before, where men say it is impossible, and highly unsuitable, to go. But what frankly can one say about the man who just wants to go as far as he is pushed?

Wilson's "New Freedom," the name he gave to his program of national "readjustment" when he assumed office, was really a "Back to the old Freedoms," not a "Forward to new Freedoms," movement. "The American people," speaking in Kansas City, 1911, he declared, "are a naturally conservative people. . . . What we must devote ourselves to now is, not to upsetting our institutions, but to *restoring* them." To restore the old freedom, not to invent any new ones, was the plan. So the adjective "new" was a hoax. It was the opposite of what in fact was planned.

There was no hypocritical slogan or soggy platitude that was not to be found in his political repertoire. "Service" was the word most often on his lips. "Service is the ultimate of life, not success."

When he, a sick man, in his fifties, went after the Governorship of New Jersey, as a first step to the Presidency, he was impelled to this step by a consuming desire to *serve*. Ambition did not enter into it at all! "Success" was the *last* thing he prized. He would have preferred to have failed: had he not *known* (owing to one of those intuitions so common with the upright) that his country sorely needed him, and he would make a better President than anybody else!

Even were he not to take this step of his own accord, it would have got about somehow that all this superlative merit was being wasted in petty actions, like his closing of the Tiger

96

Club, and other resorts of the campus snob. No, *he knew his duty.* He took the path of duty with regret. Had his conscience not prevented him, he would have prayed for defeat!

But to plumb the depths of self-deception of which this order of mind is capable is a task for the psychologist or perhaps for the psychiatrists. The Leader with a capital *L,* the Führer, feels the call. The man of destiny is sitting, say, in his peaceful college study, an open book upon his knee. There is a faraway look in his eyes: he watches abstractedly a hummingbird out of the window. The missionary spirit without warning enters into him. The life of contemplation is at an end: the life of action begins!

It is not *power* he wants—perish the thought! No, he desires only to serve. But in order to serve, he has to *lead.* This, alas, will mean power. A heavy burden to carry for a man already threatened with paralysis. But let us listen to him again.

"Men recognize genius in no other field as conclusively as in the field of *leadership.* They are eager to *crown* it with *power* and responsibility, eager themselves to *follow.*"

A revealing group of words, which I have provided with italics. Well, Wilson knew he was a Leader. At last it was revealed to him that he was called to lead the nation itself. It was revealed to him by Woodrow Wilson in person, with much dubious wagging of the head, and reminders that his health was delicate.

There is perhaps something odd about the whole affair which falls, it is possible, as I have suggested, within the field of the psychiatrists. His aggressive and autocratic temper at Princeton had involved him in a number of disputes. He was not cut out for that type of action: when he did not have his way, a health breakdown ensued. This brought him near to paralysis. After his return from convalescence in Bermuda he was unable to use his hand to write with. As a man he was unable to tolerate successful opposition to his will. In 1906 a blood vessel burst in his eye. As President of Princeton University he failed, but would not accept defeat in the field of action. After his failure as President of the United States, he treated everyone as an enemy, even his relatives and personal friends, showing a malignant aggressiveness.

Such minor actions as his attempted centralization of the life of the university were too much for him physically. Yet he plunged incontinently into practical politics, of which he had no experience, and the far more exhausting role of President of a nation, rather than merely president of a college, dragging his wife and family (protesting) at his heels.

His wife was depressed and alarmed by all this. Her letters of this period are sad reading. They were suddenly uprooting themselves, leaving the professional environment to which they had been used for so long. She naturally had no love for Princeton: but her common sense told her that Washington was likely to be worse, and to be worse for the same reasons.

But even Wilson himself regarded what he was doing as mad. For the whole of the six years of his brief political career (up to his seizure at Pueblo) he was on the verge of breakdown. His letters are full of dark premonitions. Again and again he refers, in a tone of dismal foreboding, to his political triumphs.

The death of his wife in 1914, the year following that in which they moved into the White House, was, for him, a critical event. Friends of the Wilsons of long standing described her as acting as a check, with her good sense, upon his exaltation. However this may be, shortly after her death an alarming change became noticeable, it appears, to his advisers and those most in contact with him. "For some considerable time before the end of the war competent observers, close to the heart of events, knew that something had gone wrong with President Wilson. Exactly what had happened to him is not clearly known to this day." No doubt a number of people possessed information that was not made public. There may even be some clinical revelations which have not come to my notice— though what everybody knows, the outline of which I have given, is sufficient evidence.

"There was for some reason" (to continue the above quotation) "a striking change in his personality during the World

War. He lost the keen logical quality that was his distinguishing trait in his earlier years. He was possessed by idealism as one is gripped by an incurable disease. His sense of leadership grew out of all reasonable bounds. In the secret recesses of his mind and heart he may have looked upon himself as a political messiah."

That the unenviable role of his wife was to modify the transports of this political messiah we may accept as likely, and that her removal from the scene had the effect one would expect. But his wife had not been able to stop him from suddenly deciding to become a politician. His nervous system had suffered some lesion from battles at Princeton, where already the messianic taint was apparent.

A short while before he left Princeton for Washington, Wilson remarked to friends: "It would be the irony of fate if my administration had to deal chiefly with foreign affairs." And that was, of course, exactly what happened. He had only been in office a year and five months when the European War started and Wilson's opportunity to prosecute his "New Freedom" plans were at an end. Henceforth all his time, or most of it, was occupied in trying to keep out of the war, just as McKinley had attempted to do: and there was, oddly enough, the same man there to "jog" him into it as taunted McKinley (the "chocolate éclair"). The Germans, however, with their customary diplomatic finesse, sank ships carrying Americans, and did everything calculated to make it difficult *not* to go to war.

There is one thing that is quite certain: whatever his messianic ambitions may have been, they did not lie in the direction of war-leadership. He seems to have been strangely free from that weakness. He was extremely annoyed, in fact, that these alarms and excursions interfered with his plans for bogus domestic reforms. Since he knew as little about European politics as he did about economics, since he was as old-fashioned a "progressive" on the domestic side as he was half-hearted as a crusader upon the other, it did not matter particularly which he did. But Fate had picked him as a war-President. That is a death warrant for any man.

The war terminated, he was in his element again. His "New Freedom" could now have a far vaster field for its deployment than he had glimpsed in his most sanguine dreams. He was beside himself at the prospect. He had only intended to save America. But behold, he had been chosen to save the world!

By means of "open covenants, openly arrived at," all the nations of the earth were going to sit down at a great big table, a happy and at last united family—he of course presiding, dispensing sweetness and light, the savior of mankind.

With great suddenness the whole edifice collapsed. America would not listen to whatever he had to say. In September, 1919, he had his public seizure, and vanished from sight. It was whispered that he had lost his reason and become a gibbering mental wreck. He lived practically incommunicado until he died.

Woodrow Wilson had his principles. War revolted him. His Christianity had taught him it was wicked. Nothing, for him, seemed to make it anything but wrong. But when Bryan saw that it was impossible to avoid war, that far more honest politician resigned his office in the Wilson administration. Wilson preferred power to his conscience, and stopped where he was. Eventually—with suitable high-minded attitudes—he allowed himself to be pushed into war. In conclusion, it must never be forgotten that, the war over, he turned down an appeal for the release of Debs, who had been sentenced to ten years' imprisonment for expressing his abhorrence of war. Debs, who was as gentle as Wilson was aggressive and arrogant, and who (the church-attending faculty aside) was a hundred times better Christian than his jailer. Further, he was one of the original "muckrakers" of Teddy's days, an authentic practitioner of that "radicalism" which Wilson found it so useful to affect, in the emasculated form acceptable to his richer patrons.

13 THE POWER OF THE PRESIDENT, AND THE CAUSE OF THE "PRESSURE-GROUP"

What is the moral of this tale of three Presidents? It is that it became almost a recognized function of the Presidency to integrate the "progressivist" and "populist" ferments of the nineties and earlier by the theft of those thunders, the pinnacle of power in the State installed as a lightning-conductor to protect the whole Constitutional edifice of power against storms of popular discontent. Since the 1914–18 war and revolutions, new and more violent tensions supervened, and they complicated the nature of the Presidency still further. Some Presidents stress this side of their office and some do not.

The power to be derived from appeals to popular impatience, with things as they are, is so much greater than the power derivable from the backing of the stand-pats, that any particularly ambitious President in this century is certain to play the radical, however big a Tory he may be.

Since, however, this "progressiveness" is almost of necessity insincere (for both Parties are loaded with rich men) the "messianic" act I have been attempting to describe obstructs rather than otherwise the advent of authentic change. The American people could have anything it wanted, all the things it wanted, overnight, if only it could find its way out of the maze, break the spell of politics. These Presidents were political spell-binders; they were guardians of the maze.

This official radicalism is one of those artificial growths of which I was speaking: dangerous substitutes for the real, symbolical monstrosities.

From my summary of the characters of the three Presidents chosen for discussion, it will be evident that, were I compiling something like Comte's *Positivist Calendar,* the last two would not find a place in it. Franklin Roosevelt would qualify, though I feel he was not so much a great man of action as an impresario of genius.

Any Calendar of the Great would be incomplete without the names of Jefferson, Hamilton, and Lincoln; as incomplete as if it were to leave out Pericles, Marcus Aurelius, Richelieu, or Pitt. But no American in this century would be there except Franklin Roosevelt. Such is my opinion. None have measured up to what, in twentieth-century America, they logically should have been. Their country deserved better than the "big-stick" gentleman, or he of the Fourteen Points, or, I think it must be confessed, than the co-author of the Atlantic Charter in one or two respects.

Power is unquestionably the trouble of too many of those who become President. Of Jefferson, Woodrow Wilson wrote, "It was not pretense on his part or merely love of power that made him democratic." With that we can agree: but there is more than sufficient evidence to show that Wilson's own "progressiveness" was both of those things, as I have endeavored, in the small compass of a chapter, to show.

Great as the power obtained in this way undoubtedly is, it is by no means as great as it looks. Charles Beard says: "President Wilson overestimated his power and was broken in the contest of power." For in a democracy there is no straight power. It is always something that is balanced and usually overmatched by something else.

Anyone wishing to inform himself about the nature of the executive power in the United States, or any other question relating to the Constitution of that country, would do well to go to the fountain-head, and consult what is obviously the supreme authority, namely *The Federalist, or the New Constitution* (1787–88). The power of the President, at the time hotly debated, was the subject of Alexander Hamilton's predilection: and in No. lxvii (*The Executive Department*) that remarkable advocate of maximum personal power begins the series where, in article after article, he argues tirelessly in favor of a strong and independent Chief Magistrate. He reminds his readers even (No. lxx), that the Romans did not shrink from Dictatorship, when the need arose.

"There is an idea, which is not without its advocates, that a vigorous executive is inconsistent with the genius of republican government. The enlightened well-wishers to this species of government must at least hope that the supposition is destitute of foundation, since they can never admit its truth without at the same time admitting the condemnation of their own principles. Energy in the Executive is a leading character in the definition of good government. It is essential to the protection of the community against foreign attacks; it is not less essential to the steady administration of the laws; to the protection of property against those irregular and high-handed combinations which sometimes interrupt the ordinary course of justice; to the security of liberty against the enterprises and assaults of ambition, of faction, and of anarchy. Every man the least conversant in Roman history knows how often that republic was obliged to take refuge in the absolute power of a single man, under the formidable title of Dictator."

In practice, of course, a general war does automatically transform a President into a Dictator: and Hamilton and his friends worked so well that neither Lincoln nor Roosevelt II were exactly wanting in executive power, or at the mercy of the legislature.

I have mentioned Beard, and there is no better guide (with this advantage, that it is in the contemporary idiom) than *The Republic* to the intricate power-pattern of government in the U.S.A. This is a book published in 1943, at a time when Americans were wondering, as never before, exactly *how* they were governed; the principles upon which the machinery of government in the U.S. had been constructed. Beard gave them, in a popular form, all the answers.

Like the English monarchs prior to Victoria, a U.S. President can appoint or dismiss ministers at will: and F.D.R.

got a lot of fun out of *that*. When asked by the hypothetic Smyths, in *The Republic,* to describe the powers of the President, Beard answers by a catalogue of negatives.

"Can the President alone regulate intercourse with other countries at his pleasure?" The answer is *no.* Yet this is the field of foreign affairs, in which he is supposed to be left great freedom of action. Can the President regulate immigration? *No.* Decide the size of the Army and Navy? *No.* Set up ministries and consulates in other countries? *No.* Can he make treaties? *No.* Can he declare war? *No.* And so on.

He can use his influence, and the great prestige of his office, to persuade other people to do these things. But all along the line he is checked by a Constitutional interdict, if he reach out for *absolute* power.

The words *at his pleasure* were not, I am sure, used accidentally by Beard in the question with which the preceding paragraph opens. For they awaken a historical echo. The laws promulgated by a sixteenth-century French absolute monarch always ended with the words, *"Car tel est notre bon plaisir."* This was the principle of imperial absolutism, as practiced by the Roman Emperors, and adopted by the Kings of France (as earlier it had been adopted by the Italian tyrants). Whatever this individual human being *pleased*— happened to want or approve of—automatically became the *law.*

Such is personal power: and such the U.S. Presidents do not possess. They can do what they will to a very great extent: "get away with" a great deal. But like so many other things in the United States, it is in a sense as law-breakers that they function. They can "get away with murder" and other things besides. But all the really enjoyable, first-class power of a U.S. President is stolen power: highjacked or bootlegged. And it is done under the usually complacent eyes of that Constitutional policeman, the Senate.

If it should be that a man just can't live without power, as some cannot live without much alcohol—if he so thirsts for more power, he could find greater satisfaction, probably, in a more restricted field: as the superior of a religious order, say: or perhaps the czar of a big newspaper syndicate. In these cases his subordinates are not organized into contending groups, and they have not voted him in. The ruler of a totalitarian State is in another category altogether, exercising a god-like authority, with power of life and death over everybody. That for the power-addict must seem like heaven.

It is a recognized historical fact that the power of a king (unlike the power of an oligarchy) always reposes upon the people. So it is with an "elective king." Franklin Delano Roosevelt was able to flout the Congress of the United States because his power was anchored in the broad mass of the people, who would stand by him, knowing that he, more than anybody else, could be relied on for a square deal.

But the American people is not an undifferentiated mass of voters. It is absurdly over-organized, as we have seen. Socially it is first of all a dense mass of clubs: Rotary, the Lions, the Elks, and so forth, which represent, too, a hierarchy of wealth, it being more desirable to be a Rotarian than a Lion. Politically, however, Party (to return for a moment to that, and to cognate questions) is not the only form of organization that exists. There are other large and influential groups which have far more direct influence in politics, because they stand for real, rather than for artificial, values.

Under these circumstances "personal rule" leaves little to the personality of the ruler. It is popular rule, rather than personal rule. The individual ruler today is swept, pushed, buffeted along. It is a very arduous performance to be a personal ruler, as Woodrow Wilson found, especially if the supposed protagonist insists too much upon his personal will.

F.D.R. had the right temperament for it. He gaily rollicked along on his back, delivering sly kicks as he went to right and left. His master, Wilson, had the wrong temperament. He did not rollick along. He believed he had been called to assume the robes of the philosopher-king. Had he been a better philosopher he would not have succumbed to that temptation.

The amount of personal power exercised by the head of a

government is in inverse ratio to the degree of organization attained by the respective groups within the State—labor, management or capital, sectarian, racial, etc. This is a law—in a democracy, where these groups possess real independence: so the power enjoyed by any democratic administration can be easily computed by an inquiry regarding the degree of independent organization existing in the democratic mass.

Such organization is, of course, undemocratic, in a certain sense, though it can only exist in a democracy. Parliamentary democracy should be all of a piece—or if the sub-divisions become too strongly defined and differentiated, they should at once emerge as *Parties*. Even the Party, when too elaborately organized—too powerful—usurps the functions and preroga- tives of government. Party, in fact, may be regarded as an artifice, the object of which is to forestall or prevent the formation of authentically differentiated groups in the body of the population. As it is, the President *presides*—that is all—at the bitter debates proceeding outside the official Two- Party racket. It is possible to divine which forces are gaining the upper hand at any time, by the attitude adopted by the official weather-cock at the White House, pushed about as if by the pressure of the wind.

Class does not officially exist: it is "un-American." To take any notice of *race* is "un-American" (everybody does so, of course, more than in any other country). Anything labeled "un-American" flourishes, because it is supposed not to be there, leading the immune existence of a very vigorous "in- visible man." Labor, however, in the person of its militant unions, plays an increasingly decisive role in the elections.

Since it is not a "Party," and so is eternally outside and "in opposition," or in a state of armed truce, its power is more real. I mean that it is uncontaminated with the stale unreality of routine Party-government—when the latter has become merely a traditional drama of the "ins" and "outs," staged by those who wish "public life" to remain an empty ritual.

Congress contains no laboring men: nor is the enormous Negro vote evidenced, after each election, by the appearance of a lot of dusky faces in the Congress. Women appear there, but the female voter has derived no particular benefit from that fact.

Because of the great poverty in which most colored people live, so many occupations being barred to them (their war-time affluence in some Northern cities was mainly the result of a "Jim Crow army"), and because of a universal social discrimination to which they are subjected, they are radical, like the majority of the working class. This submerged black mass of outsiders weighs more heavily in the scales every day: more than it would have done had it been invited inside. (Which, of course, is not an excuse, in a *democracy*, for keeping it outside.)

Religion, like race or class, has no separate identity: it would be "un-American" of it to suggest that it was there, as a political issue. But the Catholics, who certainly could otherwise furnish a powerful Party, such as they possessed formerly in Germany, no doubt recognize the advantages of not being visibly present, as a body, among the law-makers. There is a great reservoir of Catholic votes which answers the purpose just as well or better. The "pressure-group" is a concomitant of this situation. Finally, as a distinct "interest," is another invisible power, the big financial houses and corporations, the "economic empires." They are not visibly represented, of course, but their pressure-groups are more powerful than a Party; their money hangs like a millstone around the neck of a "reforming" Chief Executive.

The *states* of the U.S.A. are united. A war was fought, they are now indissolubly one, that is settled. But these *other* states-within-the-state—"economic empires" and powerfully organized counter-imperial groups—are *not* united. They are divided into great camps—quite as irreconcilable as were formerly the slave-states and the North, prior to the Civil War. The U.S. President is not *their* ruler, though they all, as "Democrats" and "Republicans," assist at his election. In so far as he is loyal to the Constitution he belongs to one camp rather than to the other. The Constitution, as understood by its framers, was not a "document which put human rights above property rights when the two conflict." That is the demagogic rhetoric only of a later day. But Jefferson *solus* would have written the Constitution quite' differently. And it would have been a Constitution more in harmony with twentieth-century thought, with the so-called Socialist Age.

14 AMERICA BROUGHT TO ITS SENSES BY THE MULTIMILLIONAIRES

The situation I have been endeavoring to describe had its roots in the last century. Happenings in the late nineteenth century, when the American People had a great shock, and their general outlook suffered a profound alteration, were responsible for it.

Not to go back to "the Great Strike" of '77, things really came to a head in the eighties and nineties. Capitalism had then reached its full stature: men had begun to feel themselves threatened with imminent destruction by this new steel-age mastodon walking the earth, with as little care for mankind as if they had been blades of grass. The Civil War was a victory for the corporative principle of Union: simultaneously it was a triumph for Northern Capitalism. A quite new America was there all around them suddenly, totally unlike what the pre-Civil War American had known: unlike, as a matter of fact, anything experienced before by man.

The Democratic platform of William Jennings Bryan in the nineties was in a sense the model of the missionary fervors of the Roosevelts and of Wilson: for Bryan was not a social revolutionary, but that rare thing, a good-hearted politician, who wanted to reform what was there rather than break it up and erect a new social order upon its ruins.

The banks were perfecting the method of first expanding credit and so tempting everybody into irresponsible buying, then suddenly calling all the credit in, and producing a nation-wide slump, in which everything could be bought up at rock-bottom prices. Bryan's famous phrase, "You shall not crucify mankind upon a cross of gold!" which electrified America, referred, of course, to the devastation resulting from bank-usury and its new techniques. And the inflationary "free silver" movement was a simple-hearted attempt to create cheap money, and so cheat the deflationary practice of finance.

Bryan was never President—there was always some spurious reformer, like Wilson, to put in instead of him, or some other way of stopping this dangerously sincere, though otherwise fairly harmless, individual. In reading the private letters of men of wealth writing in the jittery nineties, one is astonished at the bitterness of their diatribes against the free silver men.

But Bryan was the first routine politician verbally to molest the rich. Lincoln and the nineteenth-century Presidents generally did not specialize in attacks upon wealth. Wealth was not then an issue—certainly not *the* issue. That is new. That is twentieth-century democratic technique. Even the term "democracy" applied to the political system of the United States was not universally recognized until this century, to which point I shall return in Chapter 17.

Messianic leadership was a natural result of the building up of the American State-religion, after the Civil War, and the high-priestly function of the Chief Executive. But also it is the constitutional corrective for the discontents attendant upon a highly organized capitalist economy.

Post-French Revolution America, impelled thereto by Thomas Jefferson and his adherents, followed the abstract, Gallic, ideologic path. Then the constantly expanding empire, to which Americans became committed, drew them into a sort of jingo imperialism of their own, in the sweep and surge of which the early idealism foundered.

Their traditional habits of thought were excessively sanguine and self-confident. Then, as I have said, came the impact of this new force, and the rapid and fundamental change in their outlook. One day, as usual, Yankee Doodle went to town: but this time Yankee Doodle faltered, and turned back.

Most Englishmen are at least sixty years out of date in their idea of the typical American. The American they see in their mind's eye died sixty years or more ago. Certainly there is enough of exuberance left in a small number of Americans to sustain the illusion. Of course, too, much "brashness" and noise accompany all the activities of the publicist and publicity rackets: that is misleading. But the general run of people in the States are quite unassuming, and quite modest about their destiny, as they are anywhere else. They awakened from their pipe-dream long ago. When, in the decade or so preceding the Boer War, or the Spanish-American War, their old jingo confidence and complacency abandoned them, or began to do so, the long-accepted libertarian jargon was, they began to growl to each other, "the bunk."

Even, it occurred to many of them, it might be a rich man's trick, designed to conceal from them how imperfectly free was, nevertheless, the lot of most Americans. That their hereditary right to say "Shake" to their President, if they happened to be near him, meant that he was right at the heart of the hoax. For at all times numbers of inventive and intelligent people were to be found in this swarming population: living in a society where honor and power go to the least desirable type of human being, equipped with the simian cunning of the three-card-trick man, is depressing, at the last, for such minds. Demoralization set in. A new social-consciousness was born.

The recovery from the wounds of the Civil War had been slow, and the South, of course, became a slum, and such it has remained. The lavish proportions of the newly settled continental expanse, as it stretched away, across great prairies and over the huge, inhuman Rocky Mountains, to the Pacific, was responsible for the mammoth fortunes, which gave America its reputation as a land of millionaires. The era of the Vanderbilts and Goulds had come: it had the stimulus of mere scale. Everything was *big,* as it is in a Vachel Lindsay poem.

But there was a reaction from this living in capital letters. It ended by making men feel smaller, not bigger, than formerly. Liberty, as I have said, came under suspicion, began not to look so good; for Liberty is so *enormous* a figure—like the portentous female guarding New York Harbor—that it dwarfs and is inhuman. Supposed to symbolize man's privilege, instead it dominates him, as was to be expected of a goddess, whatever name she bore.

As to the excitingly big millionaire, at first a heroic symbol of America's great size and power, he, too, came to be more exactly, less sentimentally, apprehended. "From the same prolific womb," quoting from the platform of the Populist Party, "of governmental injustice we breed those two great classes, the tramp and the millionaire." (The date of this caustic utterance is 1892.)

In the eighties, in the Middle West, the working man began to separate himself from the general democracy: to organize outside it. Then came the giant Slump of 1893. As many as 574 banks failed: hundreds of thousands were ruined. The United States, as a good place to live in, for the first time came in question. The original American optimism was dead for good, the bubble of vanity of the dweller in "God's own country" was pricked. His vanity and boastfulness at one time were so remarkable that they are still a legend among other nations.

Hard times, in conjunction with the advent of the multimillionaire, publicly wallowing in vast wealth, resulted in a growing sense that it wasn't such a grand thing to be an American as once it had been—that the rich were too rich, the poor too poor. "What was wrong with the United States, that it had to suffer these recurrent crises? The Democratic tariff, said the Republicans; gold, said the Populists; capitalism, said the Socialists; the immutable laws of trade, said the economists; the wrath of God, said the ministers." But of these, *capitalism* is the answer that has survived to this day. Disillusionment ensuing upon the *first* economic blizzard has been my subject, but that was long ago. Although during F.D.R.'s rule class-consciousness flourished in all directions, since his death the scene has changed beyond recognition. The American workman, generally speaking, exists upon a plane of well-being so superior to that of his opposite number in other nations that he is a fortunate man. Of this he is pleasantly aware.

112

15 AMERICAN HISTORY

The history of America is compact, because so short, and—in consequence of America's remoteness—not mixed up with that of other peoples. Up to the "shot that rang around the world," or more formally, up to July 4, 1776, when America declared its independence, Americans were Englishmen. In recalling himself to the Princess of Turn and Taxis, Gouverneur Morris writes: "The lovely princess will perhaps recollect *der gute Engländer* who retains a deep sense of her kindness." He did not say "the American."

The new State duly came to birth in the year 1776: it was an English civil war, a Whig Putsch against George III, engineered by a group of ambitious English colonists. The colonists participated, as Whigs and Tories, in English politics. When the King's army was defeated, the American Whigs drove out all the Tories—the "fifth columnists" of that day—and confiscated their property.

Prominent colonists, among them some educated in England —all fine gentlemen, in the eighteenth-century English style, in wigs, lace, and knee breeches, bowing gracefully to one another, making sweeps with their hats, and taking snuff as they conversed—met at Philadelphia: these were the so-called Founding Fathers, who provided the new country with a Constitution. This sacrosanct State document is venerated as if Jehovah had stepped out of a cloud and handed it to General Washington. Its terms have been religiously observed ever since, by Swede, Swiss, Pole, Chinese, Jew, and even by the

Irish. Only Lincoln acted as if it were not there and paid with his life for this sacrilege.

As history, that of the Americans is fascinatingly simple. For practical purposes it begins in 1776—for it is easy for anyone to imagine what happened before that: how, in rat-infested little ships, numbers of people got there, cut down the trees (with which the whole country was covered), grew food (since their descendants are still there, they must have done that): and in the end built cities, like Philadelphia, Charleston, Boston, and New York, which, as near as possible, resembled cities in England or Holland. As the mode of dress changed in England, from the flat curled hat to the top hat, and from that to the bowler, and next to the hat of cloven felt which prevails at present, so it changed in America. Vice versa, if there were two-quart beaver hats back there, you would have found them in England likewise. The great landmarks are 1776, when the U.S.A. started, and 1861–65, when the Civil War occurred. The next big date is 1914–18. Everything in between is just a story of bigger and bigger, and of more and more. (One cannot describe it as a story of better and better.)

The Republic, with its "rigid" Constitution—except for this big hiatus in the sixties, given over to fratricide—has run smoothly along: chopping down trees, killing Indians, and building up larger and larger factories, taller and taller houses. The "wild land" of the interior gradually became covered with cities—all much the same. There is, in fact, so little complication that you can concentrate upon the economic and political birth and development of this titanic State-organism.

Alexis de Tocqueville recognized this uniqueness. "America," he wrote, "is the only country in which it has been possible to witness the natural and tranquil growth of society, and where the influence exercised on the future condition of states by their origin is clearly distinguishable."

For a political mind, it is one of the most attractive histories of all: it reads like a lesson in politics. It is as if the history of France began with the French Revolution; only instead of throwing up Napoleon—and getting mixed up with the history of every other country in Europe: instead of its intermediate story being packed with restorations of the monarchy, coups d'état, empires, communes, one after the other in baroque disorder—instead of all this, it is as if it had gone forward steadily evolving from a set of rules laid down at the time of the Revolution by the pundits of the Tiers, the Abbé Sieyès and the rest of them, gathered together at the Constituent Assembly.

Then, perhaps, we should have seen in France the original body of political doctrine, blotted out with two or more fungiform overgrowths of Party. To this ungainly structure, we should have seen added barnacle-like parasites of corporative economy. Giant trusts and cartels would have adhered, in sinister arabesque—had France possessed the physical opportunities of the United States. The political scenery, in a word, would have assumed the appearance of the most involved and nightmarish arboreal recesses of the Brazilian rain-forest.

At the foundation of the American State, when many very able minds contended with one another in this initial act of creation, the theory of human government is brought into a clear, distinct light. We see the State built up from the bottom as if it were a demonstration in political science.

The Federal Constitution—the primary rules by which all the subsidiary states must abide—is not there all by itself, without any further clue to the intentions of its signatories. This Constitution was explained to the American people at the time by means of what eventually became the *Federalist Papers*. This (from which I have quoted) is one of the most deservedly famous publications in the world. It was described by Guizot as being, in its application of the elementary principles of government to a particular case, the greatest work known to him. This book is the master key to American politics, and for the study of the problems of free government everywhere, the *Federalist Papers*, and the historical situation that brought them into being, offer a heaven-sent model.

The English student is less acquainted than he should be with American history. But as an American woman journalist remarked, the only people in America who take any interest in England are the fashionable rich, the only person in England who evinces an interest in America is the common man and the even more common woman. The latter can inform you upon the sentimental history, or "love-life," of contemporary screen actors and actresses: which may tell one something of the way this State is progressing, but nothing as to how it began, and the great political principles by which its life is governed.

American history has a further advantage: namely its provision of a perfect political polarity, in the persons of the two most important Founding Fathers, Jefferson and Hamilton. (Washington is not important, except as a symbol.) Right at the outset come this faultless pair of opposites. The former is the model radical, the latter the model conservative.

All American politicians today are in theory Jeffersonian, in practice Hamiltonian. It is highly confusing for the European. These sonorous professions of the most altruistic principles, ringing denunciations of the unrighteousness of foreign governments, on the one hand; on the other hand, and in stark contrast, behavior replete with a tough and strident commercialism. The foreigner should get to expect this duality (it is not always duplicity) from the American, and learn to take no notice whatever of the ethical transports and confine his attention entirely to the (often unethical) actions which accompany them.

Both Thomas Jefferson and Alexander Hamilton would be ornaments to any age: both were men of the highest intellect and (what, in the case of Hamilton, has caused much surprise to everybody) honesty.

"The secret of Jefferson's power lay in the fact that he appealed to and expressed America's better self: her idealism, simplicity, youthful mind, and hopeful outlook, rather than those material, practical, and selfish qualities on which Hamilton based his policy."

So says an excellent American history (given me by a grandson of Theodore Roosevelt as a reward for a small

116

service I was able to render the Porcellian Club at Harvard).
But Woodrow Wilson thought somewhat differently, it is
interesting to note. "Jefferson's writings lack hard and practical sense . . . un-American, in being abstract, sentimental,
rationalistic, rather than practical." This "un-American"
character he attributes to his being steeped in French philosophy. But Jeremy Bentham, for exactly the same reasons, had
a great dislike for Jefferson's Declaration of Independence:
not of course condemning it for being "un-American," but
because it was (though he did not say this) un-English. For
"the doctrine of the indefeasible rights of man has never been
quite at home on English soil," any more than it has on
American. It should be added that the theology, too, which,
in the Declaration of Independence, is introduced to provide
those "rights" with a Divine origin, conferred a further metaphysical complication upon this document.

However, the influence of Jefferson, though both his philosophy and his theology might be called exotic, does generally
pass for "America's better self." It did certainly inject into the
classical politics of the United States all that is unworldly, and,
if you like, sentimental. That so few people practice it, though
professing it with such unction, might be said to prove it un-
American. But like Christianity, it is very difficult to practice.

It was Jefferson who insisted upon a Bill of Rights, whereas
Hamilton typically opposed it, in *The Federalist* (No. lxxxiv),
comparing such a document to "a treatise of Ethics." His
words are as follows—he has been quoting some passages from
the Constitution, which, he argues, answer all sensible liberal
requirements. "Here is a better recognition of popular rights
than volumes of those aphorisms . . . which would sound
much better in a treatise of Ethics than in a constitution of
government." For him *ethics* had nothing to do with *government*. But for Jefferson they had everything to do with it.

Alexander Hamilton, however, strangely enough, was an
"idealist" too. But all his ideals were diametrically opposite
to those of his rival—also he and Jefferson were bitter opponents and in the end he was killed in a duel by a partisan of

117

the other faction. The latter ruffian, immediately after this feat, was entertained with great warmth in the capital by Jefferson.

Mr. David Loth describes Hamilton thus—at the Convention, where, with his extreme authoritarian doctrine, he stood almost alone. "Erect . . . the still rosy cheeks flushed with enthusiasm, the eyes starry with love of an idea . . . Hamilton appealed deliberately, with all the fervor of eloquence, patriotism, high-minded virtue and studied idealism, to the basest impulses of mankind."

The next three chapters continue and complete this account of the two most influential figures, always excepting Lincoln, in the political history of America. The term "Federalist" may offer difficulties to some readers. So here is an explanatory note.

In the dictionary you will find, in definition of the word "Federal," the following, or something like it: "of the polity in which several States form a unity but remain independent in internal affairs." The "Federalists" were a powerful faction, of which Hamilton was the leader, who stood pre-eminently for national unity; for America becoming one sovereign nation, instead of a more or less loose confederacy of thirteen sovereign states, the latter being the arrangement desired by most Americans at that period.

Hamilton was a great centralizing mind. Jefferson, on the other hand, was a "states-rights" politician. He was averse to too much central governmental authority. He wanted Virginia, the state to which he belonged, to continue to govern itself. States-rights, Executive authority, the individual's rights as against those of the State; these were not the only matters upon which he and Hamilton differed, but were the major issues of that opening period of American history.

16 THE BEAUTIFUL POLARITY OF HAMILTON AND JEFFERSON

Alexander Hamilton was not an American. He was born in the West Indies; to the last *government* meant for him a King and a Queen, a House of Lords, and a House of Commons. It was an obsession.

At the period when the "Federalist" faction, for which he had been responsible, was in decay, in a letter to his friend Gouverneur Morris, he wrote as follows: "Every day proves to me more and more that this American world was not made for me. You, friend Morris, are a native of this country, but by genius an exotic. You mistake if you fancy that you are more of a favorite than myself, or that you are in any sort upon a theater suited to you."

Or again, to another friend: "Is there a constitutional defect in the American mind? Were it not for yourself and a few others I would adopt the reveries of De Paux, as substantial truths, and could say with him that there is something in our climate which belittles every animal, human or brute." (This is from the *Works* 90–91.)

Hamilton is gently reproaching Morris in the first of these extracts with his aloofness, when he says that his friend was mistaken if he supposes himself any more popular than the rest of them. Where he speaks of him as an "exotic," he probably had in mind the fact that Gouverneur Morris's mother, like his own, was French.

As to the second extract and his reference to the process

of "belittlement," attendant upon the functioning of the democratic ethos: Hamilton was a man who craved authority —which he never enjoyed except by proxy, when he was propping up the massive figure of the first President of the United States. There was this further thing: unselfishly, he was for Authority; he wished it to exist and prevail in the world, armed with all the force it is possible to mobilize in its support. Then, when he bent his mind to the problem of government, he at once, with alarm and antipathy, saw the "common man" in a slovenly mass: swarming noisily in the streets and clamoring for something it ought not to have: which, if you gave it, might mean your budget would remain unbalanced, or you might find it impossible to buy yourself a vessel of war.

The Many, he felt, was a wild animal, of uncleanly habits and rough disposition, that should somehow be shackled and restrained. "The mob, sir, is a beast!" In the picture-box of his mind he saw a glittering, a nobly thoughtful, group of "wise" and "virtuous" men, a political and social elite, the heaven-ordained leaders of the nation: or, alternatively, he saw One person, a model of virtue, deserving of all men's veneration and unquestioning obedience. This latter ruled all that unruly Mob, as a splendid horsemaster sits a vicious steed, steel on his heels and steel in his eye: ready for anything, but calmly master of the situation. Hamilton was himself a handsome little man, as neat and bright as Jefferson was dim and untidy: an effective speaker, whereas Jefferson was untidy in his speech as in his gait and dress: excellent in debate, while Jefferson always shunned it (getting somebody else to do it for him; keeping in the background, unwilling to be dragged into action).

In his beautiful wig, court suit, and lace cravat, and elegant calves above the buckled shoes, eyes of Gallic blue shining with fanatical purpose, that of fitting a strait jacket upon the furious Many, and establishing upon a firm economic basis the power of the Few, or of the One, Hamilton dominated these early American assemblies of notables. His confrères listened, fascinated but distrustful, nibbling suspiciously at the bait he offered, eying this opinionated little financial wizard as dogs do a novel food, however wholesome. He wanted to make them into nobles—Washington into a king. In the end they firmly shut their ears against him: but Washington never quite shut his. Nor did "Lady Washington."

For a man of this authoritarian temper, it is obvious that in the end he must feel that America "was not made for him." Even in the pages of de Tocqueville, who is one of the greatest admirers the Americans have ever had, one can discern a doubt, never set at rest, regarding the effects of the systematic leveling. "The gifts of intellect proceed directly from God," says that admirable Frenchman, "and man cannot prevent their unequal distribution." But—"There is no family or corporate authority, and it is rare to find even the influence of the individual character enjoy any durability . . . Men are there seen on a greater equality on a point of fortune and intellect . . . than in any age of which history has preserved the remembrance." De Tocqueville, of course, applauded this absence of privilege in any form at all. Yet even so he would feel that equality "of fortune" and equality "of intellect" are not exactly the same thing: that the man who is more intelligent than another should not deliberately dim down and extinguish the intelligence (a "gift proceeding directly from God") until it be so dull and weak that the moronic, even, could not feel a speck of envy. Indeed, later on he writes: "but there exists also in the human heart a depraved taste for equality which impels the weak to attempt to lower the powerful to their own level and reduces man to prefer equality in slavery to inequality with freedom." Nor would de Tocqueville or any sensible man consider that fact, that the "individual character" enjoyed so fleeting an influence, as a national asset exactly.

Even down to the present time the United States is probably the worst country for a man of exceptional intellectual endowment to be born in; though what today is accountable for that is vastly more complex, and of a different order.

121

These are not necessary accompaniments of democracy: it is not at the mercy of all that is impoverished and wanting in charm. A beautiful girl should not have to disfigure herself in order to put herself upon a proper democratic basis. The race would soon become debased if that were so. And intellect is as important to the race as is physical beauty and health.

Of all this type of shortcoming in the American civilization of his day—fifty years earlier than de Tocqueville—Alexander Hamilton was acutely aware. But it was not because he looked upon it as an aberration of the democratic spirit: it was because he mistook it for democracy. "In America, the aristocratic element has always been feeble from its birth" (de Tocqueville). It was the absence of that, the "aristocratic element," which distressed Hamilton. He was simply in the wrong place, as he said in his letter to his friend. An "exotic": who happens to be one of the two main pillars of the American social and political system.

I am not about to assert that *both* of the two most prominent Founding Fathers—the two main pillars of that giant structure known as the "American way of life"—were "exotics." But we have seen that so respectable an authority as Woodrow Wilson described Jefferson as "un-American." You will recall that he looked upon this ideologue, steeped in French philosophy—being a man susceptible to ideas—as "rationalistic," "abstract," speculative—rather than a man of practical common sense as is the typical American—by no means representative of his country. He might certainly have concurred, had one inquired if, in his opinion, the word "exotic" could be applied to him. That was, in other words, what Wilson was calling him.

Jefferson was a "cranky" thinker. He looked like a Lakes Poet, and mooched untidily about the palace at Washington in his slippers. In this condition, and at his dirtiest, he received the British Ambassador, who, in all the gilded trappings of eighteenth-century protocol, had come to pay his respects to the new President. He wasted years rewriting the New Testament. Everything attracted him—Philology, Zoology, Archaeology, Architecture, Theology, Literature, and, of course, Politics. His treatises on the pronunciation of Greek, or the Anglo-Saxon language, are said to have been as crankily amateurish as his biological theories, which required the presence of an animal twice the size of the elephant in the Polar regions. No such animal had ever been reported, but he was sure it must be there: just as he was sure that there was a Mont Blanc made of salt in the upper reaches of the Missouri. Credulous and idly inquisitive, he pottered about with a hundred things: rather like some old farmer of an ingenious turn of mind, who constructs a clockwork scarecrow, or a primitive milker for a cow: only, being a super-farmer, he, on a Bouvard and Pecuchet pattern, ransacked the Arts and Sciences.

He was a little the sort of man who is the laughing-stock or scandal of an English countryside—works on his estate in old dungarees, or builds himself a "Folly." Democracy seems to have been one of his cranks: for there is little evidence that he was consumed with a passion for Freedom. He was no Count Tolstoi with his Negro slaves, and never seemed to mind being rich. It was just one of those lucky things, for America, that this very gifted man—very fortunately placed—with an itch for everything original, himself *"un original,"* as such get called in France—should have included what was at that time known as "democracy" among his many interests.

At Philadelphia he was socially ostracized, because of his "democratic" opinions. But this Virginian landowner did succeed in living like a member of the leisured class. His beautiful country house, Monticello, a pastiche of the Hôtel de Salm in Paris, had some of the attributes of an Ivory Tower. He had a tunnel built under a hill between Monticello and the slaves' quarters, as he liked to keep the darkies out of sight. Thomas Jefferson might be seen strolling about Washington with his arm through that of Tom Paine. And one only has to mention that name, and it becomes easy to explain whither my remarks have been tending. Tom Paine, as I am not the first person to point out, is the authentic fountain-head of American freedom. Jefferson was never a revolutionary of that

123

type. The *Common Sense* of Paine was the Bible of the American Revolution, regarded as an ideologic event.

The comparison has often been made of late between this bitter English doctrinaire and Lenin. That Jefferson and he were good friends is as it were a certificate of sincerity, if that were needed. But no one has doubted the soundness of this Founding Father. The most he has been accused of is "affectation." There are degrees of intensity, however: beside Paine's the libertarian flame of Jefferson looks a little smoky. It is a peasant's oil-lamp: Paine's is a neon light.

The particular brand of democracy known as "Jeffersonian democracy" is the strictly agricultural conception of the free life. His ideal State would be not too large, inhabited by a population of small farmers. In other words it would be Virginia, or something remarkably like it, minus big landowners. And there would be a Jefferson there, on top of a hill, in a romantic château, made to his own design—an untidy, dreamy seigneur, with "advanced ideas." He not only admitted no democracy except that enjoyed by the agriculturist, he held the very strongest views upon the alternative—the kind of democracy, namely, which mainly exists at the present time.

In a letter to Madison he wrote as follows upon that subject. "I think our government will remain virtuous for many centuries, as long as they are chiefly agricultural: and this they will be as long as there shall be vacant lands in any part of America. When they get piled up upon one another in large cities, as in Europe, they will become corrupt as in Europe."

Could Jefferson drop into Pittsburgh or Detroit today it is easy to imagine his feelings. He would find them "piled up upon one another" far more than anything he saw in eighteenth-century Paris. He would find "them" eminently "corrupt." He would see at once that democracy as he understood it was at an end.

Here is a quotation from the *Notes on Virginia*.

"While we have land to labor, let us never wish to see our citizens occupied at a workshop or twirling a distaff . . .

Let our workshops remain in Europe. It is better to carry provisions and materials to workmen there, than to bring them to the provisions and materials, and with them their manners and principles . . . The mobs of great cities add just so much to the support of pure government as sores do to the strength of the human body." This last shows a remarkable community of view with Hamilton.

Marxian Socialism would be anathema to this particular Democrat, for its doctrine postulates a society of industrial workers. Jeffersonian democracy was that of a Swiss canton or of the early American farmer, in his mountain valley.

The main purpose, of course, of this part of my political narrative is to lay bare the binary roots of what we see on the political scene at the moment of writing. Mr. Franklin Roosevelt and Mr. Woodrow Wilson, and now Mr. Truman, are Democrats: they trace their political descent from Jefferson, the "states-rights" man, whereas the Republicans go back to the Federalist power-doctrines: to the great original centralizer, Hamilton.

But Franklin Roosevelt was the most consummate centralizer since Lincoln. If you are a "states-rights" man and favor a decentralization of power, you would at present derive a little (a very little) more comfort from the Republicans than from the Democrats.

Now contrast for a moment, one after the other, a few of the leading principles of the Jeffersonian doctrine, and the corresponding attitude of Franklin Roosevelt upon the same topics.

Jefferson said, "I am for a government rigorously frugal . . . and not for a multiplication of offices and salaries merely to make partisans."

But Mr. Roosevelt, as I outlined in an earlier chapter, built up a formidable army of Federal agents and appointees beholden to him. He "made partisans." And as to the national debt!

Jefferson was a "states-rights" man—a decentralizer.

But Mr. Roosevelt was the arch centralizer.

Jefferson was unsympathetic to the industrial worker. "Consider the class of artificers as . . . the instruments by which the liberties of a country are generally overturned." The farmer, the agriculturist, was the man he liked.

But Mr. Roosevelt favored the workshop as against the farm, and among the farmers were to be found his bitterest enemies.

Jefferson, like Jackson, disliked banks and bankers.

But Mr. Roosevelt—like Mr. Wilson—got on pretty well with bankers.

This catalogue of violent contrasts could be continued indefinitely. In all respects except one Mr. Roosevelt was in fact a disciple of Hamilton, and diametrically opposed to Jefferson.

That one respect in which Mr. Roosevelt resembled Jefferson was that both announced themselves protectors of the common man (though in Jefferson's case he insisted on his client being an agricultural laborer). What for Hamilton was "the mob" was for Mr. Roosevelt "the forgotten man." In leaving Jefferson let us salute him as a serious statesman, whose instinct was for what is just and rational, but who gave his name to a utopia. Virginia, at that time, was in its way an idyll. Virgil's *Bucolics* could not be made into a political system, however: he should have seen that this momentarily happy condition, of a small farming community, in a virgin country, was too good to last: that the theory that all the disagreeable things, such as wars, slums, and insanitary congestion attendant upon factory life, could indefinitely be confined to Europe, while America led a privileged existence—far away from the smoke and grime and violence which had become the lot of Europe—providentially spared from "corruption" and cut-throat competition, was untenable. This was a short-sighted, even a self-righteous, nationalism.

When it is said that Jefferson stands for what is best, most idealistic and youthful, in America, we must accept that as substantially true. Had it not been for Jefferson, America would have been a far less attractive place. On the other hand it is a legacy of unreality, like the dream of a golden age. It serves to deepen the nonsense supervening, when tough politics and cut-throat business masquerade beneath the homespun of the simple farmer, candid-eyed, strayed out of that delectable Rousseauist democracy of Jefferson's imagination.

This isolationism was not confined to the Democratic faction, however. Gouverneur Morris, an arch-reactionary, used almost the same words as Jefferson; only whereas Jefferson insisted that the United States must at all costs remain agricultural, Morris, an advocate of industrialization, considers the development of industry essential, in order to secure for America the same blissful isolation preached by Jefferson. "Our produce," he said, "becomes daily more and more abundant . . . from the cheapness of living and of raw material [we] shall make great and rapid progress in useful manufacture. This alone is wanting to complete our independence. We shall then be a world by ourselves, and far from the jars and wars of Europe. Their various revolutions will serve merely to instruct and amuse, like the roaring of a tempestuous sea, which at a certain distance becomes a pleasing sound."

This last comfortable image, replete as it is with a rather repulsive egotism, has, even up to the present time, been too often the attitude of isolationism in the New World. On the other hand, if the Americans desired to be left alone, it was only by becoming an industrial nation that they could achieve that end.

There is another circumstance I might add to this brief description of Thomas Jefferson, namely the founding of what was known as the Virginia Dynasty. He handed on the Presidency to his friend Madison, who in his turn passed it on to Monroe. This latter reigned until 1825: so the first quarter of the nineteenth century was filled with Jefferson's Virginia Dynasty.

The government at Washington developed into a comfortable little oligarchical tea-party, then in the year 1812, at the time of war No. 2 with England, the New England states were in a highly excitable state and secession was seriously threatened. For Washington, D.C., was in the South (as the result of a deal between Jefferson and Hamilton) and Southerners had a monopoly of power. In 1814 Gouverneur Morris wrote to his nephew, David Ogden, to suggest calling together a convention to "consult on the state of the nation." The convention was to be shown how the administration (it was that of Madison) would perpetuate its power "by Negro votes and Louisiana states." These "gentlemen Jacobins" of 1814 (Jefferson and his friends) aroused precisely the same feelings as did the New Dealers of the thirties of this century. "Democrat" was a term that, for the reactionary, carried the same implication as "red" at the present day: whereas France, as a nation, stood exactly where Russia stands now. In Morris's words, Mr. Madison, the President, was "full of French feelings." This was the same as saying, in our time, "He is Russophile."

"What chance is there," Gouverneur Morris petulantly asks, "of better rulers if the Union is preserved?" Secession alone would cure this ill, it must be the knife, the time had passed for physic. The Virginia Dynasty had been going then for a decade. Jefferson lived into the twenties—all the time it was no better than if he had been personally in charge, since he remained for the Presidents that succeeded him the supreme oracle: and Monticello was uncomfortably near to Washington. It was the same situation as Franklin Roosevelt's protracted tenure of office: and Gouverneur Morris had come to the point where he felt that nothing short of secession—and a tolerably bloody one at that—would "save civilization."

For the proposed secession of the New England states and of New York he had fixed the future frontiers, more or less. "It will be for you therefore," he writes his nephew, "to say of which section you choose to be the frontier. Pennsylvania . . . may be led to cover with her broad shield the slave-holding states: which, so protected, may for a dozen or fifteen years exercise the privilege of strangling commerce, whipping Negroes, and brawling about the inborn inalienable rights of man."

(This was, of course, an ironical reference to Mr. Jefferson's document, the Declaration of Independence: "that all men are created equal; that they are endowed by their Creator with certain inalienable Rights: that among these are Life, Liberty, and the pursuit of happiness." All of which Gouverneur Morris would have classed as did Wilson—French ideologic abstractions.)

To show how near the United States was to secessionist warfare at this early date, let me quote again from Morris (the same year, 1814): "And when matters came to the issue of force, superior force and skill must, under the Divine direction, prevail. But I hear some of the brethren exclaim, 'O Lord! O Lord! why, this is civil war!' And what of it? Kind souls, could you, by weeping and wailing and the gnashing of teeth, prevent civil war it might be safe, if not wise, to weep and wail. But Eastern patriots will not ask you permission to defend their rights, and, however much you may be disposed to cushion yourselves in your easy chairs, the prick of the Yankee bayonet will make you skip like squirrels!"

Mr. Morris on his Northern estate entertained feelings of extreme ferocity about Mr. Jefferson, on his Southern estate. So did others in those parts. The Northeastern bloc came near in consequence to seceding at that time: only they had been making so much money out of the war with England that the impulse was not quite strong enough. On the contrary it was Virginia, the Old Dominion, which fifty years later seceded, on April 17, 1861, about the same time as the other ten Southern states. But the issue in that case was no longer social revolution.

The title of this chapter—"The Beautiful Polarity of Hamilton and Jefferson"—is descriptive of what, for all practical purposes, exists. These were two men who thought very differently. The issue that separated them so profoundly was that fundamental one of the "Haves" and "Have-nots." But this chapter will, I hope, have a double purpose: (1) to stress the beautiful symmetry of this cleavage; and (2) to show how,

129

if we could drop all these people down into the midst of our twentieth-century life, the cleavage would disappear. Jefferson would be a Tory, just as much as Morris: Jefferson would be so violently against the social conditions prevailing in his new surroundings, that he would begin talking rather like Morris.

17 AMERICA ESCAPED A KING BY INCHES

America might have had a king. He would have had the same name as George III, King of England. For he was none other than George Washington.

I do not think that anyone has ever claimed for Washington military ability such as that possessed by General Lee or General Grant. That he was a keen land agent and good businessman seems established. He ran a large farm property intelligently. Otherwise he was one of those men whose great place in history is fortuitous: in a non-military country he was at a given moment the nearest thing to a military man. He was "the man on horseback" of that place and time.

Once the American colonies had formally announced their separation from the mother country, and they had to set up a government of their own, it might be supposed that the natural thing for them to do was to elect a President and become a republic. That, in fact, was not the only alternative open to them. For instance, they had the example of the Polish Republic, which had an elective king, to follow, if they so desired. Technically they could become a republic, and still have a king. Or they need not be a republic at all. They could, though a new country, elect a king, either for life, or invoking the hereditary principle. An American dynasty would thus have begun its checkered career.

Republics had a poor Press: they were considered a rather second-rate State-form. Many serious objections could be brought against them, so people would be apt to do a great deal of thinking before selecting a republican form of government. Even those Americans who had lived in France, like Benjamin Franklin, would hesitate about a republic. Franklin, who was old, had associated in France with the followers of Voltaire and Rousseau, from whom he would have learned to advocate constitutional monarchy upon the English pattern, not a republic. England was the universal model in his day, whereas in Morris's it was with many Frenchmen the United States. By that time American republicanism had, in part, taken the place of English constitutional monarchy.

However—very hard as this is to believe—Jefferson, when consulted by his revolutionary friends in Paris (Lafayette, Barnave, etc.), set his face against a republic for France. Even *he* had not much belief in a republic, though committed to republicanism at home. Defiantly he named his Party the "Republican," which was regarded as daring, almost reckless. This name was intended, however, to convey anti-monarchical, rather than republican, sentiments.

What, more than anything else, however, was decisive, and made it more likely than not that the Americans would favor a republic without a king, was that they were Whigs. England had been more or less ruled by Whigs until George III came to the throne; and, instead of satisfying his thirst for power over in Hanover (which was what, by all the rules of the game, he was supposed to do), concentrated his attention upon England, and took as his model the French autocracy. This was a disaster for the Whigs. At the time of the American revolution their fortunes were at their lowest ebb in England. The Whig leaders described their cause as hopeless. Then came this Whig insurrection in America—and it was engineered by a Whig majority: those of their Party in England watched it spellbound, believing their own fate to be wrapped up in it. The colonies might turn the tide. The defeat, even, of their fellow-partisans in America might be the signal of their proscription in England. The Duke of Richmond had made arrangements for his flight to France, in that event.

In the House of Lords the Earl of Chatham denounced the war in a series of impassioned addresses. On January 20,

1775, he moved an address to the King, in the Upper House, appealing to George III to send orders to General Gage in America to remove his troops as soon as possible. "For myself," he cried, "I must declare and avow that in all my reading of history—and it has been my favourite study . . . no nation or body of men can stand in preference to the General Congress at Philadelphia. All attempts to impose servitude on such men, to establish despotism over such a mighty continent, must be vain, must be *fatal*. We shall be forced ultimately to retract; let us retract while we can, not when we must!"

In 1777 came an even more eloquent onslaught upon the policy of the government, in a speech in which the Duke of Grafton considered he had surpassed himself. "My Lords, you cannot conquer America. You may swell every expense and every effort still more extravagantly . . . If I were an American, as I am an Englishman, while a foreign troop was landed in my country, I would never lay down my arms— never, never, never!"

All Englishmen did not feel like this; the Whigs were in the minority, just as for that matter there were doubtless more of the leading citizens in the United States against Washington than for him. It was, like our present wars in Europe, a civil war. In 1776, for instance, the Whigs in the House of Commons, to mark their violent disapproval of the American policy of the government, practically seceded. They ceased to attend. The victory of the American Whigs was hailed in England as a great victory for whiggery, or liberalism, everywhere, as everyone now understands it to have been. (And American school histories would be none the worse, or less "American" if they gave a suitable prominence to these facts, without which it is impossible to understand the true nature of the birth of that great state.)

In the silk and gilt squalor of the Stuart Courts—as well as in bleak hillside conventicles—grew up a Party of resistance to autocratic rule known as the Whig. The Whig Lords were not always the same—they passed from Party to Party a little. But in a general way the Whig Party had its roots in Crom-

133

well's armies: they came from the same side of the fence as the Puritans and others who formed the bulk of the first New England settlers. Some of their great aristocratic leaders were, ultimately, the product of the upstart Tudor nobility. But, in whatever degree, they were the ideologic first cousins of the colonists—could see quite well why they had taken their departure for the New World, rather than struggle along in England—the victim of religious intolerance and arbitrary government.

Washington, the leader of the Whig insurrection, was, however, a very broad-minded man. If the Americans had asked him to accept a crown, no misplaced bigotry would have caused him to say no. Indeed, his monarchical and military aims—for he was in favor of a standing army, among other things, as men of that period saw it, a sure sign of a despot— were recognized and disliked, certainly by many people. Mackay, a member of the early Congress, expresses a wish in his journal that Washington might go to Heaven at once. Fearful lampoons and verbal attacks upon him came incessantly from the direction of the "democratic" camp. At one time in Philadelphia a mob ten thousand strong—crying for war against England—threatened to drag him out of his house. He was openly accused of having wished to negotiate a peace with the English during the War of Independence.

The nature of the charge brought against Washington by the Jeffersonians was—to put it in the language of today—that he was a fascist. He was a "political general." He was a military man who ran a kind of Court. There is a very interesting book in this connection with the title "The Court of Washington"—it describes his ceremonial habits, and those of "Lady Washington," as she was called: the State-barge in which he was, with much pomp, translated from the Jersey shore to Manhattan, the military and diplomatic etiquette, the levees and drawing-rooms which developed, after his inauguration.

All this made excellent political ammunition. Alexander Hamilton was responsible, of course, for the regal build-up.

134

For the whole plan of the Federalist faction consisted in accumulating power in the hands of the Federal administration, emphasizing its importance at the expense of that of the states.

Washington himself was for strong centralized authority. He believed in authority—he enjoyed authority. There were no political Parties, naturally, to start with: only factions. Washington's was a One-Party State. It was Jefferson who broke away into open Party opposition and so inaugurated the Party-system in the U.S.A.

Even during the War of Independence Washington was hardly a very popular figure. The Congress throughout that period was so hostile to him, as a Military Man (a typical British form of prejudice) that they almost lost the war. At the Valley Forge period, and before that, Washington was kept without supplies; to such an extent that numbers of his bedraggled, famished militia deserted to the English. His bitter comment was that he felt himself in an enemy country. The farmers hid their stuff from Washington's foraging parties; all this time abundant supplies were brought in and sold to the English army.

These were the unpropitious backgrounds: it is not surprising that when Washington became the President of the United States, the first thought of most of the leading men was to restrict, and keep within bounds, his personal power. Their second thought was, of course, directed against the People. Better a little bit too much personal rule, than no rule at all. There must be *somebody* to keep the Many in order, lest they try to attack the Few. A peculiarly disquieting case of mob-law happened round about that time up in New England. General Washington benefited in consequence—for these notables were easily frightened.

After years of Opposition—of invective and Party-polemic —Jefferson stepped into Washington's shoes. It is little wonder that as President—obliged himself to be the reverse of what he had once accused Washington of being—he was a model of informality. He introduced into the presidential "palace" at Washington (as the White House was called prior to 1812) what he described as "the principle of *pêle-mêle*."

Were a civilian insurrectionist, having liquidated the Colonel, to place himself at the head of a regiment, his first act would be to scream at the rank and file, "No more marching in step! Walk along just as you please, boys!" This was the "principle of *pêle-mêle*," of course. And it emphasizes what is tolerably clear about Jefferson: his "democracy" was what we should describe today as "anarchy." (Morris called it anarchy, too. But by "anarchy" that fierce Tory meant something different.)*

Anarchy of that kind was what America needed. In 1801 Jefferson was inaugurated President. This date was considered by him of great historical moment. He had saved America, so he thought, "from monarchy and militarism."

1801 is, in fact, one of the key dates in American history. How these dates—for orienting oneself—go (to improve on an earlier table) is 1776, U.S.A. born (but it was born in an English monarchical and aristocratic mold). 1801, Jefferson, the great Democrat, becomes President. (The English Tory influence, for which Hamilton, and in a lesser degree, Washington, stood, is finally routed.) 1828, Andrew Jackson becomes President. (Spectacular confirmation of democracy— though Jefferson disliked this latest Jeffersonian. Still pioneer days, and Jackson and Lincoln, the last great figures of the old kind—unless he and Lincoln are something half old and half new.) 1861–65, the Civil War (Abraham Lincoln). Then comes, more or less quickly, the scourge of Super-Capitalism: half-smothered, Democracy struggling against this new dragon, as once it struggled against a rather stupid Man on Horseback, not unwilling to wear a crown.

Words—the *terms* used in the initial organizing process when

*It is legitimate to inquire whether Jefferson did not, in his desire to promote states-rights, deliberately, if not degrade, at least not too much enhance the authority of the Presidency. What can be said, is that, unlike "King Andrew" who went in as a "states-rights" man, but succumbed to the lures of power, Jefferson was not attracted by power or authority for its own sake.

a new society is taking shape—are of tremendous importance. So before proceeding I will trace the strange history, upon the North American continent, of the two words "republican" and "democratic."

These two words played hide-and-seek with each other for a long while. They combined, flew apart, changed places: vanished and turned up again. The word "republican" has at one time been used by Jefferson, at another time by Hoover. It was Andrew Jackson who finally effected the transformation of "republican" into "democrat": the discarded word drifting off, eventually being used to describe a political principle the opposite of that of its earliest patrons.

We need not trouble ourselves with those intricacies. The odd fact which is worth our while to take particular note of is how the two great political Parties of today both bear names which were originally of ill-repute or small esteem. Indeed, the word "democratic" has only been admitted into currency of late years though its sister term, "republican," of course, has been respectable much longer.

Charles Beard is my authority in this instance. I will quote directly, however.

A majority of the men who used the word [democracy] in the convention that framed the Constitution continued to view democracy as something rather to be dreaded than encouraged. Until well into the nineteenth century, the word was repeatedly used by the conservatives to smear opponents of all kinds. . . .

Thomas Jefferson, unless my eyes failed me, never used the word in any of his public papers or publicly called himself a democrat. . . . [This in spite, apparently, of the "Democratic Societies."]

After the Jefferson-Jackson Republicans took the title "the American Democracy" in 1844, that phrase, to the public, simply meant the Democratic Party. It is true that many writers by that time spoke of the United States as a democracy, but that description was not universally accepted. . . .

If the indices to periodical literature are any basis of judgment, there was little general interest in democracy as the dominant, characteristic name or symbol of American political and social faith between 1860 and 1917. Republican Presidents still shrank from using the term in this broad sense. When James Bryce published his great treatise on the United States, in 1888, he entitled it *The American Commonwealth*. He did not use the title American Democracy, as Tocqueville, the French writer on America, had done fifty years before.

Nothing like official sanction was given to the idea that the United States is first and foremost a democracy until Woodrow Wilson, in making the war against the Central Powers a war for democracy, gave the stamp of wide popularity to the idea that the United States is, first and foremost, a democracy. In the circumstances, even Republicans could scarcely repudiate it without acquiring a subversive tinge. . . .

. . . Finally, by a long process, the idea of democracy, which had been spurned, if not despised, in the early days of our nation, by a majority of the people as well as by practically all high-born and conservative citizens, became generally, though not universally, recognized as the definition for the American way of life and our political system.

The word "democrat" at the beginning was abusive. As to "republican," most of the conservatives entrusted with the framing of a Constitution were willing to give this displeasing form of government a trial. After all, the alternative seemed to be to install Washington as king. Benjamin Franklin described it as a temporary expedient, saying that in the end, of course, the United States would be a monarchy. (When Washington had passed out of the picture? Probably.)

Quite at the beginning people were not allowed to refer to the United States as a republic. That is very strange, is it not? The idea was, supposedly, to leave it an open question for the time being as to what kind of government they had, in fact, brought into the world.

Jefferson it was who insisted on the name: he obliged his colleagues to refer to it as a republic. As Minister he was pulled up sharply by Washington when he first began employing the word "republic" in State papers.

"On May 23, 1793, Washington called his [Jefferson's] attention to the word 'republic' in the draft of a State paper, with the remark that it was a word 'which he had never before seen in any of our public communications.' " However, a little later Jefferson had the satisfaction of seeing the alarming and subversive term "republic" make its appearance for the first time upon an official document. On November 28, 1793, "the expression 'our republic' had been introduced by Attorney General Randolph in his draft of the President's speech to Congress." Washington "made no objection." So finally that point had been gained.

There was one point upon which the Federalists were very firm: the United States and the republics of the ancient world must on no account be confused. "The true distinction between these [republics] and the American Government lies in the total exclusion of the people in their collective capacity from any share in the latter."

You would have thought that these men had been born in the topmost drawer, instead of which in many cases it was the bottom.

The only part of the Congress of the United States which the Founding Fathers took seriously was the Senate, modeled upon the House of Lords. Since unfortunately the common people—the *canaille*—must come into the picture *somewhere* (no way of avoiding that!) the House of Representatives was provided as a horrid playground. They were given practically no power, of course. Just a place in which to disport themselves.

How these earliest Americans regarded a city-state of antiquity resembled the jaundiced standpoint of Jefferson regarding the European city. What they saw in their fancy was a dense mass of greasy and ill-smelling people milling around, electing tribunes and city-magistrates. That was all very well for Athens, but it was not how things were going to be done in the New World.

18 THE REACTIONARIES

It was necessary to make Washington's position clear, which I think I have done: for he was the patron of Alexander Hamilton, without which stalking-horse it is doubtful whether the latter could have functioned. One piece of additional information I may as well supply: it is this. The President, as fashioned ultimately by the Founding Fathers, was (in spite of *Federalist* no. lxix), an almost slavish replica of George III, with a few of that peccant monarch's powers modified to suit the case. The American system of government, like its legal system, was in no way novel, but was taken over, lock, stock, and barrel, from the British. It was called a "republic" and its king was elected for a short term and called a "President." That was the only difference.

The ideas of the other people involved in the framing of the Constitution differed from Hamilton's not so much in kind as in degree. They had no wish to dissociate themselves from the English way of life: only to be free to manage their own affairs. Commercial considerations weighed with them more than anything else. Gouverneur Morris and Alexander Hamilton were not political oddities. They represented the majority opinion of the more prosperous citizens of the United States at the beginning of hostilities with England. Many "Tories" were so violently opposed to these seditious goings-on that they left the States and went up to Canada, or back to England. Morris and Hamilton, being young, became "patriots."

Alexander Hamilton was a "stranger"—a foreigner—and

was usually described by the "gentlemen Jacobins" as a beggarly little creole who knew who his mother was but not his father: that Hamilton was the name he went by, yes, but God alone knew if it belonged to him. These uncharitable suggestions have never been, I think, either proved or disproved entirely: though as what happens out of wedlock is so often productive of better results than what occurs in it, and since grace and intelligence are at least as common among those not of great estate as those who are, it is not impossible that the detractors of this gallant little man were right. He managed while still very young to get to New York, to obtain the best education that was to be had, and to marry into an important patroon family. These were feats which testified to climbing ability of a high order. When at first the trouble blew up, he favored the British side—for if ever there was a Tory it was he, whether he came into the world in a flophouse or in a ducal bed. Both Hamilton and Morris were at one time denounced as "collaborationists" or "fifth columnists." Later Hamilton joined the Revolutionary Army and became a general. The war over, he practiced law in New York City.

This Founding Father was odd in more ways than one, and in none more than in his military pretensions. Even his violent death is not unconnected with that. The fact is that he was not obligated to accept Burr's challenge. Everyone knew he was as brave as a lion: and Burr was one of those men it was not necessary to take too seriously. But here was the motive, a laughable one, that weighed with him more than life itself—more than the thought of his wife and family, who were left destitute. He believed himself destined to play a role upon the North American continent similar to that of Napoleon in Europe. He regarded himself as a great man of action, endowed with an extraordinary genius for war: not as a great economist, nor as a Founding Father: just as the coming Napoleon, although by this time he was quite old.

Jefferson—as the situation had been analyzed by him—was the Mirabeau, who would be driven out and would disappear: the anarchy his weak rule would bring about would fatally lead

141

to the arrival of a Robespierre. *Then* would come Hamilton's turn—the military genius would take the helm. In the end, no doubt, he would be crowned Emperor of America.

A standard pattern for all history had been evolved and accepted by these politicians, derived from their reading of Aristotle's *Politics* and so on down to *L'Esprit des Lois*. In this respect they were not unlike a group of undergraduates. Their minds were dominated by a rigid, cut-and-dried pattern of political cause and effect. In Paris Gouverneur Morris writes about somebody with whom he was discussing the Revolution: "I tell him that it seems probable that despotism will be re-established as the necessary consequence of anarchy." So, seeing this was the law, and that in France a civil despot had been succeeded by a military despot, and seeing that from the democratic phase in America nothing but anarchy could ensue, Alexander Hamilton calmly awaited the sequel, till his hour should strike.

No one was better acquainted with Hamilton than was Gouverneur Morris. They were close friends from their early twenties. The Federalists were called by their enemies "the English Party." Morris, like his friend, was pro-British; like him, a Federalist, though he had declined Hamilton's suggestion that he should contribute to the *Federalist Papers*. Mrs. Morris tells us that her ancestor "was no pronounced Party man." He writes himself: "In general the policy of the Federal men was agreeable to me; but they did some things which I cannot reconcile to my notion of political economy." On the political side their views must have been nearly identical, except that he did abandon all ideas of a king for the United States, as did most other Tory sympathizers.

Alexander Hamilton "was indiscreet, vain, and opinionated." It was his friend's *indiscretion* which seems to have disturbed Morris more than anything else. Like all his contemporaries, Morris testifies to Hamilton's perfect honesty (but, even there, the reason for his honesty is found to detract from the good marks which otherwise must have accrued). When as Finance Minister his enemies thought to entrap him, the

142

investigation into his management of the Federal finances proved that not so much as a cent was unaccounted for. What seems almost inconceivable (according to modern standards) in the case of one so favorably placed to enrich himself, he died in debt. As Morris said: "General Hamilton was of that kind of man which may most safely be trusted; for he was more covetous of glory than of wealth or power." He however adds: "But he was of all men the most indiscreet." So even his honesty is seen by Morris as the diagnostic of a vice of character, not as a positive virtue.

"Speaking of General Hamilton" (this was after his death in 1804), "he had little share in forming the Constitution. He disliked it, believing all republican governments to be radically defective." Morris does not go into this: but Hamilton first advocated a monarchy: that meeting with no support, as the next best thing he proposed a President to be elected for life, with power to appoint governors for all the states (a power formerly exercised, of course, by the Crown) and with many other extravagant suggestions.

This he was, of all things, proposing to an oligarchy-in-the-making, who naturally turned it down. The argument used by Hamilton for the bestowal of these vast powers was that if the power were insufficient "to carry the business honestly," then a corrupt understanding between the dominant faction in the Congress and the President would be the inevitable result. Total independence must hence be secured to him. This extreme theory of personal power, and the efficacy of rule by a single individual, whose judgment and whose will should be made the law of the land, found few supporters. Which it should have been obvious to Hamilton must be the case. So why did he so relentlessly persevere?

Morris chides, in retrospect: "He knew that a limited monarchy, even if established, could not preserve itself in this country. He knew, also, that it could not be established, because there is not the regular gradation of ranks among our citizens which is essential to that species of government, and he very well knew that no monarchy whatever could be established but by the mob." In other words, what was the use, Morris was saying, of suggesting a king to the notables of the Convention or of the Congress, who had no desire to give themselves a master? They themselves wanted to be the only master.

As to the mob, which alone could have brought about what Hamilton desired: "When a multitude of indigent . . . people can be collected and organized, their envy of wealth, talents, and reputation will induce them to give themselves a master, provided that in so doing they can mortify and humble their superiors." He adds: "Fortunately for us, no such mass of people can be collected in America." One could, of course, object that should such a popular revolution occur, the "mob" would hardly be likely to set up a Constitutional Monarch. A Protector, a Consul, a President, but scarcely a Hereditary Monarch. However, he is perfectly right in insisting that it is absurd to suppose that a business oligarchy could be persuaded to do so: more especially since, as he observes, they had no reason to fear the masses, and so needed no great principle of authority around which to rally.

Fully aware as he was of these things—for though a fool in one or two ways, which is what Morris is asserting, in general he was a man of great intelligence—"he never failed on every occasion to advance the excellence of and avow his attachment to monarchical government. By this course he not only cut himself off from all chance of rising into office, but singularly promoted the views of his opponents, who, with the fondness for wealth and power which he [Hamilton] had not, affected a love for the people, which he had, and which they had not."

In his angry retrospect Morris places his finger involuntarily upon what was essentially Hamilton's greatness. In his very criticism, he shows us why this man is one of the two or three most venerated figures in American history, and still today is as much an object of controversy as ever. Hamilton was sincere: one does not have to hesitate, to weigh this and weigh that, one just puts it down as one could write, "Napoleon was short of stature," or "Mr. Wilson wore glasses." In the same manner one says: "He was not corrupt or selfish." But Hamil-

144

ton was by no means the only person who wished to see a Constitutional Monarch in America. Morris was in favor of that, as an earlier quotation showed. More were against it than for it, and the advocates of monarchy did not succeed.

So why, Morris asks, did he *insist:* after it had become quite plain that that issue was dead, why continue his futile propaganda?

The answer (one that Morris would not have understood) is simply that he believed sincerely—as stated above—that a republic necessarily becomes a democracy, and that a democracy necessarily is a corrupt and disorderly type of government. Of the political philosophers by whose works he had become mesmerized, none except the Athenians knew very much about democracy. Most took it at second hand, as he did, from antiquity. There are few of us today who share Hamilton's belief. We consider that democracy, if not in one form, then in another, is workable. Any kind of monarchy we regard as a barbarous survival. But the ideas of Hamilton represent one of the cardinal beliefs in political science: that popular government, namely, is a decadent State-form. It is a belief that has been held by most of those whom we agree to regard as "great thinkers." It is therefore not necessarily either wicked or stupid to entertain such a belief. It is unpopular now, and was unpopular at that time in America, that is all.

Jefferson, Madison, and the rest were shrewd and sensible, says Morris, where the Federalist leader was wrong-headed, and in some ways a fool; they—though of course no great lovers of the people, less so, in fact, than was Hamilton—being smart politicians, *affected* to love the "common man," and reaped their reward. Power and respect were their lot: whereas poor Hamilton, killed in a one-sided duel by one of them (by one who was in at the birth of Tammany, and Vice-President in Jefferson's term of office) because he would not trim or desert what he regarded as the road of "wisdom" and "virtue," died as the leader of, in Morris's words, a "proscribed" Party.

We always come back, in Morris's account, to what he regarded as a fatal shortcoming of Hamilton's: namely that

145

absence in him of a "fondness for wealth and power." It was, nevertheless, as I have suggested, precisely this indifference to power and lack of interest in wealth, combined with his great ability and steadfast adherence to a principle, which make Hamilton so pre-eminent a figure. Most people engaged in the promotion of monarchical or aristocratic forms of government are by no means averse to a little power themselves, and money is by no means the thing farthest from their thoughts. So Alexander Hamilton was one of those great curiosities—a man whose politics were not traceable to a personal motive.

Morris does report, among other things, that, of late, he had been somewhat more sensible: though by that time his Party was hopelessly discredited. "In maturer age, his observation and good sense demonstrated that the materials for an aristocracy do not exist in America . . . taking the people as a mass, in which there was nothing of family, wealth, prejudice, or habit to raise a permanent mound of distinction—in which, moreover, the torrent of opinion had already washed away every mole-hill of respect raised by the industry of individual pride." In his youth, as a foreigner accustomed to expect "permanent mounds of distinction" everywhere, Hamilton hardly noticed that no such mounds existed in America, where "leveling" had got rid of even the smallest "mole-hill of respect." He imagined himself in socially quite hilly scenery. Always he in fact seems a little hallucinated.

There were signs far earlier than Morris dates it that he had begun to see reason. When he was Washington's "mentor" (as Jefferson called him) his illusions as to bringing these bumptious and quarrelsome colonists to an understanding of the beauties of ceremonial and etiquette had weakened. We find him, to our great surprise, advising Washington against any departure from the drab democratic norm, as in his eyes it seemed.

To say a final word or two on Hamilton—though all that I have been doing, it is realized, I hope, is to pick out what is of most interest in each of these figures for the furthering of my argument. Personal motives—the term I employed above—

146

cover so much. A personal motive of sorts can nearly always be found. So let us, for the sake of greater accuracy, agree that Hamilton socially was more attracted to people with nice manners, living in handsome houses, than by people in poor circumstances.

I should not think that the "forgotten man" occupied a very prominent place in his mind. But neither did he in Jefferson's, except as an eighteenth-century abstraction—the simple, "virtuous" farmer. It is impossible to attribute all of that fidelity to an idea, to social snobbery: Hamilton was a man susceptible to ideas, in the way the French are. If, much later on in American history, his economic authoritarianism, his dreams of power (for others), his mercantilism, in contrast to the agriculturism of Jefferson, his violently centralizing doctrine—if in consequence of this rigid polarity and fierce partisanship he became an obvious historic symbol for monopoly capital now to avail itself of, it is not entirely fair to this man of so utterly different a time.

Lincoln was at least as much a centralizer as was Hamilton; they both had the same guiding principle—Union and Power. Jefferson Davis was a kind of political descendant of Jefferson: Jefferson would have been a very violent Southern partisan, had he been alive in 1861. Both these latter men cared less for the idea of a powerful State, for which great unity is necessary, than for some principle of freedom, and for the privileges of the individual man. If we banish from our minds what was absurd about Hamilton—his tiresome monarchism, his Napoleon-complex—then we have a great figure. Who would not rather be Jefferson? But there have to be Hamiltons, too. He was a rather attractive Hamilton.

Mr. Henry Wallace, I believe, has compared Franklin Roosevelt with Hamilton. This comparison would be far-fetched, if it were seriously advanced. Had it been possible, by means of some sorcery, to cause the warring spirits of Jefferson and Hamilton to inhabit one body, the result might be vaguely reminiscent of Mr. Roosevelt. All by himself, Hamilton would seem to repel that attempt at equation.

147

I will now turn to Gouverneur Morris more particularly. He is just a late eighteenth-century American clubman, with a few talents not usually possessed by men of that type. He is a historical specimen piece: not of intrinsic interest, as was his great friend. He is selected for portrayal because he was very close indeed to Hamilton: and, in his Paris diary and letters, is a great source of enlightenment upon the contemporary American mind, brought out wonderfully in that foreign environment.

Morris's uncle, Robert Hunter Morris, had been Governor of the colonies of Pennsylvania and New Jersey. His brother, General Morris, was an officer in the English Army and married to the Duchess of Gordon. He had not been a "poor boy," therefore, like his friend Alexander Hamilton.

In 1775 when Morris was twenty-three, a rupture seemed imminent between the mother country and the colonies. He engaged in "appeasement" activities, was a member of a committee formed to settle difficulties with Great Britain or to promote a better understanding—something on the lines of the Anglo-German Fellowship, immediately prior to 1939. In 1783 he was accused of being involved in a monarchist plot. Although on the whole far more "discreet" than Hamilton, his aversion for democracy was equally great, and he hankered after a monarch, too, as has been said, in his less doctrinal way. In 1781 he writes to Nathaniel Green: "I will go farther, I have no hope that our Union can subsist except in the form of an absolute monarchy."

Whether we find Morris in New York, dismissing his servant for objecting to ride behind his carriage, or in Paris, his wooden leg stuck out, sitting beside Mme. de Flahaut in that lady's bedroom, while M. de Talleyrand goes out to get her warming-pan heated up, it is a figure that is out of place, a sort of premature anachronism—if a "rich American" can be out of place, even a century before he is supposed to be there. Whenever we have a vivid glimpse of him it is of a dull "mound of distinction"—defending his mound and his money, threatening everyone with "despotism." Paris elicited all that would in

New York have melted into the landscape. He was almost too round a peg in a round hole: insufferably gallant, hobbling from boudoir to boudoir. At twelve in the morning we discover him sitting beside a lady in her bath—milk had been mixed with the water, so he was debarred from seeing more than the head and shoulders of the scintillating countess involved: at two he would be at the bedside of another patrician beauty—a *belle malade* and probably a marchioness—reading her some lines of his own composition, verse of a soggy elegance, full of trite insinuation, enervatingly amorous.

His stump—he refused to acquire a more civilized type of wooden leg—conferring upon him a certain chic; frilled and powdered and with a flow of appropriate French, his days as American Ambassador were spent laying ponderous siege to, or plunging into greater gloom with his dark sayings, or irritating by his aristocratic principles, a long array of great ladies —the Marquise de Ségur, Mme. de la Suze, the Comtesse de Frize, the Marquise de Chastellux, the Comtesse de Puisignieu, the Comtesse de Flahaut, the Duchesse d'Orléans, Mme. de Staël. As the envoy from the queer new Republic far away in the New World, about which everyone was full of curiosity, and for which many had a romantic admiration, he was everywhere warmly received.

Quite half these people, with high-sounding names, were a great deal more republican than he was: the Comtesse de Tessé, for instance. This was one of the women he was fondest of engaging in missionary work with—trying to convert her to aristocracy.

"All at once, in a serious tone [I ask]: '*Mais attendez, madame, est-ce-que je suis trop aristocrate?*' " Mme. la Comtesse de Tessé replied, "with a smile of gentle humiliation, '*Ah, mon Dieu, non.*' " But all the aristocrats thought he was far too aristocratic.

Or again, "dine with Mme. de Tessé—republican of the first feather. The countess, who is a sensible woman, has formed her ideas of government in a manner not suited, I think, to the situation . . . and there are many such." Indeed at first these noble persons shocked him very much. It was reciprocal — he shocked and astonished them. His ideas of government seemed not unlike those of the reigning house of France: but after decades of Enlightenment, of Voltaire and Rousseau and hundreds of little *philosophes* circulating round the salons, absolute monarchy had little attraction for them—especially as absolute monarchy had long ago robbed their order of its political power and turned them into Court lackeys. They could hardly understand what he was talking about (though he spoke admirable French), his politics were so violently archaic. Yet—and they could not make sense of this—he came from America, and the American Revolution had had a tremendous influence upon the French mind: it had played a decisive role in their own revolution, which was just getting under way.

Shortly after his visit to Mme. de Tessé's republican salon, Morris met Mme. de Lafayette, who told him coldly that she regarded him as "an aristocrat." This, of course, was a term of abuse, like "fascist." His effort to convert Mme. de Tessé was taken very amiss, for that lady had been active for years attempting to procure a constitution for France, and to break down the autocracy.

With M. de Lafayette he had many a brush: as when, in 1789, also at Paris, he notes as follows. "At dinner I sit next to M. de Lafayette, who tells me I injure the cause, for that my sentiments are continually quoted against the good Party. I seize this opportunity to tell him that I am opposed to the democracy from regard to liberty." That care for "liberty" has a familiar sound! He knew quite well what class of person were the beneficiaries of that type of liberty; he was speaking to Lafayette as one aristocrat to another. But the latter declined to look at it in this light and would have been highly insulted had you called him an "aristocrat."

As to the priesthood, the same shock awaited him there as among the aristocracy. They also wanted a constitution. Morris is, for instance, at the château of M. de Norrage. There there is as usual an abbé, who "declaims violently against moderation

150

in politics." Morris appeals indignantly to a gentleman who is near him, the Comte de Pelleux, and suggests that the latter ask this priest *what he wants*. The count shrugs and says: "He wants a constitution." But *what* constitution? However, a number of people present do not regard the abbé's attitude as strong enough. Morris becomes more and more scandalized. He is surrounded by a lot of *reds!* The greatest names in France, and they half of them talk like soapboxers!

Then there was the Bishop of Arras. You would think you would be safe with a bishop. But not a bit of it. He "tells me our new American Constitution is the best that has ever yet been found." Now, as Morris happened to have written that document, you would suppose that this remark would have caused him a great deal of pleasure. But it was quite the contrary: it warmed his heart as little as *his* eulogies of aristocracy pleased the republican countesses and princesses.

When the first mob violence occurred in Paris, and the hotel of the Duc de Castries was pillaged, Morris stumped round to his club. It was the Club de Valois, one of the most exclusive. There he was much dismayed to find that this act of the populace met with by no means universal disapproval.

This was the Carlton Club of Paris, of the last days of the Ancien Régime. The only people, he found, who *liked* being aristocrats were the "stuffy" ones. So there was really no one with whom Gouverneur Morris could share his enthusiasms for the caste system—for "mounds of distinction." This is perhaps why he did not feel it so deeply as one would have expected when a good few of these people had their heads cut off.

The proximate cause of this first mob outrage, even, provides another illustration of the anomalous state of affairs, so disappointing and baffling to Morris. The Duc de Castries had wounded a gentleman called M. Charles de la Meth, who belonged to the regiment of which he (the duke) was the colonel. A M. de Chauvigny had come to Paris to challenge M. de la Meth to a duel, because, he said, the latter had fomented mutiny in the regiment. But de la Meth refused to meet de Chauvigny before he had settled accounts with the

Duc de Castries; for it was the duke who had put de Chauvigny up to it. The Duc de Castries at once came to Paris, the duel was fought, and de la Meth wounded.

Here were some "aristos" fighting political duels, some of them leftists and some rightists. Charles de la Meth was very popular indeed with the Paris populace, so they sacked the hotel of the Duc de Castries, who had wounded him.

One more instance of the sort of difficulties encountered by Morris, in his enthusiasm for European courts, and of that aristocratic life of which there was so little in America. He had gone to Versailles to see the King welcome the States-General in the Salle des Menus. After the ceremony, being "tolerably hungry" he decides to find some place to eat. So as his horses are not yet harnessed he asks for dinner at a *traiteur*. At the table-d'hôte he finds that "some of the Tiers are sat down to it." The Tiers are, of course, "the People," or more usually with him, "the mob." Thereupon the same situation he is always confronted with, wherever he goes, declares itself, in the person of an anti-aristocratic aristocrat. But first he gets into conversation with the Tiers Etat.

"We enter into conversation, talk of the manner of voting. Tell them that I think when their new constitution is formed it will be well for them to vote *par ordre,* but in forming it to vote *par tête.*" (This means, return to the caste set-up, you varlets, once you have got your constitution, understand!) "Those who best understand the thing incline to this opinion." He finds himself agreed with only for a moment; these fellows are from Brittany and one of them (the insolent Hodge!) attacks hotly the tyranny of the nobles (forsooth!). Upon which they all veer round. One, "a noble representing the Tiers, is so vociferous against his order that I am convinced he means to rise by his eloquence."

The French Revolution was the work of the French middle class or bourgeoisie, it is generally said. For Gouverneur Morris, who consorted only with the aristocracy, it looked like a job for which the "lower orders" were responsible, aided and abetted by the aristocracy.

So much for these pages of Morris, and the firsthand evidence derivable from them. There were American Federalists and Tories, of course, more intelligent than Morris, who would not have presented so clownish a figure; yet their inner reactions would have been much the same as his. The spectacle of numbers of revolutionary aristocrats, who had lived for years in the full glare of the Enlightenment and wanted a king in France just as little as Jefferson wanted a king in the New World, would have repelled them. They would have thought, just as did their enemy, Jefferson, that France would not be France without a king.

For perhaps a majority of the French aristocracy their minimum demand was a Constitutional Monarchy such as the English had, and such as Montesquieu and Voltaire had taught them to believe in. It was the revenge of the aristocratic class for their ruin at the hands of French imperialist absolutism. But Morris was, in fact, something more than an "aristocrat." He was, like Hamilton, an absolutist. Those responsible for the "economic empires" of the U.S.A. have sometimes exhibited an absolutist spirit which would have done credit to the most arbitrary of the Roman emperors.

19 CONCLUSION OF PART I
(REGARDING CHARLES STUART)

As a witch says her prayers backward, I have moved from that superlative political conjuror, Franklin Roosevelt, back to the alien English "foundation" of a nation not destined to remain English, in an age that was more remote from the twentieth century than it was from the Rome of Cicero. Endeavoring madly, as at moments he was, to break out into the open—into the universal America of tomorrow—we met Roosevelt first. Going backward, we at last found ourselves with one of the earliest representatives of reactionary America, hobbling round the tottering boudoirs of the Ancien Régime, inhaling the last fragrance of an epoch in which America had been born.

Atomic or nuclear energy apart—which puts in question everything—the permanent revolution which scientific techniques entail makes our politics look absurd, like an archaic buggy upon an autobahn. What figure we can find to describe our *economic* system I hardly know. An ox-drawn cart making its way up Fifth Avenue will have to serve, though really that is far too snappy a conveyance at all adequately to represent what is meant. Gold is the arch-symbol of the barbarous nature of our twentieth-century institutions. All that is not technique stands still. Not only science, but scientific thinking, stops at the doors of our banks, and at the gates of our parliaments.

Human societies are engaged in a perpetual struggle to disengage themselves from a chaos of superannuated laws. The accelerated tempo of mechanical evolution makes things much

154

worse. We suffer from no superstitious attachment to a primitive type of automobile. But it is quite a different matter where government is concerned. A bundle of old statutes, or the medium of exchange hallowed by long use, has us bewitched. There a superstitious fixation makes of our political and economic life one vast "bottleneck."

We raise temples, even, like redoubts against change. "Be sure wherever you see an ancient temple it is the work of error," Voltaire asserted. And if you look inside and discover a bronze politician instead of a cross-legged idol, enthroned there, you can be no less positive of that. Error he may not have represented at the time, but you may be sure the deified politician does so now.

Revolutions are required, to satisfy the sanitary requirements of our social life. Yesterday's refuse has to be expelled generally with *brio*. It is idiotic, but we have discovered no more practical and orderly method. What should be discarded at brief intervals is allowed to accumulate, because of sloth, greed, or superstition. So the explosions have to be so big they shatter our society.

Could a new body of laws be enacted every week end, and the old ones thrown out, that would guarantee the efficient functioning of the national body. For a law is after all not a thing of beauty. It is of no more than transitory usefulness. As a rule, it is a mediocre prescription given us by a none too gifted doctor. Obviously the more often we change the laws, and the less superstitious confidence we develop regarding the lawmaker, the better for the body politic. In a free society of men competent to govern themselves (assuming such a society to be possible) a politician would not be a person of any great importance. The machinery of justice, civil and criminal, is there functioning daily, without our taking any more notice of those engaged in it than we do of the dustmen who remove the rubbish twice a week. We do not make heroes of those sorts of magistrates, nor ideally should we of the politician, or that other kind of magistrate, the Chief Executive himself.

When kings and queens were superseded by politicians, the

understanding was that importance of that kind was at an end. The People became the King, and politicians were the People's servants. The politician's task was supposed to be a quite humble one. Otherwise why not have carried on with the kings and queens, emperors and empresses? So, if you notice that a superstitious veneration is shown for politicians, you may be quite sure that undue power is once more being exercised; is vested in the ruler or rulers. That is, of course, if you believe in the possibility of "popular sovereignty," and do not regard that as just a beautiful phrase.

In effect we know—however much we may believe in the ultimate possibility of full "popular sovereignty"—that at present to say that "men are competent to govern themselves" (see my above proviso) does not agree with the facts.

A law made in a free society by a quite unimportant functionary—a mere politician—would be a day-to-day affair. Our society admittedly does not quite answer the description of free. Nevertheless, with conditions altering all the time, as is the case just now, and with such rapidity, laws require to be overhauled incessantly. This is not subservience to our techniques; the radio, television, the flying machine, and now atomic energy are not easy to ignore. It probably saves time to conform—be "subservient." And the most portentous of statutes is only a technique which should be scrapped with as little compunction as we do an obsolete mode of locomotion, or a lighting and heating system.

Yet the stark contradiction remains between more and more rapidly modified conditions of life—vastly multiplied power of production, etc., on the one hand, and the inherited rigidity of law on the other.

Men move into a new country or continent and take their laws with them, as they do their personal belongings. Yet if a man is moving from a very hot country to a very cold one, he provides himself, if possible, with warmer garments, and vice versa, should it be from the sub-arctic to the sub-tropic. Not so with laws. They never change until they drop off us in a state of advanced decomposition.

America offered to start with, and still provides in many important particulars, a striking example of these contradictions. It may be recalled that I quoted de Tocqueville, who bestowed much attention upon this subject. He discovered in New England an inherent contradiction: these people quite unconsciously had brought over from England in their baggage a full complement of reactionary laws. The brutal property laws of the English penal code came over side by side with Trial by Jury, the Writ of Habeas Corpus. Good and bad, there was all the bag of tricks by which the English were governed. When they surprised one of their fellow-colonists in the act of stealing a horse, embezzling, or committing bigamy, the lawyer who had come with them was consulted, and naturally went to work on the culprit with the legal tools he was used to handling.

But I will again quote de Tocqueville: "The . . . religion and the customs of the first immigrants undoubtedly exercised an immense influence on the destiny of their new country. Nevertheless, they could not found a state of things originating solely in themselves: no man can entirely shake off the influence of the past; and the settlers . . . mingled habits and notions derived from their education and the traditions of their country [England] with those habits and notions that were exclusively their own." With these latter habits and notions, of course, they began to build up a new personality, which eventually emerged as that of the American.

"Laws and customs are frequently to be met with in the United States which contrast strongly with all that surrounds them. These laws seem to be drawn up in a spirit contrary to the prevailing tenor of American legislation; and these customs are no less opposed to the general tone of society." You will, perhaps, remember that the cause of such anomalies was to be sought, de Tocqueville believed, in the fact that only lawyers knew anything about the law; and it was to their interest "to maintain them as they are, whether good or bad," simply because these men had, with much expense of time and energy, acquired a knowledge of this particular set of rules, and had no wish to be compelled to acquire a new set.

But if this is the case with law, and with lawyers, so is it also with economy, and with economists: though with these latter a factor is present of a quite different order. Monopolistic interests, with all the great power of which such interests dispose, set their face against any change in an antiquated system which has served their purpose so well, and has so many advantages from their standpoint over a new model.

This fairyland of bank capital and grandiose universal usury, out of which region a dense fog of unreality forever drifts over into politics, and makes them even more unreal than otherwise they might be, is an arcanum, of the very existence of which the average educated man is ignorant. It is relatively of recent date: for in the eighteenth century you or I would not be paying the monthly tradesman's bill by check, for then such things did not exist. The fairyland of Credit had not yet been built.

Only passing reference is being made here to this subject: it throws light upon the puzzling question of the seeming impossibility of bringing back rational standards into politics, so it cannot be left out. If politics came out of the bow-and-arrow stage, obviously economics would have to do so as well—to abandon its golden cave. So many interests, alas, prefer to confine us to a primitive and childish plane, whether in politics, or economics, or even in art. It is preferred that Alice in Wonderland should remain as she is, with her sublime candor unimpaired—rather than that she should grow up into a strong-minded political woman, such as the political hostesses with whom Gouverneur Morris had such difficulties in the Paris of the Revolution: that same Paris that is witnessing today the transfer of the banks from private hands to the guardianship of the State, the French being the first European government to take that obvious and necessary step.

Before very long all nations, such are the portents, will, as did the Reich, divest themselves of the competitive system of so-called "free enterprise." (This does not in any sense involve their turning to Communism.) It is no longer of such importance, therefore, to pay special attention to the casual trail where it is found to disappear into the massive portals of a bank.

All that need be said is that the great artificiality of politics, which in these pages I have been endeavoring to describe, is at least equaled, if not outdone, by the artificiality of economics. This is true of England as much as of America, though the United States is now the headquarters of the world of finance. The meaning of Bretton Woods was sufficiently aired in the Press, and the general public must have gained some insight, however slight, into these mysteries.

Is it possible that that inertia, or superstition of which I have been speaking—which results in the political capacity of mankind seeming to be so feeble, compared with its scientific and technological aptitude—is imposed upon the majority? Is there sabotage, in other words, where political techniques are concerned? To answer that question would be very complicated. But we are not obliged to do so here. The "sense of the State" is, as Professor Laski has said, one of the rarest of attributes; although it might be objected that in a free society—or where people are persuaded they form part of such a society—men tend to take no further notice of the activity of their politicians. They take it for granted they are doing their job to the best of their ability; as political technicians. They trust their lawyer and their plumber, not because they regard lawyers or plumbers as necessarily very trustworthy, but they have not time to acquire those techniques themselves. So with the techniques of statecraft. Perhaps in a "free society" people have less "sense of the State" than in an unfree one.

Even if the extent of the political paralysis (the prostration before obsolete formulas, the growing unreality of all ostensible government) may sometimes, in its fatuity, seem deliberate, it is undeniably a true image of mass-conservatism and confused thinking.

As to the backwardness of politics, millions of people ruling themselves (in so far as that exists) is an operation of a different order from one man designing an airplane, or bombarding the atom in his laboratory. In the nature of things, "science" is more efficient than politics. We hate the sacrifice of "popular sovereignty" it involves, the curtailment of liberty: but necessarily a Council of Ten, or a Politburo, or any small group of men controlling a State, works faster and better than where the machinery of power is very much more complex. Whatever the type of government, social engineering has for its material human beings, not steel, aluminum, or wood. It is the view of the democrat that when the Statesman begins to compete with the automobile manufacturer, or to treat men as if they were electrons, he has failed. And the sign that a human society was approaching its vital perfection would be the disappearance of government altogether.

Were I to return to this earth five centuries hence, and discovered a country the size of Great Britain ruled by a "Premier" and half a dozen secretaries, I should know that the "free society" so often said to be there was at last in actual being. But its citizens would have to be very differently trained from those composing any national group today. It should be our endeavor to assure the eventual arrival of such an ideal society. But we should never pretend it exists when it does not: for that is the way to postpone its arrival indefinitely and to encourage the exercise of lawless power, as mischievous as hypocritical.

2

We have seen how the United States was born out of the Whig revolution in England, and the Whigs were men of rank and influence under the Stuarts who availed themselves of that great reservoir of political power in the domain of religion represented by the Sectaries, Non-jurors, Quakers, Brownists, and the rest, to overwhelm the kingly power, which power they proposed to transfer to themselves. Swift's account of the Whig Lords—whose clients were the black-garbed hosts who had originally sprung from Wycliffe's Bible, and at last had set up a "Bible religion" against a "Church religion"—is very illuminating. They were a much more clever set of Lords than their Tory confrères.

The fidelity of Americans to the Whig formula of defiance of authority has confined the American mind in a conventional mold, though the mold was expanded and adapted to accommodate the bitterness of the Irish immigrant mind, inflamed by that last great injustice, the Potato Famine; a mind for which the name of Cromwell held a very different connotation from what it did for the Puritan. So Rome and Geneva appeared finally clamped into the same formula of "rebel" religiosity, under a flag that imitated the firmament.

The incubation of America in these revolutionary ferments when the Renaissance and Reformation had refashioned England; and especially the perfervid *fixity* which is such a characteristic of the traditional in America, has tended to freeze Americanism in an unprogressive "progressiveness." To start life as a rebel, knowing nothing else than attitudes of defiance and disrespect—perfectly expressed in "the American at the Court of King Arthur"—the vicious side of which is a kind of willful vulgarity, and aggressive common-mannishness, is probably not so good as the inductive road, of direct reaction against presumption and abuses of authority.

We must, I think, attribute the rather old-fashioned type of attitude, the sentimental radicalism among Americans, to the fact that their vision has been narrowed down, because of their political pieties, to one set of pictures in the past: a manner of Jack the Giant Killer fairy-tale. For the Puritanism has faded out, but the rather musty rebellion remains. Not in order to weaken impulses to combat injustice naturally, but to render the mind more elastic, some benefit might be derived from a study of an iconoclastic philosopher of the days when America was being born, but who was extremely reactionary where it came to questions of government.

David Hume was a great eighteenth-century philosopher who became also a notable historian. He was as far removed from a Whig as a man may get and still remain on the earth. Everything that made a man a Whig he heartily detested, and the authoritarian principle, of which the Stuarts were such pedantic but ineffectual exponents, recommended itself to his intellect. It was in its support that he turned to history. As he stated so unequivocally: "I must confess that I shall always incline to their side who draw the bond of allegiance very close."

(Incidentally, had a Stuart king been there in place of George III, the revolt of the American colonies would have occurred, if anything, earlier.)

The fact that the United States of America was born in Whiggery could not but "incline" it to the opposite extremity of the political compass to that occupied by David Hume. It must forever "incline to their side" who are violently divesting themselves of all authority: to the "rebel" side, in short. The beauties of Authority (for it has its appeal, not only for Hume, but many intelligent men in every age) are, in the abstract, for the average American something inconceivable. Yet, *in practice,* there is no country in which so authoritarian a type of government has flourished (apart from openly despotic States), and because, in America, kings have been *elective,* they have none the less been kings. The "rebel" fixation of the American has prevented him from seeing that he was ruled in that way, that is all: or that demands upon his allegiance often have been excessive.

We now all of us know—and even many Americans share this knowledge—what students of politics have, of course, always known, that the problems of "liberty" and "authority" are not so simple as they have seemed to the majority in America, and, with less blind emphasis, here in England. Everybody (or perhaps I should say a lot of people) are now aware that the King (traditionally the tyrant, for an American or, more mildly, an Englishman) is not the *only* kind of tyrant in the world. Under Western governments as at present constituted, we still enjoy more liberty than we could be certain of enjoying beneath a single ruler invested with divine right. But the old simple-hearted democratic picture is no longer intact.

It was, for instance, in the course of struggles against the

162

encroachments of the Crown and of personal power, that Englishmen evolved such historic safeguards as Habeas Corpus. So powerful an instrument the Writ of Habeas Corpus has proved, that no mere king or queen would, for three hundred years, have dared to defy it. But we have found that what a king or queen would not have ventured to do, a "people's government" has never thought twice about doing, in years of "national emergency"—namely, when indulging in the "sport of kings," or when against their will obliged to engage in it.

In the atmosphere of messianic politics, which have in Europe, as much as in America, prevailed everywhere during this century, the puny safeguards of democratic liberty have been swept down beneath the impact of emotional tides, either of nationalism or class-conflict, from the Right or from the Left. The legal barricades erected by the Weimar Republic against the despotism traditional in Germany were disposed of by National Socialism in the twinkling of an eye. And arrived at power, Socialism, with us, even seeks to govern as a Trade Union, and Trade Union government would remove the ability to strike. As likewise, if that government assume authoritarian powers, the guarantees of civil liberty, of which Habeas Corpus is the supreme example. This is, of course, because there is supposed to be no need for them any longer, any more than you would feel nervous, I imagine, about your valuables while staying with a clergyman.

No one today, or very few, would place themselves at the side of David Hume, in his veiled advocacy of the Stuart view of government. As between Charles Stuart and such determined individualists as Hampden and Eliot, or Holles, or Selden (the "great dictator of learning of the English nation") or Benjamin Valentine, there would be no hesitation. We are all against tonnage and poundage: all of us loathe onerous taxes, to the imposition of which Charles Stuart was so prone. Yet we cannot but notice that the twenty shillings odd which John Hampden was asked to pay (and which led to his famous legal battle with King Charles I) is a bagatelle to the kind of taxation which today we are burdened with, in spite of the fact that we have long ago got rid of despotic kings and queens, and enjoy what is described as "popular government."

Or again, who would hesitate—unless they really enjoyed being fleeced and soaked by rapacious governments, and welcomed the fining and jailing which ensued in the event of non-payment—who would not place himself immediately at the side of Pym, or Coke, or Rudyard, rather than beside Charles Stuart, and promptly set his signature to the Petition of Right, which makes memorable the year 1628?

Where in that Petition the King is reminded that "your people have been in divers places assembled, and required to lend certain sums of money unto your Majesty," and that when the money was not forthcoming, these same people had been "imprisoned, confined, and sundry other ways molested" —why it is plain enough to everyone that these gentlemen were thoroughly justified in exacting from a man of that sort a promise to desist from interfering with his subjects, and to refrain from asking them to part with their good money— however beautiful a war the said monarch might be contemplating against France, or against Spain, which could not be launched without additional revenue.

We are all against Charles Stuart, and understand how such behavior should in the end have led to his losing his head: and it is difficult to understand how David Hume should waste a tear over so extortionate a person (whose execution, it is generally considered, was decreed by the City of London, whose hard-boiled capitalists resented these tendencies of Charles more deeply even than the squirearchy). But today our great sympathy with the strong-minded gentlemen who so successfully defended their pocketbooks is even exceeded by our amazement at the mildness of this tyrant, and his lack of all real power. For our contemporary tyrants are made of so much sterner stuff. In our times, Hampden's head would "roll in the dust" with great dispatch; the twentieth-century tyrant would not wait for Hampden, or his friends, to strike *his* off.

It was easier for a man of 1913, say, than for anyone today, to feel strongly about kings and queens. Their royal wars, which more often than not were comparable to very expensive and ornate football matches, costing a fraction of what ours do (which leave us utterly ruined), their clippings and debasings of currency—seeing how debased is our own; their arbitrary imprisonment, where with us justice loses more of its beautiful impartiality every day: about all these things in retrospect we are acquiring a sense of proportion.

The American, off on his lonely continent, is probably too far away for his reactions to have been brought very much up to date. He has not suffered as have we in Europe either: even compared with Canada, his taxes are inconsiderable. So he does not feel as otherwise he would, that kings have been overrated, as historical bugbears. They have been a sort of childhood obsession of his: as the symbol of arbitrary power they so monopolized the emotional field that in arming his soul against that particular monster he has left other parts exposed to the great variety of new monsters, nearer home perchance, with which the modern age is so well stocked.

As to his Presidents, they have been no tyrants, certainly. Yet his attitude toward them would have been entirely different had they been dressed differently. Eliminate all the glittering paraphernalia of kingship, and everything is different. A king in a seersucker suit, who is called a "chief executive," is completely disarming to the romantic "rebel" mind. He could do all the nasty things that kings do—levy taxes and make war —and no objection would be taken.

For the above-mentioned glittering paraphernalia, if I may speak for myself, I feel a considerable distaste. I am very glad that that barbaric type of ruler, with his tiresome crown and scepter puppetry, is extinct. I am impatient to see the title "lord" dispensed with as a reward for very doubtful services to society: and the fewer Lady Jingle Joneses there are kicking around the better pleased I shall be. This brutal statement I trust will carry conviction—but I am speaking of today. Three centuries ago, I think that a king—even poor Charles Stuart—was not necessarily a worse type of ruler than a number of Whig lords: it is difficult to see how men who had grown rich by pillage of Church lands, or later by robbing the peasantry of their common lands, perpetuating their criminal eminence by a law of primogeniture, and, impressively titled, exercising a snobbish mesmerism over their dupes—how such are, ideally, a great improvement on a king, no more prone to taxation than they would be. All rulers are taxers.

If modern politics is to be understood, superstitious thinking has, of course, to be superseded by a more objective type, which takes no count of how much, or of how little, gold braid the potentate displays. And intelligent Americans by their use of such expressions as "economic royalists" reveal a clear understanding of the essentials of the problem. What it remains to do, in order to go to the heart of the problem of political liberty, is—having grasped the fact that the title "king," "mogul," "shah," or "czar" is not important, nor the clothes a man wears, nor the weighty incrustations of gold and lace— to go on from that to a further bitter truth: namely that when great *wealth* is eliminated, but great *power* remains, human liberty is no way advanced. It is power, not money, that is important.

The object of these observations, since that point where I introduced the Whig-hating figure of David Hume, has been to show how difficult it is to bring political thinking up to date if a foundation of emotional prejudice underlies the national mind. In America, that, unfortunately, is what we find, in spite of the great numbers of emancipated intelligences—more, I dare say, than are to be met with in England—who counteract, on the fringes, the archaic fixity of tradition.

Because the Americans have embalmed their Whiggery, along with their "Bible religion"; because they make exhibition of so noisy, if superficial, a radicalism, they look more progressive than they in fact are.

PART 2

---

20 INTRODUCTORY

Up to now my feet have been firmly planted in history. From this point I am moving into a more controversial region. We know a lot about the future, we can see into it a short distance very clearly: but there is plenty with us here in the present, substantial evidence of what is to come, to enable us to go much farther than that narrow belt, into the darkening time-tract ahead. There is a fatality, too, that is written all over a country, if you know how to read it. America seems charged with it, to bursting-point. A curse upon a race is a familiar enough phenomenon: I am speaking of a fatality of that sort. But this looks to me more like a *blessing*—the thunderous murmurs of a cradle-song are audible. Something is being born.

I am conscious, however, that all I shall be saying in this second part of my study will at first seem to be flatly contradicted by my first part. How can the universalism celebrated in the second part be born out of that very parochial Party-system of British origin?

Intrenched in every big city or town of the United States is a small group of rich families, all blamelessly Nordic. The country clubs, Junior Leagues, etc., are their preserve. They are surrounded by a sea of underdog "foreignness," outnumbering them by a hundred to one. How can you "melt" *them?* Will this universalist future be a miracle-birth into Cosmopolis? Will an animal that is jet-black waken one morning and find itself snow-white? Or will two animals, one white, one black, awake one morning and find themselves both a beautiful dusky yellow? Will the concrete become the abstract from one day to the next? Or can what was not so long ago an English colony become the cradle of the first race of cosmic men?

I set out to show, after a certain fashion, America as it has been, is, and is about to be. In *what it is* is so implicit what it soon *will be:* and that is so much the opposite of what it so recently *was,* that I know the European may be a little incredulous.

The first two of this past-present-and-future chronologic triad I have produced for you—as I have said, in my own way. I have shown how the English Whigs in these Atlantic colonies defeated, in armed rebellion, George III (as their English brother-Whigs would have dearly liked to do), drove out all the Tories and "collaborators," and set themselves up as masters of the "New World": a Whig World modeled upon England in almost every particular. But the New World is a mercurial, electric continent of great size and great climatic range, responsible for alligators in its Southern part, and black sub-arctic squirrels and sub-zero weather in its Northern part: it began at once to make their correct, well-articulated, perfectly balanced State-edifice of checks and balances look like a mirage.

It began to distort and to caricature the original British political, legal, and even religious framework (neither Sectary nor Peculiar Baptist, in Stuart England, nor the members

168

later on of the Holy Club, would have been edified by a "Camp Meeting." Even the wild miners of Kingswood were not so savage as that). And then it quickly became an empire which filled up as if by magic with people from all the countries of Europe, and from elsewhere. Asia began to lap over into it on the west in a discreet Celestial tide: and, branded and herded, Africa already was established from early days. That gave America its music. The bagpipes of the Irish competed with the jungle tom-toms: the tom-toms won. Even something Indian remains: Mexico is peopled by aboriginal Americans, and when the Indian culture of Mexico melts into the great American mass to the north, the Indian will probably give it its art, as the Negro has its music.

As it is, a Mexican Indian called Rivera has massively transferred into pictorial terms, in his splendid murals at Detroit, the titanic glories of American industry. It took an Indian to understand the tropical shapes of the great steel labyrinths. He, Orozco, and others are the best North American artists. Mexico City promises to be the future Paris of the New World, where the big *ateliers* or *estudios* will be situated, the Aztec and Mayan cultures for a background, instead of the Greco-Roman. At cafés on its boulevards art students will spend happy nights under the Aztec moon, after the manner of George Moore and his friends long ago in "the great moon-lights of the Place Pigalle." If only the Papacy were to establish itself at Quebec, as it is rumored that it may, that would assist the symbolism of American universality. The new involvement of the United States in Asia will have for its result the Asiatic element numerically competing with the Negro in the States.

In earlier chapters I stressed the wizard speed of its waxing, so characteristic of America—the mass-power of its Technic rushes everything into being with magical suddenness. There-fore, all about which I am speaking are things many of which may have come to pass only a few years after the ink is dry upon this page. Others will take longer; but none so very long.

Alexander Hamilton, his small stockinged legs elegantly crossed, one finger pressed against his brow, taking up his copy of Seneca, or of Cicero, to cull a brave phrase or two, can scarcely have foreseen what kind of society he had been called to found. The hard glare of the Manhattan sun outside his study windows should have warned him that this was no place to which Tory England could be transplanted, or where anything English could subsist for very long.

A young Harvard instructor was once talking to me about the eary French explorers. America was the Dark Continent, and the French, *voyageurs* and adventurous aristocrats, with incomparable daring, moved up and down its uncharted rivers. La Salle, I think it was, who was descending the Mississippi, to which no Anglo-Saxon had yet penetrated: several men were left by him to build a boat. When he came back he found the boat only half finished and his compatriots had vanished. Upon the timbers were scrawled these words: *"Nous sommes tous sauvages."* They had gone off with the Indians, and the young Harvard pedagogue gave it as his opinion that all foreigners should bear in mind that message, scribbled upon a half-finished boat in the wilderness.

This is much too romantic. The savagery melted away before the impact of British civilization. But the invaders could not melt so great a wilderness without themselves losing to it much of their personality. Not the human "savageness," however, of the romantic imagination, but the alien waste of nature is still there underneath: the "wild land," as they formerly called it, very imperfectly covered up.

There is a logic and congruity, I think, in this vast place, so recently a kind of *tabula rasa* physically, this world that is still new, being the cradle of a new type of man: not a man that is Mongol, or African, or Celt, or Teuton, or Mediterranean, but the sum of all these. Its situation—an island with Asia on one side, and Europe and Africa on the other—is propitious: whereas in a historic State like Germany, the Ukraine, or England, for so long identified with one type of man, the very trees would offer resistance to so promiscuous a suggestion.

In this second, and shorter, part of my book, accordingly,

I indulge in a prediction as to the political and cultural future of the North American continent. I treat of the present, too, a little: but only that I may demonstrate how the future is being prepared. The present is not a thing for which one can make any very serious claims: in fact, if America had only its *present,* no one, except for statistical reasons, or to be informative, would feel particularly impelled to write about it.

The use of the word "cosmic" is open to criticism. There is, however, no reason why, because of its fatal attraction for fakirs and mountebanks, it should be shunned. Cosmopolitan has associations of another and trivial order. World or earth are not promising substitutes for cosmic. So I have given the word "cosmic" precedence, and that is what I generally use to describe a society, the preliminary stages of whose incubation may be studied in America.

21 ANGLO-SAXON UNIVERSALISM

In a pamphlet of mine, published in 1941, I analyzed the Axis propagandist attacks of that time upon "Anglo-Saxon maritime universalism," as they termed it. Mine was counter-propaganda: but much of the argument has a validity beyond the special pleading of the moment.

Coming from the sea, and now the air as well, we poke our noses—so went the Axis argument—into every corner of the earth. Settled and ancient earthbound societies, replete with pieties of *Blut* and of *Boden,* are obliged to suffer this intrusion.

The average European lumps together, beneath the label "Anglo-Saxon," all whose tongue is English. Circumstances of late have done nothing to dispel this illusion. During the war, from the Mediterranean to the Pacific, Yankee agents, if not armed men, swooping down from the air, or disembarking from ships, became ubiquitous, in a way that Germans and Russians, or Frenchmen, Italians, or Greeks have never been— none, in fact, except the British. Indeed the Americans out-matched in global ubiquity even John Bull.

"With all that the ocean and the air take with them of elasticity and freedom, of intangibility and in a sense *root-lessness"* (I quote from my pamphlet), these great maritime nations—erroneously confused because of their common tongue —had introduced a new, as it were, abstract and fluid principle into world affairs. Such was the Axis picture, designed to be a crushing indictment.

In my war-pamphlet, I pointed out how the English were

of all people the least susceptible to racial doctrines, or even to thinking in terms of soil, or rootedness. Their roots being as much in the sea as in the land, and having regard to their phenomenal dispersion, it is but natural that should be so.

This accidental sort of universalism, possessed of no philosophical background, is not of much significance—except that it has saved the Briton from certain manias. It certainly is not the species of universalism I am talking about here: though it might provide a not unuseful groundwork for an international outlook. Whereas with the American it is quite another matter. In him we should expect the nearest approach to an international outlook it is possible to find, in a world still given over to nationalist rivalries. It grieves me to say that this is not the way most Americans look at the matter.

We are clear as to what the expression "good European" means. As to a good American, he, it appears to me, cannot but be a universalist (the term internationalist is conditioned too much by its past use to be a feasible alternative, though if you are not a nationalist, you are surely an internationalist of some sort).

To make of America merely another nationality, neither more nor less—like the German or the French—would be an ambition limited indeed. The destiny of America is not to be just another "grande nation": but to be the great big promiscuous grave into which tumble, and there disintegrate, all that was formerly race, class, or nationhood. That the average American is unaware of this peculiar destiny is true, as I have observed. He does not regard himself as a solvent—he does not even realize that it is largely through American action, in the last war and the last but one, that what had endured in Europe for two thousand years has almost overnight been dissolved into a bubbling chaos. That that Sickle which resembles the Crescent should fly over Vienna and over Berlin seems to him just a news-item like another. But this unawareness in the rank and file is not important. A cat and a reindeer are not *aware* that they are those things.

It is what happens that is important. And, of course, that

it had to happen this way: that the great abstract reservoir of human beings labeled America (black, white, and yellow, Irish, Polish, Syrian, Swedish, Russian, German, Italian), the first great "melting-pot," should be instrumental in bringing about the melting of *other* pots, where the various elements had so far remained obstinately intact.

Two average Americans, however, had displayed awareness of their peculiar destiny: the late Mr. Willkie, in his simple Hoosier fashion: like a starry-eyed bear, who had been taken a breath-taking trip around the globe, and found it was not much bigger than a football after all: and then Mr. Henry Wallace, who always seems good-naturedly bubbling over with the good tidings of international brotherhood, rather like an old-fashioned type of English labor-leader, before they all became the yes-men of the Opposition. Many, more philosophically endowed, needless to say, possess this awareness. In such men as Wallace or Willkie, meanwhile, may be seen the enlightened villager, become aware of, as it were, a novel Cosmopolis. Not a Utopia; just somewhere in which armed groups are not incessantly menacing each other, and throwing all ordered society back into a primitive savagery every few years.

Of course, Willkie, and still more Wallace, had in mind other advantages besides the absence of war. They saw that many other evils might be superannuated likewise. But the more and more destructive wars by which our life is at present stultified is the most timely issue.

Now for a long while I thought a great deal about peace. I even as a writer took action—as one would if one saw a child applying a torch to a building in which one knew many people were sleeping. I am now conscious that I thought too much about peace—detached, that is, from those things by which it is conditioned. A society in which children are not encouraged to play with torches should occupy our thoughts: one in which men are not encouraged to remain children all their lives, and mischievous inhuman children at that. That is the way to think about peace.

Never trouble even to think about peace at all until you have abolished the principle of "national sovereignty." The equivalent of state sovereignty for the individual man would be the right to counterfeit, to murder, to rob. No one will have to rack his brains how the peace may be kept once national sovereignty has gone.

But what about *planning for peace,* someone might inquire —seeking to devise machinery to maintain it? Is that quite useless too? Perpetual disappointments are not good for morale, and it leads nowhere to discuss peace in isolation. Planning for peace is to put the cart before the horse. War is so much a part of the structural pattern of the old system, that and all other forms of competitive savagery, that to call a conference, where a group of men prepared to use force if they do not have their way, their pistols beside them on the table as they debate, sent there to outsmart their neighbors at all costs, that, on the face of it, is unpromising. Yet all conferences between sovereign States are fundamentally of that order.

With the coming of peace we find that it is proposed to reassert the sovereign rights of all nations, irrespective of size or other limitations. We should, of course, instead of this, be insisting upon small States merging themselves into larger units, not the perpetuation of insignificant polities, the accidental creations of a world very different from ours. To go into any conference insisting that Russia and Santo Domingo possess the same voting power, as we did at San Francisco— so that two Santo Domingos outvote the Soviet Union—is as dangerous as it is silly. The fact that the Soviet Union is rapidly absorbing a number of small States is, because of the coercive methods employed, justly a subject of reproach. Otherwise, as a giant step toward political monism, what could we do but applaud? A World State can only come piecemeal. It will never be the result of a fiat.

A Middle West educationist of note has placed at five hundred years the interval that probably separates us from a single social system for the entire planet. Half a millennium seems too pessimistic. This computation is based, I suppose, upon a consideration of the backwardness of most communities. (That point I shall take up presently.) Or it may be the outcome of a rough guess as to how long it will take for all small sovereignties to be absorbed, by the process of war and revolution, into one great sovereignty—as we see today Estonia, Latvia, Lithuania, Poland, Rumania, Bulgaria, Yugoslavia, Persia, and doubtless quite a few other States becoming a new group of satellites in the European and Asiatic State-system known as the U.S.S.R. It is certain that in East Asia the influence of Russia will grow. So great a body as that will represent must continually attract more satellites.

It is in all likelihood by such a process as we may now observe that the universal society will come about. When there are only two "sovereign" monsters left, they will, judging by all precedents, attack each other. But all wars today are, as Mr. Lippmann has justly remarked, "wars of domination and annihilation": not wars "of limited objective," as formerly in Europe. They will be more like wars between small African kingdoms, as described by Mungo Park, in which the defeated community was incorporated as serfs by the victor. In the end, one monster will gobble up the other. Then there will be *one* political body there, throughout the world. But nuclear energy is going to hasten all these processes.

I have been treating these increasingly large States as if they were celestial bodies. I might know that a certain star contained a race of beings imbued with principles of social justice, whereas another neighboring star, threatening to collide with it, contained nothing but a race of Yahoos. Nevertheless, as far as the question of the collision went, what degree of civilization was to be encountered among the parasites of their respective bodies would have no relevance. And when States get so large, it is their mass, their size, and weight we have to consider, as if we were physicists.

To return to nuclear energy, the rate at which weapons of greater range and destructiveness are being designed suggests to me that the ultimate pacification of the earth may be much nearer than the pessimistic estimate above quoted.

As regards the gigantic proportions being assumed by Russia, nothing can be taken for granted: the death of Stalin might be productive of a great convulsion. The U.S.S.R. as the result of violent rivalries could break up, though I have no reason to suppose this is likely, indeed it appears to me improbable. Meanwhile, this rapidly waxing aggregation is so violent in its action, that it must drain of its ancient identity what it absorbs. There might even be as many as six powerful and violent political monsters in existence at a time. But at last they must, it would seem, coalesce.

I indulge in such guesswork for no other reason than to combat the discouraging estimate of five hundred years of war. One hundred years or less would be my guess; although if the present tempo of scientific development is maintained, is not even that very slow-going? There will always of course be a certain amount of scuffling around. But the end of the era of great wars is already clearly in sight. It would be very optimistic to suppose there will not be another huge war.

To be the cradle of this novel principle, to be the ante-chamber of a world-state, the United States of America had to be very large. Its area is, in fact, so considerable that "regionalism" cannot be altogether absent: though the great uniformity of thought and of daily habits reduces this to a minimum.

Mr. Allen Tate, in the 1945 *Virginia Quarterly Review* (spring number) had much to say that is interesting upon that American problem child, the "region." He himself, of course, belonging to no less a region than Dixie Land, has regionalism in his blood. The universalist is assailed with the acumen that we would expect of so practiced a controversialist. Much that he says, were things very different from what they are, I should be disposed to endorse. But while I find his excellent article most helpful in its clarity, I would like to make a few observations.

First of all, glancing through its text again, I do not think that men are so concerned with smallness and bigness as he assumes: nor with "provincialism" and its opposite. Indeed, provincialism is a word that has lost most of its meaning.

As to size, the word looks less impressive in 1948 than ever it did. It looks about the size America or Europe used to look only a short time ago. And as to culture, a universal culture—one intellectual and emotional standard in place of a plurality of standards—is with us already.

In the region of ideas, the "melting-pot" is in full operation. Further, the traditions and beliefs inhering in these so-called "regions" are subject to dissipation and decay, and, what is very much to the point, no new "regions" will take the place of those now moribund. We shall have a full-fledged universal culture long before we have a universal society, unfortunately. Nationalizing forces will still for a long time be at work, interfering with a unity that ignores their conventional frontiers, tollgates, and "alien" restrictions. A true internationalism will be in being, while an ever more rapid nationalism will affect to believe it can never occur.

Today a regionalist, in the cultural field, is a mere archaeologist. You will see how this must be if you take one by one the "regions" into which the North American continent is mainly divided. There are the New England states, the Southern states, the Middle West, the West, Canada, and Mexico. Mr. Tate was associated with a movement in the Southern states, the manifesto of which was entitled *I'll Take My Stand*. This movement produced many good things, and one of the best writers in the field of creative fiction alive, Faulkner, belongs to it. "That renascence is over," Mr. Tate tells us. And who will pretend that New England, to take that next, could flower again, culturally?

As to the Middle West, that has flowered, pictorially, and is still doing so. A painter from those parts went to Munich and came under the influence of a movement known as *Neusächlichkeit* (which stood in somewhat the same relationship to Hitlerian *Blut und Boden* as Marinetti's Futurism did to Italian Fascism). He returned to the Middle West and started building up a pictorial consciousness specifically Middle Western. There is, of course, some sense in these local, departmental nationalisms. Nature has a very different aspect in, say, Mexico, from what it has in Quebec. The visual material of a countryman of Rivera must always be most unlike that of a compatriot of Cagnon, the French Canadian, unless he chooses to inhabit an abstract universe of pure form, like Mondriaan. But standardization proceeds apace, and the inhabitant of Mexico City will in the end be indistinguishable from the dweller in Montreal.

179

In Canada "regionalism" is resented by the contemporary Canadian very much and is almost defunct. This inhabitant of a sort of icebox resents extremely being regarded as a species of Eskimo. The fur cap has vanished from Toronto, except for an occasional old-timer. The snowshoe has been superseded all over Canada by the elegant touristic ski. And when the tourist from the United States arrives, muffled up in furs for the occasion, the inhabitants of Upper Canada are apt to inquire if he feels *cold*—or did he imagine himself on a visit to the *Pole?*

Now I know that with Mr. Tate and his Southern friends a serious economic and cultural principle is involved: with some even what they regard as a religious principle. With them it is nothing climatic or picturesque. And beyond that, on the animal level, I might agree with anyone who asserted that never again would such romantic-looking beings as the *voyageurs* and trappers of the traditional North, nor as well-dressed and vivid people as the present peons at a Mexican market, be found in those places. Centralization abolishes local color; and not only color.

In the public libraries of a city in which I stayed for some time, there was a large section, perhaps a third of the fiction shelves, labeled "Western." Grown men devour these stories. For Time has its regions, too: and many prefer to live fifty or a hundred years back. They are stage-coach people: they are contemporaries of the Oregon Trail or Deadwood Dick.

Where Mr. Tate is ridiculing the "let's get closer to the Chinese" cry, and all similar political uplift, I find myself in agreement with him. But where he is combating the notion that knowledge of one's fellow-men, of other races, means that you "cease to fight them"—when he expresses a doubt as to the truth of that, he has, surely, forgotten the United States of America. There men of all colors and breeds mingle in its great cities, and they do not use tanks and bombers to express their disapproval of each other. Given *one* State, men do not do those things.

Again I seem to detect a slightly primitive assumption

in what he says next. But I will quote. "Europeans are fighting one another today not because they didn't 'know' one another."

This "Europeans fighting one another" seems to accept the notion favored by the publicist that the little children spontaneously fly at each other's throats because they are such ferocious little devils (especially Europeans, who are *always* at it). Of course, the reality is not quite like that: and if Europe were one State, as is the U.S.A., there would be no "fighting."

Whatever may be said in future of Mr. Churchill, there is one thing I am sure will be held to his credit: that is that he alone, of all modern, or as far as I know ancient, statesmen, proposed to two great States a common citizenship with his own: namely to France and to the United States. To join up, in short, and have no more nonsense. But the regionalists of France and the regionalists of the U.S.A. weren't having any. They like that nonsense, alas, too well to say good-by to it, as do, for that matter, regionalists of Mr. Churchill's own country.

I will turn now to a very different man from Mr. Allen Tate: namely, Mr. Henry Miller. Mr. Miller's "region" is the capital of France, Paris. He was born in Brooklyn, but he is far more frantically delighted with Paris than people ever are about the place to which they belong, even the most confirmed regionalist.

When I met Miller in New York in 1940 (whom I liked, I should perhaps say) he had just been shipped back from Greece much against his will—a new "region" he had discovered with a rapture that was literally timeless. For he embraced the whole of Hellenic antiquity and the present population in one indiscriminate, burning accolade. For the remainder of his days, he informed me, he proposed to live in the Orient. I could not imagine anyone exchanging Paris for Peking: but his heart was among the junks and pagodas, so it was good-by Place Notre Dame des Victoires.

However, let us listen to Henry Miller—I quote from the *Sunday after the War:* "What a curse it is for a man to trot about the Globe . . . be so adaptable that he can live anywhere, rootless, nomadic, the eternal wandering Jew who acquires everything and possesses nothing." This was a blast against the French writer called Morand, who, instead of sticking to Miller's beloved France, gallivanted about with all sorts of countries, even with the States, if you please. The perfect man should be full of "antagonisms, hatreds, and prejudices," too, he tells us: and Morand, whom I have not read, is ap-

parently one of those people who do not hate all other people—
"hate their guts," I should perhaps have said.

To be so prone to displacement as are Miller and myself
is "a curse." But that is only in the present epoch, it seems.
For he has a vision, elsewhere in the same book—he ecstatically
foresees, thousands of years hence, a world in which all this
will be contemptuously discarded, and men, mingling in
perfect brotherhood, will be as much at home in one part
of the globe as in the other—(I quote)—"The people of the
earth will no longer be shut off from one another within States,
but will flow freely over the surface of the earth and inter-
mingle."

Unless they want to be recipients of Miller's curse, "the
people" must *meanwhile* stay put, replete with parochial
prejudice and hatred. All I can say is that I, as does Miller,
prefer to step up a little the chronologic process, in my own
case; move about freely, and not remain shut in within the
borders of a single State: and I should, of course, be rejoiced
if our example were followed by the laggard multitude. I
find it difficult to understand why Miller should so incon-
sistently dissuade others from doing what he does himself. Also,
as to *hatred,* Miller himself is a very gentle person. How can
you with such a parade of fiery conviction condemn the
"cosmopolitan," and the next minute pass into a prophetic
trance, in which it is granted you to gaze upon a beautiful
scene, far, far away in the future, in which mankind had gone
cosmopolitan? *Then,* presumably, you awake from your sibyl-
line transport, catch sight of a contemporary cosmopolitan
strolling past your window, with a pair of shoes he has bought
in Constantinople, and clothes of obviously American cut,
and a gaucho hat, and you shake your fist at him and shout
your contempt of all transgressors of frontiers and hobnobbers
with other than their own home folk. All this happens in Paris,
though it ought by all rights to happen in Brooklyn.

This kind of emotional writing makes me somewhat dizzy.
But do not let me leave Mr. Miller without congratulating
him upon *Reunion in Brooklyn,* or without saying how much

I enjoyed the published fragments of his *Air-Conditioned Vacuum*. There he is at home once more in the U.S.A., and it is a lulu!

There is something that I have never seen seriously challenged: namely, this notion that to *have roots* (as if one were a vegetable or a plant) is a good thing for a man: that to be *rootless* is a bad thing for a man.

The exact contrary, of course, is the case. References to that subject are to be found in my first part: but this is the place to take it up and re-assert what to me seems very plain: to be rooted like a tree to one spot, or at best to be tethered like a goat to one small area, is not a destiny in itself at all desirable. It is a matter of surprise that the bluff of the *rooted* boys has never been called—I mean radically so, by a plain statement of the excellence of what is the opposite of rootedness.

As we have with us, in my own person, as good an illustration as can be found, I will take myself. I am just as much at home, if not more so, in Casablanca as in Kensington; feel in no way strange in Barcelona—like equally Paris, London, or New York. I feel most at home in the United States, not because it is intrinsically a more interesting country, but because no one really belongs there any more than I do. We are all there together in its wholly excellent vacuum.

The sight of the *root* depresses me; and I know in that country that everyone has left his roots over in Poland or Ireland, in Italy or in Russia, so we are all floating around in a rootless Elysium.

Never having been in the West, I cannot say what it feels like to be there. But in the Midwest and East, where I have lived, it feels just grand to be drifting around in a sea of Poles, Lithuanians, Irish, Italians, Negroes, Portuguese, French, and Indians. It is the kind of disembodied feeling that I like.

But to be perfectly earnest. No American worth his salt should go looking around for a root. I advance this in all modesty as a not unreasonable opinion. For is not that tantamount to giving up the most conspicuous advantage of being

184

American, which is surely to have turned one's back on race, caste, and all that pertains to the rooted State?

American citizenship is in a different category from any other citizenship, as I have already explained in Chapter 7. The ceremony of initiation that accompanies the acquisition of citizenship is of a peculiarly solemn character suggestive of something more (as indeed it is) than a mere transference of allegiance from one government to another. The rite is of a religious order: in becoming an American, it is not a nationality that is being assumed, but a new way of life, universal and all-inclusive in its very postulates: in a New World in which a new type of man is destined to appear.

Tolstoi had much to say about patriotism; it bore the imprint of his massive common sense, and abhorrence of the tricks by which men are enslaved. In order to demonstrate what becoming American is *not* (I mean ideally, of course, and historically), I will quote a passage from *Christianity and Patriotism,* an essay wherein Tolstoi is vigorously engaged in the task of attempting to unseal people's eyes. The myth of the starry-eyed Russian peasant and his veneration for the "little father" and so on is his target.

"They talk of the love of the Russian masses," he writes, "for their faith, their Czar, and their government, and yet there will not be found one commune of peasants in the whole of Russia which would hesitate for a moment which of the two places to choose for colonization—(1) Russia, with the Czar, the little father as they write in books, and with the Holy Orthodox Faith, in its adored country, but with *less* and *worse* land, or (2) without the little father, the white Czar, and without the Orthodox Faith, somewhere outside of Russia, in Prussia, China, Turkey, Austria, but *with some greater and better advantages* . . . For every Russian peasant the question as to what government he will be under (since he knows that, no matter under what government he may be, he will be fleeced just the same) has incomparably less meaning than the question as to whether, I will not say the water is good, but as to whether the clay is soft and as to whether there will be a good cabbage crop."

No one, I hope, would be so determined an idealist as to deny that there are *any* immigrants to the U.S.A. who have shifted themselves over there for precisely the reason described by Tolstoi in the above passage: in the pleasurable expectation of better conditions of life, better wages, less interference, less war. But should one of these immigrants suddenly take it into his head, in later years, to *leave* the New World, then there would, I believe, be something more difficult to dispense with than the Czar, the little father, or the Orthodox Faith to deter him.

How shall we define this? It is very different from pious attachment to the soil, which scarcely exists in America, or to historic tradition. No: it is attachment to the *absence* of these things. It is attachment, I should say, to a slightly happy-go-lucky vacuum, in which the ego feels itself free. It is, it seems to me, something like the refreshing anonymity of a great city, compared with the oppressive opposite of that, invariably to be found in the village. Everything that is obnoxious in the Family is encountered in the latter: all that man gains by escape from the Family is offered by the former. The United States is full of people who have escaped from their families, figuratively.

"Freedom and irresponsibility are commutative terms": such is a definition of freedom proposed by me in a book published in 1926. The more he is beset by duty, the less free a man is. I am not saying the more happy he is, nor would I resist the rejoinder that you can have too much of a good thing. Here I am doing my best to define, wherever it leads, something I have constantly felt in that country, as I have lived in its cities. London is a village compared with New York. One has a most pleasant disembodied sensation, as I have remarked, among all those herds of Italians, Germans, Jews, Irish, Negroes. You at last are *in the world*, instead of just in a nation.

There are few friendships in America such as exist in Europe. Every man is *a little bit* your friend, and will call you Bill or Fred or Jim after he has known you half an hour. But you will never become *his* Bill: there are too many other Bills for that. Friendship is a responsibility!

I am quite serious when I say that this is what heaven must be like—agreeably inhuman, naturally; a rootless, irresponsible city (for everyone is agreed that heaven is a city, so what the confirmed agriculturist will do it is difficult to see), where the spirit is released from all the too-close contacts with other people (others who get "in your hair," or are all the time "underfoot") but where everything is superficially fraternal.

Now having analyzed something I have invariably felt all about me, while in America, I will return to the citizen making up his mind to emigrate *out* of it. Where he would be going there would be no Americanism—there would be something far more solid; there would be friendships that chain down— a marriage that was, of all things, a friendship as well—there would be tradition telling you it "wasn't done," or that it *was*— saddling you with a thousand duties and obligations. Would he like all that after his prolonged immersion in this sort of ether? He would not.

My definition of freedom ("freedom and irresponsibility are commutative terms") would have, no doubt, to the dutiful ear, equivocal implications, perhaps sound like invitations to license. My "rootless Elysium" likewise would have a lawless sound: would appear to be located in an equivocal region, not subject to the moral law.

But let us, to the best of our ability, challenge the ascetic prejudice, which, if you analyze it, would ultimately be seen to deny all real freedom to anybody. Let us, if anything, go too far in the other direction, rather than surrender to that prejudice.

Then the standards that enthrone Duty at the expense of the happiness of the individual belong essentially to fiercely competitive systems. They are standards proper to a state of chronic emergency; which is descriptive of our modern societies, forever eying a neighbor known to be subject to accesses of homicidal mania and who does not disguise the fact—far from it—that he has a revolver in his pocket. The emphasis upon Duty, to the exclusion of all the epicurean values, is the natural result of such conditions.

America, however, is outside that area where nations are crowded up against each other, groups of rival diplomats engaged in that apparently absorbing game in which our lives and fortunes are the stakes. Until quite recently, rather, this has been the case: the air-age has closed up the ocean gaps. Then Americans are in the main people who have escaped, or whose ancestors escaped, from the rigors experienced in such societies as ours. They could at last relax somewhat, were able to put down their guards and be at peace, enjoy a freedom from interference they had never known up till then. They could discard the major part of duties and obligations, since what had dictated their imposition had been left behind. The Puritans, the Huguenots, the *émigrés* of '48—whether politics or religion had driven them out of their native land—all moved *outside,* out of the area of great pressure, into an area where the pressure was lifted from them and they could breathe freely. They would suddenly have the sensation of walking on air, of having been delivered of an incubus. For millions of people America has been as near heaven as they will ever get. If it did not go on being heaven, it always remained different from any other place.

Was this flight to America (a sort of suicide, as the nationalist would see it) immoral: a flight from Duty? The refugee blackens his motherland by the mere act of leaving it in this very pointed way.

Criticism is always involved in flight, from a country as from a wife: but it was usually from what they regarded as the wrong kind of duties and allegiances that men effected their escape. William Blake, for instance, typifies the spirit in which men have usually passed over into this great international sanctuary. His friend Tom Paine had gone there, and Blake, at a certain moment, was preparing to pass out through the "Western Gates," as he called them. Here is the poem, *Thames and Ohio,* in which he gave expression to his discontents, and his expectations of a better life:

> Why should I care for the men of the Thames
> And the cheating waters of chartered streams,
> Or shrink at the little blasts of fear
> That the hireling blows into mine ear?
>
> Though born on the cheating banks of Thames,
> Though his waters bathed my infant limbs,
> The Ohio shall wash his stains from me;
> I was born a slave, but I go to be free.

That is what they all have said—"I go to be free." And America is the place in which all these dreams have forgathered. Is it surprising that occasionally in the air one thinks that one detects something so far not met with; the electric intoxication of the air breathed by prisoners set free? The American air is conditioned by these immigrant multitudes, hollow with the great *ouf!* with which they have turned their back upon the European world.

(I ought, perhaps, to say that *our* America, at the opening of what has been called the "atomic age," is not any longer across the seas. Instead, it is a time, not a place: namely, the cosmic era which lies beyond the ruin and disintegration of atomic war.)

To turn back for a moment to the propaganda of *rootedness:* most of it emanates from governments, by the agency of their newspaper Press and other channels, emotional jingo purpose behind it. They desire a sedentary population, for the same reason that feudal lords wanted to be able to put their hand on their personal militia.

But the moment you get rid of the "sovereign State," you will hear no more about "roots." Cosmopolitan values will displace immediately the "root." An authentic World Government would have the desired effect, though that is only a first step, and a full world society is necessary. Then there would

189

be no further inducement to keep people fixed to one spot, nor to promote romantic values regarding their hereditary fixity.

So glorification of rootedness is bound up with conditions which have at last, as might have been foreseen, reduced us to a bankrupt slum—which is what the Socialist Government of England inherits from generations of men who have put class before country, but were too stupid even to keep healthy and intact the milch-cow of their privileged order.

The ruler is traditionally anything but a rooted person. Kings had roots in every country, just like a modern American, and so had many nobles too. It was only poor Hodge who was quite certain to have a good firm root. The higher you went in the social scale—when Europe was "Christendom" prior to the nationalist era—the less the root business would have any meaning.

Today the parliamentary rulers, who have succeeded the kings and archdukes, take every opportunity of traveling outside their national frontiers. Their roots must get frayed a good bit, from so much moving about, and this is in general an excellent sign. We should always welcome movement of any kind.

Now I arrive at the goal of these particular observations. The "rootless Elysium," as I have called it, enjoyed by the great polyglot herds in the American cities, is what will come to exist everywhere after universalism is established: after the final change-over from a plurality of competitive nationalist societies to one great cosmic society. And for the new principle of brotherhood, and the essential de-snobbing of the various racial stocks, we can depend, I suggest, upon the atom bomb. It sounds ridiculous put in that way. But all our behavior is ridiculous, and there is no rational road to a more sensible world.

When that change has been effected, it is obvious that there cannot but be an immense *relaxation* of the kind experienced by the earlier immigrant to the United States. Consider how the elimination of one great department of our political

190

life labeled "Foreign Affairs," with its corollary, "War," would revolutionize our lives. The change would be far greater than it is easy to imagine. Were we informed that our span of life was henceforth extended to an average of two hundred years —the man of forty becoming the man of a hundred—that would have a very great effect upon our lives, would it not? But hardly greater than will this change I am discussing.

Few people are conscious how much space all that stupid activity occupies, what is called "defense" or "security." Nor is it quantitative only. It does not merely with its brutal bulk monopolize the space allowed for us to live in. It impregnates and colors everything about it: the shape of our minds is determined by it. Literature, and some of the greatest of it, is filled with an obsessional tension. Men are shown there as little fighting animals, whose lot it is to fight other little animals like themselves—and nothing else. We might be bull-terriers, for all certain of our other attributes, not concerned with fighting, play a part. Philosophers whom we have been taught to regard as among the wisest of mankind are no exceptions.

All the nightmare of austerity—Duty ruling each man's life from the cradle to the grave—which was Plato's idea of a model "Republic," is an excellent illustration of this. Human life in society was reduced by him to a military problem. The only state he was able to imagine was a "sovereign State," as we call it today, all of the life of which was conditioned by *other* sovereign states, next to which its citizens dwelt in a tense watchfulness, armed to the teeth.

So grim, and cruelly dull, a pattern of a State could never have occurred to him had Plato lived in a world in which state-sovereignty had been abolished, or had never existed. He then presumably would have thought of something slightly less disagreeable. If you reply that Plato was a member of a military aristocracy in decay, attempting to introduce a super-Spartan discipline, we only come back to the same point. An Athenian Junker, who was one of the most extraordinary intelligences that ever existed, composes an account of the

191

perfect state, and as such it is laughable. It turns out to be a convict settlement. Its purpose—collective training for the slaughter of other men (probably Spartans).

Let us imagine, however, this republic of Plato's in full swing—should the conception of the State embodied in it have been adopted, and such a State been set up in Attica or elsewhere. Then let us suppose that as a result of some tremendous catastrophe (such a disaster for the human race as a war in which atomic bombs were freely used in large numbers, half of the population of the world wiped out), the "sovereign state" was at last abolished. What would happen to the republic on the platonic model, just established? An immense relaxation would, of necessity, at once ensue: an abrupt deflation of the entire social structure. Its constitution would be from that moment quite meaningless—its purpose, in the new dispensation, unattainable. For men would have abandoned the age-old habit of mutual slaughter. To train all day long so that you might be in good trim to smite your neighbor hip and thigh would be pointless. To subordinate everything in life to *that* would now, fortunately, have become criminal, just as it would be to wipe out the family in the neighboring flat, or to bludgeon to death the rival tailor, or apothecary, across the road. To subordinate free speculation, art (Plato would have abolished free speech and free creation), the delights of the family (Plato would have made women public, and so destroyed the family), and all the adjuncts of a happy life to a program of power would now be regarded as maniacal, and be dealt with accordingly. Your neighbor had unexpectedly become your brother. You might train to defeat him at bridge or chess, or excel him in the rugged splendor of your rock-garden, but you might no longer plot and prepare to take his life.

Were you a citizen of this platonic republic, it is easy to see what, under these circumstances, your sensations would be like (assuming you were not a Guardian). You would feel all your rigid little world agreeably dissolving about you. The relaxation would be almost painful—like the blood bursting into an arm long constricted: or like a Trappist's tongue beginning eagerly to move, the vow of silence suddenly canceled. All the springs that had held you tensed up, like a fierce tomcat upon a dark night, would snap.

I have been conjuring up these images of admirable relaxation to give an idea of what America has been, and to some extent still is. A fine irresponsibility and innocent egoism survives, to be a preview, in this peaceful checkerboard of races, of the world to come. There men will be able to jettison a good deal of responsibility—to gain for the advantages of their ego what the winding-up of Mars and Co. makes generally available. And, finally, one does not have to be ashamed of happiness!

On the philosophic side, the Utilitarian, as against the intuitive, is the path to take at this time. For everything that is not Utilitarian has failed us. The principle of the Greatest Pain of the Greatest Number has for far too long held sway.

It is with great diffidence that anyone today mentions such a thing as *happiness*. And the Puritan is still with us, to chide us, if we speak of pleasure. A famous American political lady, in face of the universal destruction that threatens us at the hands of Heavy Water, delivered herself of the aphorism— "Either men must love each other or die." As an improvement on that I suggest the following: "Either men must pursue Happiness, or perish." There is no middle course.

So-called "austerity," the stoic injunction, is the path toward universal destruction. It is the old, the fatal, competitive path. "Pull in your belt" is a slogan closely related to "gird up your loins," or the guns-butter metaphor. It is fight-talk language. Let us call to mind—for it may save us—the saying of William Blake: "Curse braces—Bless relaxes." Which is the moral of all my foregoing arguments.

Let us hope that in England minds will gradually turn toward the cosmic, or universalist, age ahead, and not be lured back to "big-shot" politics. Luckily we have a Socialist government, which is here to stay, and which will make this vastly more simple. My stressing of Happiness places me upon the epicurean side in this old argument. As to epicurean teaching, as that affected the destinies of Rome, "the anti-patriotic tendency of its teaching contributed to that destruction of national feeling which was necessary to the rise of cosmopolitanism." This is stupidly stated; but it will show you how any doctrine of that sort—one smoothing the way for "cosmopolitanism," as it is called by the above writer—is liable to be criticized as unpatriotic. When you hear that, all you need do is to recall the bloody path along which the great "patriots" of all great nations have led us. Let us pray for the rise of "cosmopolitanism," rather than more of the same patriotic poison. When I substituted the pursuit of happiness just now for brotherly love, I did not mean to dismiss that. Of course men have to acquire the habit of brotherly love as well.

The logic of the geographical position and history of the United States leads only, I believe, to one conclusion: namely, the ultimate formation of a society that will not be as other societies, but an epitome of all societies. If a nation, then it must be a super-nation: so inclusive of all the various breeds of men, all the creeds, and fads, and philosophies, that its unity must be of quite a different character. It can only be something more universal than the Roman Empire, because its metropolitan area is conterminous with its imperial area. It has been built or is being built from outside, many different peoples and cultures converging on it—either, as that regards the people, as refugees, or as slave or what not: people have moved in to make it, it has not moved out, like a spider constructing its web, to embrace all outside itself. Nor is it an endemic culture, moving out to modify other cultures, and subdue them to one standard, namely, its own. It has no original culture of its own (except for the Negro contribution, which is African): it is eclectic.

Of course, all the peoples of the earth will not move into North America, but in the end there will be larger or smaller segments or pockets of all of them there. Now, if, like many Americans, you aver that all the different stocks present already are not in fact going to mix, thoroughly to merge into a homogeneous mass, but instead will remain, as in large measure they still are found, isolated from each other (in great cities, inhabiting separate wards or districts, or sprinkled over the country in discrete racial and religious settlements), then that is going to be a very odd kind of nation—if it is a nation that is intended, of the usual sort.

At present all these various stocks—and even religions—enjoy an anything but uniform social status. As I pointed out at an earlier stage, race has tended to be class in America. Economic disparity, even, is not more productive of class feeling than blood. In fact, to have a son-in-law of a racial stock not highly esteemed—say a Greek, or Peruvian—would be more embarrassing to parents than to have one of "poor boy" origin.

In Canada, for instance, there is the most impassable race-barrier separating the English Canadians and the French Canadians: or the English side this is interpreted as indicative of a racial superiority, enjoyed by themselves *vis-à-vis* the "Peasoups." The fact that a majority of French Canadians have Indian blood does not improve their chances of social equality with the Nordic Blonds; and Catholicism is a peculiarly unpopular religion with the latter-day Puritans of this isolated and backward country.

The "Wop" in the States, as elsewhere I have indicated, is a much lower-grade citizen than the Nordic (especially one with an English name). The Negro is naturally out of the picture altogether, from the standpoint of marriageability, as is also the "Chink." If either of these elements moves into a street, everybody else moves out. You have to be a remarkably poor white to take a colored mate, or to tolerate a colored neighbor.

The equilibrium is, however, highly precarious. Present conditions will not survive any major shock to the political and social system—such as a record slump, or a war which rocks America to its foundations, in the way the war that has just ended has shaken the British Empire. As to Negro and white, that situation at present approaches a bitter climax. If anyone believes that this huge population of Africans is going to remain as it is, an insoluble black lump, they will fairly soon be undeceived. The Negroes of the United States

196

cannot be shipped out, as once they were shipped in, nor do even the most hostile suggest that. But they cannot remain there and continue to be treated as animals, whom you could no more marry than you could mate with a baboon.

That dark lump *will* melt, spread out, and color the entire human contents of the States, until "American" will mean somebody with that dusky intermixture. As the traditional social supremacy of the "Nordic" dies out (and the instability of American family-wealth and the violence of economic change accelerate the disappearance of this social advantage) all the other race-barriers will rapidly dissolve.

Whether America has a Big Business Fascism, or some sort of change to a Socialist economy, will not alter the outcome, except that the latter would precipitate the process of miscegenation. If it were a Business-Fascist economy, with America's penetration of Asia greatly stepped up, that must result in the impoverishment of the white population. Cheap Asiatic labor—which would doubtless be used in America proper, as well as on the spot in Asia, in affecting disadvantageously the home labor market, and in reducing the living standards of the masses—would overcome snootiness of a racial order.

The policy of both the Socialist and his enemy the Capitalist would work out identically as regards the white and colored population. The former is committed to the non-recognition of race discrimination, the latter is the natural protector of all colored people, because they work for less money.

Why one takes any interest in this so-called Pot, and the problems of its melting, is very simple. We lock ourselves up aggressively, or are locked up, in that antiquated group-pen the "nation," and pretend to be a "race," and a mighty fine one too, as did par excellence the National Socialists. But in America you have a powerful country of great size which at least cannot call itself a "race." Like everybody else, it takes on the competitive attitudes, the jingo emotionalism. But those devoutly hoping for an international order naturally see in America the thin end of the wedge. The requisite raw material is there, namely the great variety of races present— all that is needed for the manufacture of Cosmic Man.

But "Cosmic Man," as I have called him: would not the arrival of this hybrid be a bad thing? Should such creatures be encouraged? The answer is that in the event of a World Government (which man has been trying to bring about for so long, and there is good reason to suppose may now, with the help of nuclear energy—after a final conflagration—obtain) with a single government controlling all the affairs of the earth, a cosmic society would be a necessary corollary, as distinct from the mere administration. It probably would not be very satisfactory for everybody stolidly to go on behaving as if nothing had happened: it would be better for man to unanchor, and circulate. In order permanently to banish the parochial or tribal spirit, that would be the best course.

The idea of a federative World Government—which is the most popular at present, because men so hate the prospect of rendering up their identity—might involve only a mechanical administrative change, a spiritual status quo: consequently it should be rejected. War out of the way (and let us hope its twin, the profit-system, with it), very little local government would be necessary. The latter serves to keep alive the ancient territorial rivalries.

It is not enough to have a central administration alone then. Some fresh approach to the problems of living in society should go with such a change. This is where the United States is so useful. It is not interesting only because it is a "melting-pot." That might perfectly well be as dull as it sounds. What makes it so worthy of everybody's attention is the fact that in America there is, as nowhere else, the basis of a cosmic ethos. Even their gregariousness belongs to an, as it were, deep emotional fund, a sort of communal pooling of all the cordial reactions of man. But to this I will return presently.*

For a World Government when first formed to have a genuinely cosmic society there already, practicing—and preaching

*Cf. Chapter 26.

—all the collective virtues appropriate in a world-State, would be of great value. The example of a kind of universalized Everyman would prove infectious. And the new war-free, tolerant, nationless world society—arrived at last at the point reached by the forty-eight States of the Union—could do worse than take for its model American citizenship (purged of its nationalism, of course).

It is comprehensible that many people should be disinclined to accept the idea of a cosmic society, and so of a cosmic man. Human conservatism is fathomless, and when it comes to *roots*, habit is another name for those roots. But it is most difficult to see how any fairly intelligent man or woman could question the desirability of a World Government.

To take its minimum claim: a World Government could scarcely be as bad, however imperfect it might be, as a number of governments, or so-called "sovereign States." For the main incentive to be bad would be lacking. A large proportion of the crimes of governments arise from the existence of *other* governments. Just as a man all by himself, alone on the earth, would be debarred from committing most of the recognized crimes, which require the presence of two or more people (apart from ill-treating the animals, there is not much he could do), so if there were only one government in the world, it would have had removed from it the possibility of committing many major crimes. It could still, if so disposed, commit a great number of crimes against the people it governed. But at least it would have inter-governmental war removed from its repertoire of crime.

War is a major crime of government—there is none so great, where it is *total* war, *levée en masse*, with all that that entails: paralysis of all the creative functions of the community for years on end; squandering of the nations' wealth, which otherwise employed would abolish poverty entirely; brutalization of millions of men; fearful catastrophes of every kind in the private lives of "unimportant" people, men, women, and children; mental regimentation of communities; by appeals to the vanity, the causing everyone to have a stake in his own misfortune; the death in youth of multitudes, maiming, impairing of health, of opportunities in life—but I need not continue the catalogue.

A World Government appears to me the only imaginable solution for the chaos reigning at present throughout the world. Many would agree that it is desirable, but very unlikely, in their view, to materialize. Such is, and always has been, the logical goal of civilized mankind—though usually men have said, "We must give our law to the barbarian." It has been imperialist.

The Greeks had the notion of Cosmopolis, they were too power-hungry and contentious to do anything about it. The Romans made the attempt: it was the Roman World and imperial, but became highly cosmopolitan. That fell to pieces, and in succession to it a theocratic universalism was attempted. But Christendom was the reverse of a reign of peace. Luckily, they had only battleaxes and bows and arrows, instead of the weapons of wholesale slaughter which we possess, or there would have been very little left, so remorselessly did the Sermon on the Mount impel those Christians to homicide. Christianity, as a unifier, became a bad joke long ago.

With a start of surprise (followed by apathy) we find ourselves in the presence of the so-called atom bomb. Perhaps that will do what the Sermon on the Mount failed to accomplish. That this will come to pass *before long*—that the inhabitants of this planet have not only the chance, but the certainty, of again enjoying one government instead of a plurality—may, I believe, with complete confidence be predicted.

It has been suggested that probably the three governments capable of producing the atom bomb will agree not to use it, and go on as before, as if it did not exist. This is most unlikely. One of them would be sure to get so angry it would loose one at its enemy. Experience shows that, once a weapon exists, the poor ape that man is cannot refrain from using it.

A corollary of such a merging of power in a world organization would be a society where the profit-motive grew sanely domesticated: their attention no longer drawn away from domestic issues every few years by foreign wars, then all their energy absorbed in recovery from them, people would be unlikely to tolerate chronic racketeering at their expense, and licensed dishonesty under the name of "business." The ex-national frontiers again would be an invitation to leave your pen and fraternize with other peoples—trade, exchange ideas, and intermarry: they would no longer be a wall bristling with immigration and customs officials to keep you penned up, ready for the next visit of the Butcher.

To resume: the United States of America is a place where those conditions of fraternization and free intercourse, irrespective of race, class, or religion, already prevail, or enough at least for a start. Therefore it is a model for all other nations, still battened down within their national frontiers.

If it occurred to you to wonder how the Americans—without some beautiful old village at the foot of a down to love and cherish, that had been there perhaps since it was a Gesith, in the days of the eorls and ceorls—can without all that be so attached to their strange, rootless, restless, polyglot world, the answer is they like it that way. They only have a country to live in that is not much more *theirs* than the valleys and green meadows of the ocean. But the disdain of "rootlessness," they would declare, is a bluff or a superstition. *Roots* are the last things they want. Released from all the stocks of Europe, Africa, and Asia, they enjoy what is, in fact, a *cosmic* sensation. Their citizenship, about which they make so much fuss—and a justifiable fuss—is a kind of world-citizenship model A. For here is the beginning of the new world, which must one day be everywhere, when the term "American" would be as irrelevant as Polish, Irish, or Arab.

This is, I repeat, the only possible meaning of the U.S.A.—to be the place where a Cosmopolis, as the Greeks would call it, is being tried out. Either the United States is (1) a rather disorderly collection of people dumped there by other nations which did not want them—a sort of wastepaper basket or trash-can; or (2) a splendid idea of Fate's to provide a human

201

laboratory for the manufacture of Cosmic Man. It is, I feel, quite certainly the second of these alternatives.

Cosmic Man is, however, not merely being manufactured in the flesh but also in the spirit. A cosmic society must have a cosmic culture: and that is being provided for it, at colossal expense and the deployment of a fantastic pedagogic apparatus. The cultural centralization in America, for so vast a place, is abnormal. New York, with its massed publishing houses, its swarm of art dealers (as headquarters of the book-racket and picture-racket), and control of theatrical reputations (both for playwright and player), is as much the cultural center of the United States as Washington is the political center. And it is a long way from New York to Texas or to Idaho.

New York's intellectual authority is feebly disputed at times by the Middle West. You will have heard the saying: "New York is not America." For a Texas Ranger, or a man growing potatoes in Idaho, it of course is not. In all cultural matters, however, it is that absolutely. It is the Mecca of all women, who play a so much more important role in America than elsewhere, it is the headquarters of Fashion, as Paris is in Europe, and its hotels are always full of visiting provincials.

That there is a cultural melting-pot in America as well as a racial—that it melts a great deal more effectively than the latter: that it is part of a vaster melting operation, going on all over the world, not stopping at frontiers, so that the young man in Birmingham, Warwickshire, and in St. Louis, Missouri, is apt to be reading just the same books or literary reviews, and looking at photographs of the same pictures or buying the same musical records, let me repeat, before moving on to the next chapter, in which I explain how the cultural life of America functions. Science, naturally, is already internationalized, the pharmacologist or biochemist in Chicago or New York is in touch by letter with workers in the same field in India, South America, Europe. That is "culture," too, and it is enjoyed in common.

Naturally, there is nothing farther from the thoughts of most of those engaged in these cultural activities in America (most of them no doubt violently nationalistic) than a cosmic society of the future, or that they are in fact engaged in preparing the way for a "Cosmic Man"—a perfectly eclectic, nonnational, internationally minded creature, whose blood is drawn—more or less—from all corners of the earth, with no more geographical or cultural roots than a chameleon. Yet it is to that end that their activities will imperceptibly lead. They cannot be a cultural center: they can only be a place that things blow through from the outside. But in the end, so conditioned, they will insensibly produce the sum of all assimilations, a cosmic fruit, indeed.

25 THE CULTURAL APPARATUS
IN AMERICA

It would be a mistake to look for anything endemically American in the cultural ferments which give life to the fringes of the United States. It crackles and sputters at its edges: its interior is stolid and conservative, but, because conservative, the latter is not more "American." Less so, for the great thing about America is that it absorbs not only numbers of people from all the European and other countries, but also their ideas.

The incoming *people* get drafted into the interior, generally (the Poles go where the big Polish centers are, in the Middle West, the Lithuanians to the New England farms, and so on); but the *ideas* stop at the seaboard, mostly they do not get farther than New York, where they are subjected to the same process of "melting," of mixing, as are the people who come in. Only ideas "melt" quicker than people.

The true American is something that is not yet there. It certainly is not the "Daughters of the Revolution" or a Southern "cavalier" that is American, par excellence, but the contrary. Such being the case, any account of cultural developments in America resolves itself into a report of what is happening to the medley of militant doctrines which strive for supremacy in that spectacular antechamber, New York, or even on the Pacific side, in Hollywood. To those centers, no doubt, has to be added Chicago.

An eminent New Yorker of my acquaintance, however, who functions educationally in Chicago, insists that even that giant city is just a large village, as are all the other Lake cities and those scattered over the Middle West.

Size in America means nothing, you take that for granted: usually it is just more and more of the same thing. Thanks to modern industrial techniques, they spawn a city several times the size of Babylon in two or three decades. From personal observation I should, like this eminent acquaintance of mine, class Detroit, Chicago, St. Louis, Buffalo as monstrous manufacturing villages. Their culture is what filters back from New York. Those of their inhabitants with the money to do so go to New York as often as possible, for their "culture" as for their clothes.

Only Chicago is *so* large a place that it not only produced but retained Carl Sandburg, for instance, a big national figure, and in one of its suburbs it nursed and schooled Ernest Hemingway. He escaped to foreign parts. But he took with him something Chicagoan: in his violent imagination are indelible traces of its vivid gang-life. (Chicago still has first place, as producing the best gangsters. Any particularly business-like stick-up in Detroit, its nearest big neighbor, is attributed, for instance, to visitors from Chicago.)

Village or no village, Chicago must be counted in. South and inland from it, all is beneath a bourgeois eclipse, or it is pigs and cattle and crops, and nothing else. ("American Gothic," which I include among the pigs and crops, is nothing cultural.)

Let us, however, go back and qualify a little what I began by saying. I have an unshakable belief in the potentialities of that wonderful country—whose destiny, if anything, holds more exciting possibilities, as I have asserted before, than that of Russia—that I am apt to pass over what is actually there, in America, in my haste to proceed to speculations as to what *will* be there. Then there is so much that is clownish and backward, and all calls itself "American."

However, what voraciously assimilates all the new cultural doctrines and techniques is not a neutral machine, but an American mind. The Irish, the Germans, the Jews, the Italians, the Negroes, the Poles, the Scandinavians, the Indians, the French, the Chinese have merged their minds and sensibilities. There is a new man there you do not find anywhere else. He is not Cosmic Man yet, of course, he is innocent of the notion, even, of a cosmic culture. But he is moving toward that end, by reason of the logic of his position in time and space.

This man can be seen compiling books of first-rate scholarship, as an engineer creating machines of wonderful elegance and barbaric fancy: he may be seen acting in the theaters, cartooning, illustrating in the magazines and in books, designing bookjackets and posters, writing songs, in all of which skill and sometimes imagination of a high order are evidenced: he may be observed bravely cracking away in the *New Yorker,* is responsible for skyscrapers, and dress designs of a clinical elegance, he can be listened to pouring out a wealth of talent on the air, on a dozen radio networks.

This field of his activity (though taken little count of by Americans themselves) is worth detailed notice, for although not the most important, it is here that the comparison with his English opposite number is most feasible, and full of instruction. There is nothing comparable in the entertainment line to "Henry Aldrich" (the idiot youth of the small town bourgeois family and his slyly drawling, nasal friend, Homer Brown); to Amos and Andy, Jimmy Durante and his hero Umbriago—a volcano of brazen mirth; to Edgar Bergen and the sharp-witted child of his brain, Charlie McCarthy; to the Benny program, with the inimitable Rochester; and the Bing Crosby show—where all the popular songs get their first radio publicity.

The tremendous vitality and high spirits, compared with the genteel quietism of post-Victorian England, should be seriously noted by the English. Class lifts its ugly head, alas, whenever English men and women (I beg pardon, ladies and gentlemen) address themselves to the Thespian art. You have to go to the French cinema, or the German or Russian, to match the wonderful life, resourcefulness, intelligence of some American productions.

206

In England the insufferable "toffs" who broadcast what is called "news" to the abashed English are out of range of the comparative faculty. There is nothing like them anywhere. Why it should be thought necessary to produce the effect of the Public School condescending to report to the Board School such colorless fragments of news as is good for it, it is difficult to see. If you pick up the American radio at news-time, you may not get much news, but Lowell Thomas, say, does not treat you as if you were a particularly moronic house-serf, from whom he's not going to stand much more nonsense. (For usually they sound a little gruff, these great gentlemen of the air.)

If WOR or the Columbia Broadcasting System could be heard in England for several hours daily, it would be a good thing. The American radio is as good as the American movies are bad. (The news programs could easily be suppressed, if it were felt that the general public should not be told things which every possessor of an expensive short-wave receiving set can hear.) It might stimulate our own Olympian radio brain-trusters to shake a leg, to put it coarsely. All these manifestations of the popular genius of the American are not "culture," that is true. But they are its raw material.

In the last chapter I have made it clear how the background against which America must be viewed is *the future*. It can only be seen in its true light against something that is not there. It is what in the fullness of time it must become—according to causal laws the operation of which is dramatically visible—that is its real background: and in all its cultural procedure this is implicit. Its past—what I have surveyed in Part i—is highly misleading. Not only its past, but its present, requires interpreting too. For it seems violently to contradict, in many of its characteristics, this fatal promise of which I speak.

The fact is that Americans in general not only are unaware of their destiny, they actively obstruct the functioning of the "melting-pot." Culturally, this is very serious. There are bottle-necks of archaic prejudice everywhere.

To take the most flagrant cases, though it does not by any means stop there. American civilization as we know it owes

207

more, probably, to the Negro than to anybody. The colored people are the artistic leaven; out of their outcast state they have made a splendid cultural instrument. The almost solar power of their warm-heartedness has been a precious influence; their mirth, too, which explodes like a refreshing storm, often making these house-serfs the only sane thing in the white household. Yet everybody knows how they are requited by their fellow-citizens for their enormous gift to America. The colored people suffer more than it is easy to convey. Infant mortality among them is appalling. Since so many callings are barred to them, a majority live in sub-human squalor. Even Eleanor Roosevelt, in strenuous advocacy of political equality for colored people, was compelled to add that, as to *social equality*, she would not claim that for them. All one can do is to wonder why.

An even stranger superstition is that affecting Americans of Jewish origin: I say stranger because the Jewish contributions to science, the arts, economics, politics—and, after all, religion —have been so great and vastly influential that it seems almost inconceivable that a "numerus clausus" should exist for the Jewish student at the great American universities. Jewish wealth is resented—as if the Jews had not the same right as other people to acquire more money than is good for them.

Anti-Semitism, however emotionally satisfying to some people, is a bad business for all of us, like any other public feud— and this is in origin a religious one. In rebuking anti-Semitism, we are defending ourselves, not the Jews.

The wife of a wealthy Jewish merchant, living in a large Middle West city, explained to me (with great dignity—no pathos) how when her children grew old enough to understand, she had to explain to them how they must be prepared to encounter great prejudice, because they were her children. Very nice for the mother—very jolly for the children, as life opens out before them!

But these conditions produce all sorts of silly situations: as when, say, you have had lunch at the Racket Club (very select) in a certain important city; next day you are with a Jewish friend, and are about to remark: "Oh! What's your opinion, by the way, of the Racket Club? Why don't they get a better cook?" You stop in time. For you remember they would never let him inside it.

The Jews used not to be very good *melters*, but that is not the case now—though I doubt if they are anything like as disengaged from *their* superstitions as they ought to be. However, the "melting-pot" has far more cause for complaint against the Gentile and his exclusiveness than vice versa.

These are the worst of the racial bottlenecks. But since in America class is race, as we have seen, with something vaguely Nordic as the Brahmin end of the caste set-up, they do not stop at the African skin, or those congeneric with Him who is described as the Saviour of the World.

To the Wop so-called—that is, of course, one of the race of Dante and Leonardo—I have adverted already. Let me give another instance of snobbery. A German-American caretaker at a house in which I stayed in Long Island had a son of about eleven. Once when I was watching him playing (not for the first time) with some jolly little Wops who lived not far away, she was embarrassed, and explained that two days a week, no more, she allowed this to happen. And the German Americans —or hyphenateds, as they, along with the Irish-American, used to be called—are by no means first-quality citizens.

The effects of a decade of the New Deal are evident in the remotest fastnesses of conservatism. But it is still with the conservative elements that the cultural life of America outside New York has to deal. The "great manufacturing villages," as I have called such cities as Detroit, or equally the small town, are heartbreaking places for the young of literary or artistic talent. They end by going to cover in some university— these in the U.S.A. fulfilling one of the most useful functions of the monasteries in the dark ages, and the half-lighted ones. All those not interested in business, but with taste for more serious things, are huddled together in universities, museums, colleges, or schools. In the howling wilderness of unrestrained commercialism outside there is no place for them.

209

But the teaching profession is one of the most despised, as well as ill-paid, of any career in America. The members of the teaching staff in a university, all holding doctors' degrees, receive a smaller pay envelope than women teachers in a collegiate school. This is largely because they cannot as "professional" men be prevailed upon to form a union.

Having less social standing than a plumber and far less money, being thrust into a communal life with what are often a herd of aggressive hacks clawing their way up to some small preferment (for most of the inmates of a university are not poets or scholars, but the same type of man who becomes a priest) is not a very attractive alternative to office life. But it usually is taken. The luckiest are those who tuck themselves away in the museums—the pay is better.

When the State is the patron, in principle authentic talent of any kind is taken care of. In a capitalist country, however, it is upon the capitalist class that this responsibility rests, unless a "world without art" is what is desired. Well, in the States the rich classes, outside New York, are apt to be a cultural zero.

The odd rich man who has a collection of the more enterprising type of pictures, etchings, sculpture, ceramics is to be found in most places. But these pieces are generally European. So that solves nothing for the American.

The provincial bourgeoisie in the United States may be classified under two main heads. First, there are the "old families"; among these are many very cultivated people, but spare cash is not their strong point. Mostly they are comfortably bankrupt, clinging to the remnants of great wealth. Second, there are the new, or newer, rich: the families that own the factories.

The latter live naturally in large and expensive establishments. There are Afghan hounds upon their lawns, and English butlers with side-whiskers inside. But it is not the habit of the American provincial rich to regard an English butler as incomplete without a dash or two, a soupçon, of the things of the mind, in evidence in the reception rooms across which he

210

so ceremoniously moves. You just get straight butler—unadulterated gilt and plush, powder-closets, and Louis Seize.

If you went into the igloo of the Eskimo you would expect to find such objects as subserve the needs of the purely animal life, no more (a lamp of blubber oil, say, a harpoon or two). To avoid disappointments, it would be wiser to expect nothing more than this beneath the roof of a big "executive," for (though instead of oil lamps there are glittering chandeliers, and there are, of course, no harpoons) nothing more is as a rule what you will find.

If the city—the "manufacturing village"—is big, there are big universities, theaters, art schools, and a Symphony Orchestra—the latter *de rigueur*. There are large libraries, usually very good art museums (small libraries, well-stocked with books on the fine arts attached to these). The experts and officials of these public institutions are generously remunerated, and are extremely courteous and helpful, as are also the people in the libraries.

But all this immense apparatus of culture, of learning and taste, is a discreet screen to cover the void—the "air-conditioned vacuum," as Henry Miller puts it. And, of course, such things are there to advertise the city, not to promote letters, the fine arts, and science.

The young man or woman of unusual gifts might just as well have been born in Eskimo Land as in such an environment as this; better, in fact, for as Eskimos they would have been spared all these beautiful works of art, these massed books full of disturbing knowledge, produced in more propitious times and places—spared the frustrations such cultural excitements provoke.

The Carnegie and Guggenheim Foundations offer, to a few, a blessed escape for a short while. Or the talented and ambitious can take a chance and buy a ticket for the city of New York. But New York is, after all, a place of business: it is not constructed to be lived in, as was Paris or Vienna, but to be worked in. In a section known as "the Village," a filthy cold-water flat would probably absorb in rent all this student's

211

resources. Few, however, play the Dick Whittington with New York City. It is not a city to enter casually, which is thoroughly understood by the American. You approach it with money in your pocket, you leave it respectfully well before the money is exhausted.

About *Education* there is no difficulty—that is quite a different question: the most elaborate training centers abound—no need to go to New York. Every city of any size has hundreds—that is part of the cultural camouflage of which I have spoken. The difficulty (and this is the point) is to find anything to do with your skills and expressional resources once you have acquired them.

The general feeling is, among artists, that far too much is spent upon all the cultural apparatus, and nothing at all upon the potential artist. For there must be an art that is not rigidly conditioned by the profit-motive, and the vulgarity inseparable from it. But that is all you get up to now in America: for it is still so busy importing culture that it has no time for anything else. So talented contemporaries have to take their chance, or go into the import business, or education.

One university I knew had the most lavish plan for imparting a theoretical and historical understanding of the Fine Arts. The professor at the head of the art department, in his lectures upon the Renaissance painters, had two artists to demonstrate while he talked, one a painter, the other a sculptor. The former would show the class how Titian painted a picture, with the closest approximation possible as to materials. There was the correct Venetian underpainting, the "forty glazes" were simulated. The sculptor did a Donatello or Verrocchio act.

Their star-pupil, instruction lavished upon her during three or four years, left in a blaze of academic glory. She went into the book-section of the local department store: she was able to speak quite learnedly about an art-book, as she was selling it to a bourgeoise. Another star-pupil became an instructor in a girls' school.

So there is no difficulty about getting *taught* whatever you like, from dramaturgy to dry-point. But the advantages offered

212

you to *assimilate* are out of all proportion to the opportunities you subsequently enjoy to *create*. This is perfectly logical: it is what one would expect in view of the peculiar destiny of the U.S.A. Which is not to say that the activity need be quite so one-sided.

All the emphasis, then, is upon Education: in New York there is the Museum of Modern Art, the most dynamic of centers for the dissemination of culture ever imagined by man. A site in the center of London the size of Harrods, for the conversion of England to Cubism, Expressionism, or Constructivism, could not exist, any more than the lions in Trafalgar Square could come to life and start roaring at the passers-by. In Robert Barr, the ex-Director, they had the perfect man for such a task of mass-education, with his card-index mind and his neutrality as regards all modes of expression; prepared to accept anything on its merits, and tuck it impartially away in one of his mental pigeonholes.

The Modern Museum is a factory. It is designed to absorb ideas, doctrines, techniques in the Fine Arts as they flow into the States, upon every wind, and through every conceivable channel: to tidy them up, classify them, distribute them neatly labeled. Heaps of pictures and sculptures are pouring in and out all the time, the offspring of the ideas.

It would be hypocrisy to claim that this mountain of Modernity, dumped down in the center of New York City, has so far produced so much as a mouse. First-rate painters or sculptors are no more numerous in America than before it arrived. So in a report upon cultural development in the U.S.A., all that can be said is that the most modernist doctrines find acceptance, are housed in a palace of the Arts, and that even if it closed its doors tomorrow, so much visual virus has been pumped into the veins of the public that the next great artist in America will be very hot.

As I have tried to make clear, the United States, as at present constituted, does not lend itself to the development of outstanding artists, nor can it attract them from outside. A New Yorker, very prominent in modernist art circles, remarked

213

with great bitterness one day that, were Picasso to come to America, there would be enough work to occupy him for perhaps one year, no more. This was an outside estimate. New types of domestic architecture make slow progress. The rich prefer a "residence" suggestive of "background" (social): pillars, mullioned windows, gables. Something to go with the English butler.

Already newspaper and magazine art—from Virgil Partch to the best of the ads—is vastly better (far better than in England). And then, naturally, there are many other agencies of change—the Modern Museum is only one, though the best advertisement for Modernness. Also, not being profit-making, it is disinterestedly busy all the time pushing the new European ideas—those of the last thirty or forty years, that is, into and around the great expanse of what the Russian war bulletins called "inhabited places," as well as the mighty villages, bursting with capital.

But there are Americans for whom this is "foreign styles." They are cultural nationalists; Miro and Klee, for these people, are just "foreigners." And if you retorted that art, like science, is international: did they mean that Dürer and Bach should be "foreigners" to anyone except a German, Dante and Giotto "foreigners" to all but the Italians—was that what they meant? and if so, it was nonsense—*yes,* that *was* just what they meant! these people would hotly reply. New York for them would be a place full of "foreign-born agitators and crackpots" and for good measure, they might add "fifth-columnists."

I have already described the importation of *Neusächlichkeit:* the Middle West has many affinities with the germanic genius, and it is easy for an artist hailing from those parts to fall under such influences. "American Gothic" is nationalist painting, and doctrinally opposed to the "internationalism" of New York— of the Modern Museum and the "Fogg Factory" (this refers to a Harvard cultural center of internationalism, responsible among other things for Mr. Robert Barr, who was a "Fogg Factory" product).

The nearest thing in modern English painting to Middle

West regionalism is John Nash (not to be confused with Paul). Almost as if his were a foreign eye, he has a knack of picking out all that is, even caricaturally, English. The leafless tree-tops splayed out like a squat fern, against the gray cloud-ceiling customary in these islands: the damp fields, the soggy sky depress one—it is England at its worst because at its wettest. Yet it is an unmistakable likeness; just as the worst thing about the Middle West is its flatness and monotony and you get that accentuated in the regionalist.

The controversy between Benton, Grant Wood, and their followers on the one hand—the embattled "regionalists"—and on the other the pundits and painters preferring *"l'école de Paris,"* has developed in favor of the latter. The internationalism of New York being far more American than the nationalism of the Middle West or South, it of course prevails.

The regionalists are people who regard the United States as a nation of the usual kind. That assumption being incorrect, they strike us as less good Americans than they are patriotic Kansans or Ohioans. It is American to be open to all the winds of heaven, to be eclectic, promiscuous—universal.

Nobody will ever get anywhere in America by shutting himself up in a region, and trying to find *roots* there, or by the exploitation of a piety about a particular Heimat. For he belongs to the whole, to the spiritual union. That is of such fundamental importance that the "rooted" business seems grotesque and trivial.

If Education—the mechanism of cultural absorption—is essentially what we find in the United States, rather than new and original cultural forms, the mechanism is, perhaps, laid bare for us more in the Fine Arts than in Letters. But in the latter field it is the same story; except that the most outstanding American men of letters actually do not live in America at all. Instead of waiting expectantly in New York for the cultural matter to arrive—prepared for the fecundative impact (as those waiting for the latest shipload of Picasso canvases do) they take ship for Europe, and go where they can collect it—and absorb it—at the source.

Thus Ernest Hemingway, America's unchallenged No. 1 creative writer, went to Paris, the place from which all the literary influences came, instead of waiting for them to reach him in Illinois or Ontario. He went there to be where they first take shape. An American lady, Miss Stein, was permanently stationed in Paris to feed any fledgling that turned up from the States with mental nourishment and Pythian stammerings. She fed Ernest to such good purpose that he would do credit to any country. He lives in Cuba—because it has not been de-Europeanized—coming over to Europe now only for wars.

The greatest cultural influence in the United States still, and for a long time past, is the poet, T. S. Eliot. He has fed it with what it demands from London as did formerly Henry James (a quintessence of culture), or, in another department, Whistler and Sargent.

Why these people—the creative ones, for what is fed back in those cases is firsthand stuff—have to leave the U.S.A. to do their good American work is because, as I have explained, there is no place in the States where the creative life, as distinct from the purely critical or educational, can be pursued. New York is no exception to this rule. But such writers do not (as the more stupid and jingo of their compatriots suppose) cease to be Americans. It is far more American to live in Bloomsbury, London, or Montparnasse, Paris, and write, as they cannot help doing, powerful American books, than it would be to bury themselves in Missouri, and write merely Missourian books. But the word "American," as I use it here, covers a new culture, an incipient universalism—in the nature of things eclectic: not an old-style nationalism. That is why geography does not matter. Paris, Illinois, has no advantage over Paris, France, unless you are thinking in the old national terms, and the latter is a much better place to work in for intellectual workers—or *writers*.

26 ANARCHIST AND COMMISSAR

In many places in the course of this book I have extolled the wonderful social attributes of the average American, and I must come back to that again, in order to relate it to democracy. The pioneer period, of course, has something to do with it. But there are other pioneers, besides the American of the United States, both in the Americas and elsewhere: and they do not possess this attribute. It may be that the brotherly love which the early Puritan or Quaker settlers set such store by was so potent an essence that it has survived all changes and still impregnates this country. Waves of later immigration brought with them a spirit susceptible to the influences of this extraordinary gregarious piety, especially, I think, the German.

Whatever may be its cause, or causes, I should describe the survival in so powerful a form of this beautiful human impulse to befriend, to treat all men as brothers, as what is most surprising about American life. By this I do not mean that everybody goes about like an early Quaker, advertising loving charity in his quiet and friendly face. I refer to something that is widely distributed, part of the equipment of most Americans, which reveals itself in many graceful and practical ways. It is something, it may be said, that is unknown in England. In Scotland, I think, there is something of this left, or something that might remind one a little of it. It is this attribute of theirs, you will remember, which I indicated as the complement of the American "melting-pot." Without it, or something of the sort, the mere mixing of races would be of little significance: just as a world-State might be quite as bad as any other kind—on the domestic side—unless its creation were accompanied by a "new deal"—a great mobilization of the social impulses (such as only a great catastrophe could assure). And —once again—the great importance of America lies here; (1) it is a cosmopolitan society, a kind of advance copy of what an eventual world society would be—so much so, it may be said, that the global society of the future has actually started already on the North American continent; and (2) a Rotarian or Lionesque brotherly gregariousness presides at this operation— often taking somewhat ridiculous forms, but of the highest utilitarian value. Again, it may further be noted that no Socialism without this active brotherliness is much more than a Fabian middle-class bossiness, or the cold mania of a frustrated religionist. There are other varieties: but all true Socialism starts and must end as a relationship between brother and brother—not between father and children.

This strange and beautiful solidarity of which I have been speaking is quite distinct from political democracy: for it would go on existing if democratic institutions were superseded by some other form of government. Roman slaves, for instance, possessed it. Indeed, if we may identify this with the Puritan and the Quaker, then it flourished a long time with great intensity under a tyranny, until at last a system of government supervened, Republican and Democratic, with which it could associate itself, but with which it is by no means identical. Just as there have been many pioneers, but they have not usually been conspicuous for the pioneering virtue of comradeship, so democracy does not of itself promote any special increase in the social virtues.

We must, in studying the United States, group these two things in our mind: American democracy—deriving, as I have shown, in the main from Jefferson—and this profound feeling of identity with other men, no doubt religious in origin. The Jeffersonian heritage is enhanced by this association. With the last of these two things we know where we stand. But democracy (by itself) is another matter altogether: for political

218

democracy is by no means a simple thing, presenting many contradictions. Let us examine some of the pitfalls democracy, as a political faith, presents.

Is it democracy that is responsible for the somewhat anarchic paradise of which I have spoken so much and so enthusiastically? Is that disembodied sensation I have already described, that fine irresponsibility (which once I identified with freedom), attaching as it does the American to his great impersonal refuge for the homeless—is all this contingent upon democratic doctrine? If so, it is probably a short-lived paradise. For men are not born to be so happy yet awhile as all that. America as a great natural storehouse to loot was a momentary heaven of easy wealth: is that intoxicating American easygoingness and *sans gêne* a short-lived phenomenon deriving from the same set of circumstances? Or it may be a decadence: one in which a nation is giving itself up to be pillaged, and is joining in the looting of its own house? The States has often been described as decadent. Is it just that?

Again, is all that we like about democracy something ethically we ought not to like? But democracy has many meanings. Are we perchance attached to the wrong kind? I will at all events take up a few of these points. Additional light should be thrown in this way upon the subject of my earlier chapters.

For those exposed to the Anglo-Saxon tradition, "freedom" is apt to be an assertion of the ego: of the individual's privilege to act by himself, not with other men. A hangover from the Sagamen? Possibly. It is a very potent tradition, taking a great number of forms throughout the world.

According to the sober view, of orthodox political science, political "freedom" is what is left over, when all the requirements of group discipline (and they are many and onerous) have been satisfied. It is a freedom that the average man would regard with only moderate interest. For most, all freedom worth the name is captured or even stolen, not received as a ration; secured by the circumvention or defiance of the recognized code of social ethics. Only to drink as much as he *should,* to spend as much money as he *should,* to get to bed when he

219

should, to make as much money as is fair and just, having regard for the interests of every other member of his group, is not "freedom" as generally understood. It *should* be, but it is not.

In the West, the "rebel" is the most popular type of free man. What is free is felt about as something mildly criminal. In America, where the social conscience is more uneasy than in England, legislation is forever tending to classify as a penal offense anything for which men crave—such as the consumption of alcohol, or of tobacco, indulgence in the sexual appetite, or the possession of a faithful hound. There is no country where sumptuary laws blossom more naturally. And Red Tape proliferates with the luxuriance of the liana in the rain-forests. Anyone living there soon acquires the insidious sensation of being a minor criminal. When a millionaire goes to prison, he evinces no surprise or indignation. Everybody would regard it as absurd if he did.

An integral part of Anglo-Saxon freedom is the *rights* that secure it. Those rights owed much in their origin to the metaphysical notion of the inviolability of the human personality. There is nothing more empty imaginable than the words "right to life, liberty, and the pursuit of happiness," denuded of (1) the metaphysical and mystical, or (2) the contractual background. Yet the vast majority of people who, in America, repeat these words, are quite unacquainted with what they mean (or with all that they *can* possibly mean). They remain for them a mere rhetorical music. "Rights," like "liberties," are words whose potency has, customarily, no rational basis. However, the Statue of Liberty is not an emanation of ecclesiastical law. Nor is its torch an invitation to bacchanalian license. The individual's rights are not the stuff of libertarian oratory.

The *réclame* of democracy in the U.S.A. has been largely drawn from anarchic passions. It is undoubtedly in the theory of philosophic Anarchy, of which Proudhon was the father, that American libertarianism finds its most consummate expression. The full-blooded anarchist's conception of the State is one without a government. The "rule of the road" is for him a red rag to a bull. He drives his car upon the left or right side, according to his fancy at the moment. In everything he is a public danger: he is the political problem-child of today, the most clownish figure among the crowd of bitter theorists who throng the contemporary stage. It is appropriate that the adherents of the Marxian teaching, namely the Communists, and those who derive their political philosophy from Proudhon, the anarchists, are the most irreconcilable of all enemies (though excess of discipline in Soviet practice is a phase only, it is at least possible; external pressures removed, some anarchy may be re-introduced).

Jefferson, like most "progressive" men in his period, stood for *the less government the better,* you will remember. Jeffersonian democracy contains much more that is anarchical than democratic, in the stricter sense. Consequently, in the very center of the main body of American tradition is a principle that, under analysis, would prove to be anarchical. And full anarchy is the political philosophy of Paradise, not of human society. But theoretically it might quite well be the philosophy of the cosmic society of the future—or some democratic regime, with a generous admixture of anarchy.

The only theory of government consonant with the idea of political "freedom" is democracy. I should say, perhaps, at once, that I would dislike myself having to change the modicum of license I enjoy, thanks to the fact that I live in a democratic community, for any system where I had less. So, however, must all men feel—those who have no ambition to boss others. But democracy is one of those things that fade quickly: it should be constantly renewed. It can be tightened up or relaxed at will. At one end it becomes very rigid, the Soviet variety, at the other is the American.

To face at once, however, the major difficulties besetting this doctrine, I will turn now to a latter-day Federalist —who incidentally illustrates his text as much from American as from British history; namely Professor Harold Laski. He interprets contemporary politics rather as if he were a revenant of those early American days. He seems really to feel he has a new country to build up and "found." The pole toward which this latter-day Federalist, as I have called him, inclines is Hamilton. But, unlike the latter, for him the mob is not "a beast," but a rather feckless and peculiarly ignorant darling, who *should* be the repository of all power in the State. Only, since poor, "mentally idle," inattentive Demos is quite unable to use this power, why, *we* will use it for him. We who possess that "sense of the State" which Demos lacks.

Somewhere between Mr. Koestler's Commissar—the exponent of the maximum of government—and Jefferson or Proudhon, who, in their different ways, were vowed to a minimum of government, Professor Laski swims sedately down the left bank of the contemporary stream, so that it is out of the question that he will ever cross the stream and mount the right bank, yet it is never certain that he will actually stop swimming and come to rest at any particular spot upon the left.

Laski, whatever people may say, is a genuine Democrat. He is distressed and impatient with the Public, the supposed ruler of the State. One sees that he feels inclined, sometimes, in a perfectly nice way, to take this enfranchised dunce by the shoulders and shake him.

What is most people's dream-picture of democracy—in which the People are a responsible monarch of unchallengeable power—he has converted into the most diluted and unreal of constitutional monarchies. His Demos is a constitutional monarch besides whom the kings of England, as we find them today, are sovereigns enjoying an alarming amount of authority.

I will condense in a few key quotations, however, Laski's text. It is best always to have the *ipsissima verba* of a writer whose views one is canvassing, or invoking. By the method of continuous quotation, interspersed with commentary, I will demonstrate the impression made by his recital.

In our time "democratic government has become a commonplace beyond discussion," he begins by asserting. That is axiom number one. There can be no government but democratic government. But from there on everything becomes

222

"complex." "We are coming to recognize that any theory of society which avoids complexity will be untrue to the facts."

Our task is a complicated one, it is not "straightforward." "Many of the assumptions which the nineteenth century fought for seem so obvious that men [today] can scarcely realize either the novelty they represent or the anger to which they gave rise." To these nineteenth-century "novelties," anyway, we are inflexibly committed.

One of the nineteenth-century principles is, of course, universal suffrage. But here is where the complexity begins with a vengeance. Votes for Women, for instance, has doubled the number of people at the ballot boxes, but it is only too evident that it has not increased—or, for that matter, diminished—the volume of political sagacity discernible. That nineteenth-century dream has gone up in smoke, like so many others.

One is legitimately somewhat depressed. Clearly we must abandon the optimism with which the Benthamites "approached the issue." They did not doubt that the possession of the franchise would, in combination with the natural reason of mankind, build a State in which effort would secure the reward of liberty and equality. We have no such assurance now. We have been taught by long experience that the part played by reason in politics is smaller than we supposed. Indeed, it is almost non-existent.

"The mass of men and women who, at the electoral period, function as that Demos in whom all power is vested, are very impressive in their numbers, but, alas, in nothing else. They are scarcely articulate about their wants; and even when they are articulate, they are not trained to judge whether the solutions suggested are in fact an adequate response to their desires." At this point he might have added that, untrained as they are to judge whether the solutions suggested by the rival candidates are wicked or charitable, the Press and Radio step in, so that they may know how to vote; and that the Press and Radio are not such politically Simon Pure agents as they claim to be. These additional factors demand attention, to make democracy thoroughly intelligible, since, as Bryce pointed out,

223

it is impossible to imagine a modern democracy without the Press (to which the Radio has since then been added).

So we have that "basic condition that ultimate power must be confided to those who have neither time nor desire to grasp the details of its working." The bulk of those in any parliamentary democracy have quite trouble enough just living, without politics; "their capacity will be exhausted by the mere effort to live; and the search to understand life will lead them into complexities they have rarely the energy, and seldom the leisure, to penetrate. . . . The context of their lives which is, for the majority, the most important, is a private context . . . they set their wills by the wills of institutions they rarely explore. . . . They obey the orders of government from inertia; and even their resistance is too often blind resentment rather than a reasoned desire to secure an alternative."

A very promising company upon whom to bestow absolute power will be the reader's reflection all along. However, it is only in name that this horde governs. "The administration of the modern State is a technical matter, and . . . those who can penetrate its secrets are relatively few in number." It is, then, pretty obvious that the State, in fact, will be governed by these few "technicians" (or what Mr. Burnham would call "managers"), and that the "government of the people, by the people, for the people," is just a political fairy-tale. A fairy-tale told to the people to lull and please them, while the group of technicians are busy, in their inaccessible administrative fastness of power, governing, in whatever way they please.

These quotations all come from five consecutive pages of Professor Laski's book (*The Grammar*, pp. 15–19). They are not arbitrarily selected passages. What has just been quoted represents the view of most instructed men: the body of any democratic electorate is exactly as shown in the above quotations. This is not a view peculiar to Professor Laski. But the latter has the temper that is most desirable of all in a democrat, a very critical one of what *passes* for democracy. Political equality is useless, the franchise is a mockery, without social equality of *training*, that is of education. And that, in the country more addicted to "freedom" than any, the English have never had. Post-feudal class-conditions have endured up to the present time.

The above statement of Laski's could be made to look, in isolation, a cynical theory of government which is, in fact, a power-system: a statement of the case for power-politics as practiced according to a cunning libertarian prescription. The reason for this is plain. Democracy, as we practice it, is just that.

Here would be that cynical theory, put in plain language. The people are (more or less) persuaded that they are governing themselves: disarmed by this flattering illusion, you, the man of destiny, govern away to your heart's content, in your arcanum of perfectly camouflaged power, surrounded by a small group of fellow "experts." Finally, the vastness and complexity of the twentieth-century mammoth communities have made the individual of less and less importance: his will is negligible: his "freedom" a ridiculous fantasy. At the heart of this mammoth web, as if spun by some mad spider, there is a small area of relative freedom. If you can gain access to that inner ether, you can push around myriads of people, without their ever knowing quite what is happening to them. (All the while, naturally, their Press and Radio would be assuring them that they were pushing *themselves* around.)

Optimism, as Professor Laski tells us, is inadmissible. What would be called a pessimistic scrutiny is the only one that can lead us anywhere, except to the cynical conclusions of the philosophy of power, a résumé of which I have just given. As it is, all the democratic freedoms we inherited from a highly undemocratic time are being swallowed up by slumps and wars and then still more slump.

The only theory of government consistent with the popular idea of a "free society" is democracy, yes: but is such a government even possible? Is it not Utopian? And however much you call a system "utopian," that does not make it so, and you might get a series of the most hideous Utopias. My quotation from Professor Laski, taken by itself (for that is not all he says!)

would tend to suggest that democracy is a name, nothing more. But what might be termed *the right to interfere,* on the part of the citizenry (a right only existing in democracies), is of great importance. Elections—agreed—are an even less effective gauge of the true will of the people than an accurate poll. But so long as the elective machinery is there, we have something solid at the back of us. The right-to-strike is the workman's habeas corpus: the suffrage occupies the same position in the life of the community. Its votes may be ill-considered, emotional, the result of hypnotic suggestion by Press and Radio: but at least it has the power to strike back at despotism.

As very few members of the English electorate have ever opened a book by Professor Laski, they are unable to benefit by such instruction as is to be derived from the above passage. All books of that sort make their minds ache. They cannot therefore improve their chances of freedom by learning more about the brand of politics involved every time they function as electors.

All Western democracies are living upon a considerable but diminishing capital of free institutions inherited from a more vigorous or less complex epoch. While it lasts, these democracies will enjoy governments tolerant of more individual liberty than any other. But these democratic communities should understand they are in the nature of political sports.

What fantastic standards of free government men entertained a hundred years ago—how could they be so sanguine as to lay down rules for good and bad government, in the way they did, as late as J. S. Mill in mid-nineteenth-century England? Let us listen to him for a moment.

"That mankind are not infallible; that their truths, for the most part, are only half-truths; that unity of opinion, unless resulting from the fullest and freest comparison of opposite opinions, is not desirable, and diversity not an evil, but a good, until mankind are much more capable than at present of recognizing all sides of the truth . . . As it is useful that while mankind are imperfect there should be different opinions, so is it that there should be different experiments of living, etc."

226

This is high talk! Tell the politicians of our day that "their truths . . . are only half-truths," that in order to arrive at the full truth they should defer to the opinion of those who disagree diametrically with them, and see what reply you would receive! Mill, it is true, would not from the rulers of his own day have received a much more patient one. The point, however, is that no one at this time thinks it worth while to discuss government in that grand manner, as if laying down rules for the ruler. We know that the "mankind" *we* shall have to deal with is "infallible." That is why in writing a book of politics I entitled it "The Art of Being Ruled." Not so long ago it was "The Art of Ruling" about which men theorized.

We will now return to the stage reached in this argument before an analysis of democracy (or one essential aspect of it) seemed necessary. The history of English democracy is interwoven, of course, with an emotional conception of "freedom" ("Britons never shall be slaves," a jingo song which meant "Shall always be masters"). But there were "rebels," not English, who contributed to the American idea (or rather emotion) of freedom, or liberty. There are other conceptions of democracy too, besides the English, not so much involved with emotional freedom, or indeed freedom at all.

The stormy romantic emotionality that flowed outward over the world from the furnace of eighteenth-century revolution in France (and of which Jefferson made free use) was not a democratic heat. For democracy is, in fact, not hot at all. Even it can be quite cold. Let me explain this in the following way. When a student in Paris, I read the *Contrat Social,* and there I found enlightment of an unexpected kind. Had I been required at that time to supply a definition of Liberty, I should not have been able to comply. It did not seem to me that, except as a myth, it had any existence (or, as Mr. Shaw puts it, the first thing to understand about freedom is that it does not exist. I should have said that). But Rousseau cleared up the difficulty: for he showed that it was, in fact, *duty.* This, I believe, was the passage, which I copied in a notebook—though it may have come from

227

some résumé of the *Contrat*. "In consequence of the social contract, a great change was effected in man. Up to this time, desire and instinct were mainsprings of his actions: now he was guided by a sense of justice and duty. He had regard for others. Instead of natural liberty, which found its limits in the measure of his own strength, he now enjoyed the civil liberty whose limits were established by the will of all."

When Rousseau advanced this idea of a contractual basis for liberty he was on sound historical ground. In Maine's study of "Ancient Law," we learn how, in the civil law of primitive societies, Contract is conspicuous by its absence, "the greatest gap in ancient civil law will always be caused by the absence of Contract, which some archaic codes do not mention at all, while others significantly attest the immaturity of the moral notions on which Contract depends, etc." The liberty of the *Contrat Social* was that as understood in jurisprudence—a moral, a contractual liberty. However, after reading Rousseau, I knew that by liberty men meant some form of duty to others. I had never realized that liberty meant anything so dull and disagreeable as a social obligation: or some carefully measured out ration of unfettered action—or, it is better to say, severely fettered freedom of action, of a specified kind. But such is the kind of liberty which, in a strictly administered democracy, the citizen would enjoy. As I remarked just now, such is the view of orthodox political science. It is obvious that the democracy of Geneva and of Whig England would be very different. But the former is the more real. And it has nothing to do with freedom or liberty, either of the anarchic American variety, or of that rebel afflatus for which the French Revolution was responsible.

So, to conclude: American democracy—which has become so complex a thing that it is, in a sense, a misleading simplification to derive it from Jefferson and Jackson—is a much less pure and less important ingredient of the American nature than those other social attributes which at the beginning of this chapter I went out of my way to emphasize. It is the latter which will go over into the future, perfected, American society.

In the course of this book, my insistence upon the future, always the future—at the expense of the past or present—my tendency to regard the America of the present as merely a laggard and uncompleted American future, is, of course, accounted for by the fact that the United States is undeniably something in-the-making: it is a forward-looking dynamism, with little time for actual accomplishment, in the midst of a welter of incessant readjustments. But everywhere change is the order of the day: and it seems to me men should provide themselves with a chronograph, to register the strange velocity with which events are now whizzing past or to record the way in which the processes of change have been accelerated.

This can be illustrated, I think, by a passage from Professor Arnold Toynbee's *Study of History* (p. 90, Vol. III). In it he speaks of "the catastrophe of A.D. 1914–18: a great war which may or may not prove to have been the undoing of our own Western Civilization." In a footnote he adds: "The generation now alive will not live to know whether the wound dealt to our Western society in 1914–18 has been mortal or not, though the truth . . . will doubtless be manifest, several centuries hence, to our descendants."

It was quite unnecessary to wait for several centuries for enlightment on that subject, as it has turned out. This volume of Toynbee's is dated 1934. So we only had to wait a decade to be in possession of this information. Had of course this admirable historian been writing that passage in 1948, he would have written it differently. Western society, as that term was understood by the pre-1914–18-war European, is in dissolution.

The enormously increased velocity of the time-machine confounds the historian. His thinking is geared to time-tables which contemporary techniques have made suddenly obsolete. Even a revolutionary weapon like the rocket-bomb alters the conservative picture entirely. The atomic bomb just blasts it to pieces. The aerial platforms, two-hundred miles up, of tomorrow, which, it seems, the rocket-men were turning over in their minds, while engaged in the perfecting of their "doodle-bugs," will, in combination with the new nuclear principle, write an even more comprehensive *finis* to history as it up to now has been conceived.

Life on earth will henceforth be lived upon quite different terms. The campaigns of Hannibal and Caesar and our desert campaign of '42–'44 will seem laughably feeble, ant-like exploits, scarcely worth recording. In a sense, we are moving out of "history." Historic time is not our time. The columnist, like the historian, shows little consciousness of this important fact. He will describe every battle and every conference as the "greatest of all time." One even declared that the San Francisco Conference was the greatest event since the Last Supper. (This, it is true, was an American columnist.)

The analogies of history become less valid every day. There is and there is not an analogy between the "parochial sovereignties" of the Greek city-states, and the parochial sovereignties of contemporary Europe.

Like Hellas at the death of Alexander, Western Europe *should,* if it wishes to survive *as Western Europe,* think in terms of Cosmopolis. It should abandon its parochial sovereignties: the national sovereignty of that ancient commonwealth, Great Britain; the French Republic; Holland, Italy, and Spain. But all these countries jabber different languages: they are even less able to subordinate their private interests as sovereign states and to combine than were the city-states of Greece at the time of Alexander of Macedon.

So, as "Western Civilization," they are doomed to perish. But something quite different will happen to them than the long decay of a degenerate Hellenism which overcame the Greek world. Consequently, the analogy is without relevance. Only half of the analogy holds.

If I am not mistaken, we shall have in the future to go to History for different reasons: not in order to attempt to read, by means of historical parallels, our own fate: we shall go to it for its scientific contribution, not for politics and prophecy.

The rising and falling of empires, budding and decaying of civilizations, the slow evolution of nations, like the English or the French, of which history is full, is a pattern that is at an end, or so nearly at an end that the rest of that little story (since the suspense is dissipated, and we could write the remainder ourselves) is of no particular interest.*

A modern Englishman or Frenchman—a very highly differentiated animal—took a couple of thousand years to produce. People have to be very much shut off from foreign influences, to cook in their own juice for a very long time, to reach the ethnical discreteness of a typical Britisher or Parisian. These conditions are not likely to be present again. That type of historic evolution is, according to all likelihood, a closed book. The historian will look back at it as an interesting curiosity, not as the contemporary historian is apt to do (see last chapter), as to something possessing a continuous relevance for the human being, evolving after a Spenglerian pattern.

When I read the life-story of the Irish, the ancient Israelites, the Norsemen—the response of these communities to challenge (or, in other words, as Herr Hitler would have put it, their *Kampf*), always engaged as they are in some lifelong murderous duel with some great Enemy, I feel I might just as well be reading the life-story of a hyena, a wild dog, a rat, or the most belligerent variety of ant. It is more complicated certainly,

*If this statement of our case is correct, it also disposes of the perennial controversy, in which "upstart Theory," as it was once called, is confronted by the opposite principle of gradual organic growth. In a very few years it will be possible to destroy in the course of a morning an organized society that has taken many centuries to create.

because he of the human species delivers interminable harangues, dresses himself up in a series of disguises, and finds all manner of excuses for homicidal exhibitions. But, speaking purely for myself, it is dull reading.

The life-story of an ant-hill would read much the same way—barring the lofty slogans and the ceremonial garments (prescribed for killing, or for engaging in the diplomatic preliminaries of killing). The turning-point of a battle would be a particularly heroic stand by a platoon of gallant insects who had taken up their position behind a clod of earth. Disguised as blades of grass, an attacking party of the enemy, selected for their beautifully developed antennae, would steal out from behind a leaf. But the intrepid platoon would advance to meet them; they would rout the attackers, killing at least half, which little engagement would be the turning-point of the battle (and perhaps of the molehill—the "greatest molehill of all time"). A "V.C. show," if ever there was one! However gory the details, one can soon have enough of such reading. Even if in one ant-hill a new technique were invented by some particularly resourceful leader, involving the rolling of rows of heavy pebbles before an attacking force—even if some formic statesman succeeded in drawing a group of ant-hills into his people's orbit, for "security" reasons, and isolating another ant-hill which he feared: yes, even if one particularly subtle ant succeeded in stirring up the workers of a neighbor against their drones! Obviously the workers *ought* to be stirred up: but it should be routine ant-hill practice. As history it would be dull.

No, the life-story of *communities,* which is full of screams and bellows and bangs, recriminations and shrieks of triumph, in contradistinction to the life-story of *individuals,* in which the reason plays at least a modest part, is a dull business, to my thinking. The State, the community (unlike the individual), is backward. It is still in the "state of Nature," as the seventeenth- or eighteenth-century moralist would put it.† Un-

†"The relation of several states to one another is like the relation of men in a state of nature; one of enmity." Spinoza, *Tractatus politicus.*

232

like the individual citizen, the State indulges in brutal reprisals, in thefts of property, in blackmail, forgery, and periodically in wholesale homicide (upon this let us continue to insist). It has a variety of very primitive habits indeed, has the State. I cannot get up much interest in its goings-on as history.

If States were men, they would be cave men. Yet we, *collectively*, are, of course, the State. The State, in fact, is our great weakness: it is the lowest, not the highest, thing about us. The State is our badge of servitude and often of degradation; for we cannot do without the State, any more than we can dispense with the water-closet. And the Statesman is deserving of admiration only in so far as he identifies himself with the people, and not with the State—not with such a state as nine out of every ten prove themselves to be.

Why the State should lag behind in this manner was not explained by the above-mentioned moralists. They accepted that as a fact, just as, until Jean-Jacques Rousseau came on the scene, they accepted social inequality without trouble. It seems natural to Locke that Lord Shaftesbury should have a lot of servants, and not the servants a lot of Shaftesburies.

These reflections upon the State have a somewhat bitter ring, I fear. It could scarcely be otherwise, however, at this time. A Frenchman, a German, or an Englishman, looking back down the years, upon a century and a half of *States*, has such a portrait gallery of either morons or monsters to delect his saddened gaze with, that he could hardly, if asked what he thought of "the State," find anything very flattering to say. "It" is either a half-human shape, with a brain so diminutive that Neanderthal Man would scorn it, who plunges the nation it represents into slough after slough of Despond: or it is a homicidal lunatic, clutching in his sweaty fingers bunches of human beings and thrusting them with a snarl into gas-chambers it keeps in its lair for that purpose. And these lunacies are infectious. The State is always angry with some other State; at their best, when not over-adrenalized, they are lethargic, and have as much care for the welfare of the men they rule as a camel for its fleas.

233

The State is here being considered in the past tense: thus States have always been, with few exceptions, up to this time. For they have been *sovereign* States, which has been the main trouble with them, as again and again I have pointed out. The Socialist State, on which novel form England has embarked, is a state of a different order, and its function can only be as soon as possible to divest itself of its sovereignty, and to take England into a world-society—a cosmic society—where these monsters I have been describing will be as extinct as the dinosaur.

In Chapter 23, I referred to the exclusion of the poets from the platonic State: books and their writers are never popular where a population is to be strictly controlled (controls being directed sometimes to one end, sometimes to another). An article by Miss Dorothy Thompson, dated July 19, 1945, has just been brought to my notice. It is so *à propos,* I should like to quote from it. It is especially useful as Miss Thompson is one of the most popular columnists, and cannot be accused of being "an intellectual." It is an article written upon her return from Germany, jeering at all the solemn nonsense about "re-educating" the German.

The Institute for the Re-education of Germans [she writes] has decided that the United States must make unavailable to the Germans "all books glorifying war." I hope we have thought that one through, but I am afraid not. Are we to copy Hitler's book-burnings? Are we to turn over to a commission authority to raid German libraries under some general directives? . . .

It is impossible to suppress all books glorifying war without sup-pressing the Old Testament; the leading classics (Homer, Virgil, Caesar); parts of Shakespeare; all the great body of English, American, and German poets who wrote in praise of the struggles for freedom—Byron, Shelley, Whitman, Schiller, for instance; Marx, Engels, and the Communist writers who preached the class-struggle; the histories of the British, French, American, and Rus-sian revolutions (many of these suppressed by Hitler!), and, in fact, most of the existing histories of the last 2,000 years, and almost everything written in any country during these war years, including the speeches of Churchill, Stalin, and F.D.R.; most United States films; many United States comics, and the speeches of General Patton.

She winds up with a playlet which is very much to the point: how re-education would work in the Reich under present circumstances.

Whatever measures are taken to suppress books, will, I suppose, be carried out by military authorities. I imagine a conversation between—let us say—four-year-old Hans and his mother:
Hans: Mama, what are those men doing?
Mother: They are removing dangerous books that might fill your mind with war!
Hans: And why do they wear such beautiful clothes and brass buttons?
Mother: Because they are soldiers.
Hans: What are soldiers, Mama?
Mother (for the sake of the argument): People, dear, who make peace.
Hans: Mama, I want to have a suit like that and make peace. Where can I read about soldiers?
Excuse me, while I go out and have a nervous breakdown.

Plato is quite as bad as Homer—indeed, worse—and in any plan of political censorship one would be disposed to ban very nearly all the books mentioned by Miss Thompson, for fifty years or so. The Old Testament, or the Norse Sagas, as much as *Western Stories,* should be banned for school or university reading, in association with an interdict upon the manufacture of toy pistols and leaden soldiers; all that has to do with imperialist war. Marx, perhaps, is in another category. It would be irresponsible and meaningless violence—killing men as you go duck-shooting—that one would seek to discourage.

Fifty years would be enough. At the end of that period, during which everyone up to the age of fifty would have been nourished on other ideals, the ban could be lifted. For by that time no one would want, any longer, to read about the stupid ruffians that Shakespeare portrayed so much better than Homer, in *Troilus and Cressida*. Or they would only regard them as swashbuckling clowns, to be laughed at, not imitated.

Had it been a very common thing for our ancestors of, say, two centuries ago, to murder one another—neighboring streets or villages, even, given up to feuds in which dozens would be killed—civilization meanwhile maintained (much as it is at Broadmoor) with Opera, State Balls, etc.: and had then a cure of that sick society been effected, by now their better books would be quite safe reading.

No list could be too comprehensive, if right education is our aim. The demilitarization of the German mind would be a great boon. The romance of physical violence should be exorcised in the case of the American—speaking in Utopian terms. Wholesale re-education in, and out of, Germany and Japan is imperative.

I have been led into a digression by the vistas of censorship opened up by Miss Thompson as earlier by Plato. To return to my remarks about history: a pure lack of interest—not a religious or sentimental objection—is what I experience for the material of history, as action, not of course as the record of the growth of civilization. The destructiveness of war is hair-raising, but not more so, nor is it more imbecile, than all the other things that go with it, which collectively we call "peace." The pacifist is a man who can see only one thing at a time—war. You cannot isolate war in that fashion. It is just the culmination of peace, of such peace as we get. So there is another kind of book that should be banned, just as much as books advertising war and senseless violence; for millions of men and women in periods of peace are being killed too—slowly poisoned with bad food, starved with inadequate food, exposed to disease (where the rich are not), improperly cared for when sick, allowed to die like dogs when old, fleeced by insurance companies to obtain a proper burial—but I need not enlarge upon the horrors of peace. All books that condone or consent to these conditions—or treat sympathetically the lives of people who are conspicuously responsible for their continuance—should, of course, be banned. They are at least as numerous as those books which make war the big thing in life, the "great adventure."

28 REGARDING A FEW OF THE TERMS USED

In Chapter 26, as you will have noticed, perhaps, two contradictory impulses were under discussion at once: for in America they are found in such intimate association as to make it impossible to speak of them apart. They would, in isolation, lead to very different ends. One is somewhat anti-social, the other is highly social. One tends to glorify the human personality, the other to exalt the group, in a warm human benevolence. And I have never been in a country (except perhaps for Germany) where man was so tolerant of man, as if he were his favorite animal; where, when a number were together, their eyes all seemed to shine with a light that came from a common source, their limbs seemed to move as if at the command of a single brain.

One of these two attributes I have placed far above the other in human significance, namely, the aptitude for comradely solidarity. For the future of life on earth that should have priority. The competitive principle, which estranges and separates, is the villain of our little piece, especially now that we confront each other with atomic power at our command.

My own position may not have been explained sufficiently. In this last chapter before my Conclusion, I will define my attitude in greater detail, as to what is covered by such terms as "anarchy," "freedom." Of the doctrinaire anarchist I disapprove. He teaches chaos. But for Happiness—I stand implicitly for that, as against the "austere" canon—there must not be too much order: better chaos than that. For Happiness,

238

equally, there must be order: therefore, where we find both these conditions present, we applaud the happy accident—both those impulses that tend to make men mild and obliging with one another, and those which cause a man to possess himself in uninhibited union, to free himself from the chains society forges for all of us, and by this very closeness to the inner self to approach closer to all other men, who will appear to him then just as another self, shaped a little differently, that is all. Where such fortunate conditions exist, men naturally feel that in some sort their goods are held in common; you find that the American will offer another what is in his wallet as a soldier will share with a comrade his canteen: thus escape from the dark obsession of property is effected; and the rich there are heterodox. It sounds odd, seeing it is the Bankers' Olympus about which I am writing, but those people grasp the meaning of the word commonwealth far better than do we.

As to order—to return to that—a very orderly room, for instance, is not comfortable, as a room should be, nor is a very orderly society. An army is the classical example of the latter: except for a short while it is very uncomfortable. A great American city is customarily dirty and untidy. This is an asset. It is more like nature. And for Happiness we have to get as near to nature as we can, without incurring the disadvantages of the natural condition; for with straight nature, discomfort makes its unwelcome appearance again, as when at a picnic insects join us and destroy our pleasure.

These laws regulating our attitude to *order* apply likewise to government. *No government*—what the anarchist would like—would be extremely uncomfortable and savage. Government is a compromise; it is, as in the last chapter I expressed it, our badge of servitude. This boss we give ourselves we cannot do without, but *the boss* is seldom an object of love. In ideal conditions, a rather disorderly state would be the best, since it would combine the advantages of living in society, with the satisfaction of the rugged comity of nature.

Here I will anticipate a possible misunderstanding. What I am saying has no reference to the present time. Indeed, it could not have. Advocate of Happiness as I am, I see very well that in England just now to be comfortable or happy is out of the question. Until everywhere State-sovereignty is abjured, great and costly armaments are necessary; with an unnaturally large population, to refrain from engaging in competitive commerce, as need be in trade-war, would be impossible. And England is bankrupt. To that I need add nothing. It is obvious that what I have been saying can have no conceivable application to a country in that situation.* My remarks have had for their object the provision of a philosophic background for my running panegyric of that "rootless Elysium" of the American city: irresponsible, dirty, corrupt, a little crazy; a scene where the values obtaining are reminiscent of Butler's *Erewhon,* one of the most entertaining Utopias.

America has been *able* to relax. We have always to remember that. Other countries at the moment are not so lucky. None have ever been so lucky. But to claim merit for being unlucky is not intelligent.

The Russians do not congratulate themselves on having so tough a life. But the Soviet Union started poor and ill-equipped. Great austerity has prevailed, all accounts of life there agree; it is a misfortune, as the Russians, who are not sentimental, will tell you. But political beliefs of so aggressive a character obliged them to spend half their substance on armaments. The government runs the Black Market itself (why the British Government does not I cannot imagine): they have been compelled to be most severe where graft is concerned, to employ draconian laws to discourage dishonest officials. But this is because there has been a genuine scarcity

*The present Socialist Government of England struggles to effect the conversion of as much as possible from private ownership to public ownership, with such dispatch as the lamentable conditions will allow. They are obliged to that end to maintain all the Tory war-controls. Minor hardships resulting, they will undoubtedly be used against them by the very people who are ultimately responsible; for such is the legacy of decades of neglect, of policies of artificial scarcity and of profitless war. I append this lest my message be taken to the wrong address.

in Russia—not the artificial scarcity invented by us. It meant if food was stolen, somebody went without food. Under conditions of permanent rationing, in England, we can understand this better than before.

But, in the world at large, there is at normal times a great plenty of food—of stock, of corn, of rice, of sugar. And our industrial techniques are such that we could supply everyone on the earth with enough and to spare of everything—of shoes, underwear, garments, furniture, refrigerators, washing-machines, and so forth. What stops the human race from enjoying this plenty is in the main two things: war and the economy of scarcity.

The atom bomb, I have suggested, means the end of the former, and a new social order is so visibly everywhere in the making, that it would be an optimistic gamekeeper who did not feel that the economic order he represented was about to disappear. Men are perfectly capable of blowing up our planet. We are assuming this will not happen. So, once these pre-eminent obstacles to the happy life of men in general are removed, will not the conditions be present for, if not an ideal, at least a so much more fortunate society than ours, or than men have ever known, that it would no longer be ridiculous to speak of Happiness, or of that genial relaxation which is inseparable from it—or of that certain irresponsibility which is a main ingredient of freedom, which, in its turn, is necessary to Happiness? This may sound utterly improbable; but what seems tolerably certain to me is that if something of that kind does not transpire, the alternative is the destruction of our race. It has never before had the ability to destroy itself. Now at last it has. As to the probable outcome, your guess is as good as mine, as the American says. Such (with all its necessary qualifications) is my propaganda for a future life.

29 CONCLUSION

(NUCLEAR ENERGY AND AMERICA)

Once "Western Man" was the object of my particular solicitude.* He was ailing, in fact in a decline—it was denied me to foresee what would so shortly befall, and I sought to heal and reinvigorate him. He was, of course, past help, and now is dead.

He only breathed his last a short while ago, but to me he seems as far away as Cro-Magnon Man. I cannot regret him, I find, in the slightest degree. I feel no loyalty toward him. All my loyalties today are for a far more significant and imposing person, namely, Cosmic Man (or "Cosmopolitan," as they would have said in the last century). This man I have seen and talked with in America. So I know what he will be like when his day comes, and he is everywhere.

As was explained in my opening chapters, to watch, for years on end, many millions of Europeans living peaceably side by side, as they do in America—bilingual, speaking as well as English either German or Polish, Italian, Russian, or Greek; all this at a moment when these same men, had they stopped in Europe, would have been massacring one another: to be where forty-eight states—a number of them formerly possessing sovereignty, each still in possession of a bicameral legislature—constitute a peaceful and united world of their own: this, for a European, is of an almost startling logic. To what conclusion can it lead, except to a deep conviction of the inexplicable folly of these ancient States of Europe,

Time and Western Man.

which persist in their murderous habits, and, as a consequence, sink into misery and ruin? In the forty-eight United States of America we have the model and exemplar of what is required everywhere. In the fact that great numbers of people of different nationalities can live side by side, without interfering with one another, we have the proof that it is not the *people* who are responsible for the incessant disputes and armed conflicts. All that is necessary is *one* government instead of many. It is as simple as that. How right Lincoln was to fight to the death for that. The end of state sovereignties would not resolve all the problems of human life. But the difference would be so enormous than anyone might be excused for thinking of that to the exclusion of everything else. No official of U.N., however the Charter may read, should admit any other thought to his head.

From *The Times* of January 29, 1946, I quote (it is the daily report of incidents in Parliament), "Mr. Noel Baker said he had been asked whether the Government did mean to work the institutions of the United Nations in such a way that in due course we should produce the equivalent of a world government. His answer was 'Yes, that is the object we must have in view.' "

This answer should have come with greater zest: for the time is very short. But would a spokesman of the governments of the U.S.A. or the U.S.S.R. go so far even as that—or mean it if he said it, which I think we do? And those are the States today who have the deciding voice. Were all the facts put before them without bias, a referendum of the inhabitants of the earth would tomorrow produce a vote quite overwhelmingly in favor of a world government. But it is small groups of people only who decide. It is fearfully difficult to imagine these groups agreeing to such a universal merger of power at present enjoyed in isolation by each group. The chastest of women could be thought of much more easily succumbing to lascivious advances, than could powerful States be imagined parting with their precious sovereignty. And our world, unfortunately, still is divided between very hostile economic principles; to merge

Wall Street and the Kremlin seems, for a start, a sheer impossibility.

The atom bomb, and all it means, does not appear to have sunk in at all. It has bounced off, as it were, or been mentally repelled as a tactless intruder. Everyone is behaving much as they did before. It is not because of callousness that in this book I have assumed the high probability, in due course, of an atomic war. It is because it is so impossible to imagine any other solution under the circumstances.

In an article of such insight that I should like to quote it in its entirety, Mr. Stephen Spender discusses this question. He writes: "Since we have become accustomed to accepting the idea that all arrangements are adjustments of existing interests, which can be calculated in terms of power and wealth, the step before us seems almost impossibly difficult to take." We have to take this step at a time when we "have almost abandoned thinking of politics in terms of humanity."

The nature of the difficulty could not be more clearly stated. The superhuman effort required to drag up our collective foot, with the dead weight of centuries upon it, and take that step forward of which Mr. Spender speaks, we recognize, and we resign ourselves to what we know from experience is likely to occur. Whether, however, it should be looked at in apocalyptic terms, as a problem of good and evil, is another matter. All we know is that *we* collectively should not be saddled with the onus of a tremendous sin, if it turns out that way; for the choice does not rest with us. We shall have no part in it, one way or the other. We, collectively, are profoundly ignorant of all that goes on, and, in the main, God has not endowed us with great intelligence. A just God, therefore, would not be likely to hold *us* responsible—for a decision in which we had no voice (such as a properly arranged referendum alone could ensure) about a matter with regard to which we are either scrappily informed, misinformed, or not informed at all. He might as well send His thunderbolt to punish a flock of sheep as to punish *us*.

At this juncture, where literally everything is at stake, it is in vain to think of good and evil as likely to be influential in the shaping of decisions upon which we helplessly attend. If, or when, the button is pressed, releasing those fearful energies, the responsible hand will not necessarily be evil— perhaps merely a nervous or splenetic, a hasty—or just a tired hand. The fact is that, as men, we are not at all fitted for such issues as these; we are like children who have chanced upon the secret of some magical force, in an adventure story—the uttering of a password involves the destruction of the sun.

One of the more valuable of Mr. Shaw's recent pronouncements was to the effect that he had at length reached the stage where he was, perhaps, fitted for the post of secretary to an assistant under-secretary of state (I forget the exact words). This would be to propose a high standard of human responsibility; but not too high. To confide to Mr. Shaw, at five hundred, the guardianship of an atom bomb would be very rash. To work all the human fallibility, the frivolity, out of our system would take longer than that.

In anxiously scrutinizing the future, we can only calculate the chances inductively and from experience. As my own contribution, I can think of nothing more moral than starkly and without qualification to declare that atomic war appears to me almost inevitable. This statement cannot do a particle of good—people seem rather to relish the idea of being destroyed, at such odd moments as their minds lazily turn in that direction. But at least it can do no harm, as it does to hold forth the hope that men will, perhaps, experience a change of heart. They would appear resolved to ignore the existence of these apocalyptic weapons, as I have remarked, and go on with the diplomatic game of skittles as if nothing had happened.

While on this dreadful subject, let me say a few words about pacifism. Such a term as "pacifist" is obviously quite meaningless when discussing what would, in fact, as today, signify the shattering or even the complete destruction of the human race; for the weapons used against Hiroshima are no doubt already poor things to what are at present at our disposal. But at what stage, exactly, in man's progress to final self-destruction, would it be legitimate to say: "From this point on all men who are not violently against what is known as 'war' are insane, and the term 'pacifist' has no further relevance"?

I do not think I was ever what technically could be called a pacifist. It is all a question, however, as to where you draw the line beyond which war is past a joke. I drew that line at the year 1918. Any unflattering remarks for which I have been responsible regarding war, subsequent to that date, or any action taken to dissuade men from it, I regard as sanity, not as pacifism.

Today, war appeals to me no more than formerly—but war has always had a rival for first place upon humanity's black list, and I shall not again place it first on mine. (I declare this for the second time.) Should anyone say: "Don't you think this war that is coming is a little over the odds?" my answer will be, "Of course it is. But don't you think *this*" (and I shall mention something else, commenting upon the greed, callousness, and thirst for power which occasion it), "don't you think this is pretty bad, too?" We may regard war, however, as no longer there: all the great front-rank questions have merged into *one* question. All have to be dealt with together.

To conclude—speculations about the future of the world at large are imposed on one by the atomic developments which are responsible for a situation without precedent in human life—and America, the subject of the present book, is open, like every other part of the globe, to the action of these great agencies of change. But those changes are far more likely to bring about a cosmic society than any other variety.

Here are the three main factors in this connection (condensing under three heads what I have already said). (1) The possibility has been widely canvassed of experiments with this great agent of disintegration getting out of hand, and even some major terrestrial alteration being effected, which might involve the end of human life altogether. Probably that, for all practical purposes, can be discounted. (2) Atomic War.

Einstein's estimate (see an earlier reference) that such a war would not destroy more than fifty per cent of mankind, and civilization would be salvaged by the fifty per cent remaining, recommends itself as a sound guess. But it is most unlikely that they would reinstate nationalism (which certainly is not conducive to "civilization"). Such an unexampled catastrophe would precipitate the kind of future about which I have been writing, holding up America as a rough and ready advance copy of that. (3) Lastly, reason may, after all, prevail—which would again be all in favor of a type of man emancipated from the present competitive chaos. For that chaos either has to get worse, or men extract themselves from it and attain more rational standards. It cannot stay as it is. A very few years of no change-for-the-better and you have atomic war.

America is the country meanwhile where, far more than here, people have shown awareness of what this newcomer, nuclear energy, means to man. Very temporarily sole guardians of the secrets of this, from the purely human standpoint, diabolical discovery, it is natural, no doubt, that Americans should be the first to be infected with this terrible awareness.

Before closing, let me say that I trust my American friends will excuse me for availing myself of the American scene and employing their country as my paradoxical exemplar for the other nations, as yet so painfully uncentralized, as once were the states of the great American Union. All men may be very much nearer to that future which I found there, and which I hope this book may advertise, than they understand.

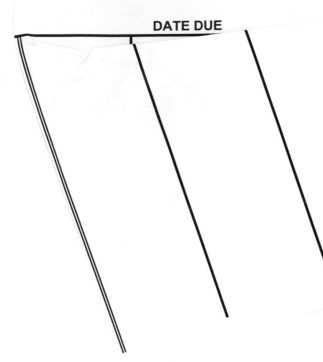

DATE DUE